D0215345

JANICE D. AURINI

MELANIE HEATH

STEPHANIE HOWELLS

THE HOW TO OF QUALITATIVE RESEARCH

Los Angeles | London | New Delhi
Singapore | Washington DC | Melbourne

Los Angeles | London | New Delhi
Singapore | Washington DC | Melbourne

SAGE Publications Ltd
1 Oliver's Yard
55 City Road
London EC1Y 1SP

SAGE Publications Inc.
2455 Teller Road
Thousand Oaks, California 91320

SAGE Publications India Pvt Ltd
B 1/I 1 Mohan Cooperative Industrial Area
Mathura Road
New Delhi 110 044

SAGE Publications Asia-Pacific Pte Ltd
3 Church Street
#10-04 Samsung Hub
Singapore 049483

Editor: Mila Steele
Production editor: Sushant Nailwal
Copyeditor: Andy Baxter
Proofreader: Derek Markham
Indexer: Avril Ehrlich
Marketing manager: Ben Griffin-Sherwood
Cover design: Wendy Scott
Typeset by: C&M Digitals (P) Ltd, Chennai, India
Printed and bound by CPI Group (UK) Ltd,
Croydon, CR0 4YY

© Janice D. Aurini, Melanie Heath and Stephanie Howells,
2016

Apart from any fair dealing for the purposes of research or
private study, or criticism or review, as permitted under the
Copyright, Designs and Patents Act, 1988, this publication
may be reproduced, stored or transmitted in any form, or by
any means, only with the prior permission in writing of the
publishers, or in the case of reprographic reproduction, in
accordance with the terms of licences issued by the Copyright
Licensing Agency. Enquiries concerning reproduction outside
those terms should be sent to the publishers.

First published 2016

Library of Congress Control Number: 2015956035

British Library Cataloguing in Publication data

A catalogue record for this book is available from
the British Library

ISBN 978-1-4462-6708-0
ISBN 978-1-4462-6709-7 (pbk)

At SAGE we take sustainability seriously. Most of our products are printed in the UK using FSC papers and boards.
When we print overseas we ensure sustainable papers are used as measured by the PREPS grading system.
We undertake an annual audit to monitor our sustainability.

This book is dedicated to the hundreds of people who have graciously participated in our research projects over the years.

SUMMARY OF CONTENTS

CONTENTS

LIST OF FIGURES

LIST OF TABLES

ABOUT THE AUTHORS

Janice D. Aurini is an Associate Professor in the Department of Sociology and Legal Studies at the University of Waterloo. She completed her Ph.D. at McMaster University and was a postdoctoral fellow at Harvard University. Her research examines education policy, education inequality, private education and parenting. Dr. Aurini has conducted field work, interviews and photo-interviews. She has also worked on several mixed methods projects. Her recent articles can be found in *Sociology of Education*, *Canadian Public Policy* and *Canadian Journal of Sociology*. She is currently the primary investigator on a five-year SSHRC funded project on summer learning inequality.

Melanie Heath is an Associate Professor in the Department of Sociology at McMaster University. She completed her Ph.D. at University of Southern California and was a postdoctoral fellow at Rice University. Her research examines marriage promotion policies in the United States, and she is author of *One Marriage Under God: The Campaign to Promote Marriage in America* (New York University Press, 2012). She has conducted field work, interviews, focus groups, and textual analysis. Her research has been published in *Gender & Society*, *Qualitative Sociology*, *Sociological Quarterly*, and *Contexts*. She is currently the primary investigator on a five-year SSHRC funded comparative project on government regulation of polygamy in Canada, France, and the United States.

Stephanie Howells is an Assistant Professor in the Department of Sociology and Anthropology at the University of Guelph. She completed her Ph.D. in the Department of Sociology at McMaster University. Her doctoral research focused on the cultural and organizational processes that lead to inflated perceptions of school violence, and seemingly disproportionate policy responses. Her research is generally centered on education, crime, violence and youth. She has worked on several mixed methods research projects, and has conducted focus groups, personal interviews, and media analyses in her qualitative research.

COMPANION WEBSITE

The How To of Qualitative Research is supported by online resources for lecturers to aid study and support teaching. These are available at https://study.sagepub.com/auriniheathand-howells and include:

PowerPoint slides for each chapter, which can be quickly adapted for use in classroom or virtual learning teaching and presentations.

Testbanks for each chapter, which include both multiple choice and short answer questions that can be used in exams or assigned as homework.

PART I

JUMP STARTING YOUR QUALITATIVE RESEARCH PROJECT

1

INTRODUCTION:
FROM WHY TO HOW
IN QUALITATIVE RESEARCH

> I want to understand the world from your point of view. I want to know what you know in the way you know it. I want to understand the meaning of your experience, to walk in your shoes, to feel things as you feel them, to explain things as you explain them. Will you become my teacher and help me understand? (Spradley, 1979: 34)

Spradley originally made this classic statement about ethnographers; yet for many it captures the broader essence of what it means to be a qualitative researcher. As qualitative researchers we are interested in describing the context and meaning of individual and group life and understanding how people make sense of the world around them. Our methodological toolkit allows us to examine how broader structural, historical and cultural conditions influence people's perspectives, experiences and choices. Interviews, field observations, and physical and social traces tell a unique story about the complexity of human development and group life.

Based on these qualities, it is no surprise that qualitative research has arrived. As studies continue to multiply, so too have the number of books about qualitative research methods. If you are new to qualitative methods, you will find no shortage of excellent books that broadly describe types of qualitative research, questions that different methods address, approaches to qualitative research, and ethical issues (e.g., Creswell, 2013; Hesse-Biber et al., 2010; Silverman, 2009). Other sources focus on a specific approach such as grounded theory (e.g., Corbin and Strauss, 2008). Complementing these books, you can also find edited volumes that provide useful overviews of the field, including discussions of competing paradigms and broad explanations of interpretive traditions (e.g., Denzin and Lincoln, 2011).

If however you are ready to design and collect qualitative data, you will not be so fortunate. In our search for the right book, we found few that take researchers from the 'what' and 'why' to the 'how' of qualitative research. *The 'How To' of Qualitative Research* fills this void and will take you from understanding what qualitative methods are all about, to knowing how to *execute* a high quality qualitative research project. We have written this book to be accessible to more advanced undergraduate students, while providing enough methodological detail to make this book useful for graduate and postgraduate researchers interested in conducting a project that includes qualitative data.

A PRAGMATIC APPROACH TO QUALITATIVE RESEARCH: WHAT THIS BOOK IS (AND IS NOT) ABOUT

You will benefit most from our book if you have already taken an introductory research methods course and are familiar with the variety of approaches, such as feminist or post-positivist ontological and epistemological positions, and types of methods, such as interviews and field research. Why? Well our book is not about is describing or theorizing qualitative methods, but rather *doing* qualitative research. That is, regardless of your 'approach', you still need to know how to design your project and data collection instruments. Our goal is to provide you with the practical tools you will need to answer critical questions such as

'What are some ways to sample potential participants?'; 'How do I construct an interview schedule?'; 'How many interviews are enough?'; 'Should I be thinking of a single case study or a comparative study?'; 'What and how should I record in the field?'; 'How do I manage participants in a focus group'; and 'What other sources of data should I consider?'.

We take a practical approach to doing qualitative research and do not subscribe to or promote any particular approach or method of qualitative research. Instead, the book is written from a pragmatist perspective (Patton, 2002), which subscribes to the philosophy that you should select 'the right tool for the job'. To do this, this book has the following features:

- We bring together exemplary technical guides and research studies in one book to offer detailed explanations of qualitative methodology and design. Drawing on the trusted sources from some masters of qualitative research (e.g., their own course outlines), along with a thorough literature review and our own experience as qualitative researchers, allowed us to distil the most salient strategies for designing, collecting and analysing qualitative data.
- Our book includes clear step-by-step instructions for developing a research design and complementary research tools (e.g., interview schedule). Our book provides some background (the 'what' and the 'why' part of qualitative research), but focuses primarily on detailing *how* you actually create and execute these techniques.
- Our book identifies the practical issues that many budding qualitative researchers face. Our book contains a number of useful pedagogical features, including boxed summaries, diagrams, checklists (e.g., creating an interview bag), and templates for organizing and collecting data (e.g., demographic survey). These tools can be used as is, or easily modified to suit the specific needs of your study.
- If you are an instructor, we offer a number of complementary teaching materials, including PowerPoint slides and a testbank. The aforementioned student exercises, templates and checklists can also be easily used as effective in-class exercises or as assignments.

Our book is about preparing you to make informed choices that allow you best to answer your research questions and make convincing statements about your data. How? Well when you have forged a clear methodological pathway you will be in a better position to build trustworthiness and credibility into your project (Lincoln and Guba, 1985). Trustworthy and credible qualitative research has the following qualities:

- **Self-Reflexivity**: You are able to show that you considered the ways in which your personal characteristics and history shapes how you approached, collected and analysed your data.
- **Transparency**: You are able to describe and document your data collection and analysis procedures in a manner that can be reviewed and scrutinized by others.
- **Evidenced-Based**: You are able to demonstrate clear connections between your data, how you answered your research questions and any conclusions you made about the focus of your inquiry.
- **Built-in Credibility and Trustworthiness Techniques**: You are able to show that you thoughtfully and purposefully built in specific credibility and trustworthiness enhancing techniques such as prolonged engagement, triangulation, thick description and member checking (Lincoln and Guba, 1985).

Trustworthy and credible qualitative research does not happen by accident or luck, it happens through good research design. This book shows you how to accomplish this by detailing the specific methodological strategies for conducting high quality qualitative research.

HOW TO USE THIS BOOK

Each chapter can be used as a stand-alone piece. If you are a less experienced researcher, you will need to start with 'How to Conceptualize Research' (Chapter 2) and 'How to Design a Qualitative Project and Create a Research Question' (Chapter 3) before moving on to the chapters about the specific qualitative methodology that will best answer your research question (Chapters 4, 5, 6 and 7). Chapters 8 and 9 will take you through the 'how to' of data analysis and writing up qualitative research projects. If you are a more experienced researcher, you will likely narrow in on different sections and chapters of this book that address a new kind of project, including the chapters on focus groups and unobtrusive methods. If you are an instructor, this book can be easily adapted for a one-term or two-term course as either the main or complementary text depending on whether it is an introduction or more advanced methods course.

This book is divided into three main parts.

Part I will provide you with the tools you need to conceptualize and design your project.

- Chapter 2 is about conceptualization, the art and practice of formulating a research project. This chapter will take you through the process of moving from a general research interest to a concrete and researchable research problem.
- Chapter 3 is about research design. This chapter is premised on the belief that the research question drives the method. To this end, the chapter outlines different types of research questions and the optimal qualitative methods for answering them.

Part II outlines the strategies and methods for collecting various kinds of qualitative data, including interviews, focus groups, field research and unobtrusive methods.

- Chapter 4 is about interviewing, one of the main qualitative data techniques used by students, researchers, and public and private firms. The chapter will allow you to make an informed choice about different interview types and methods of interviewing and hardware, software and service options. We will also provide you with concrete strategies for preparing for the interview, recruiting, developing an interview schedule and conducting an interview. Finally, we discuss transcription options and provide you with concrete tools for managing interview data.
- Chapter 5 is about focus groups. This chapter will provide you with the information you need to make an informed decision about the structure of your focus group, size, group composition and the number of focus groups you will need to answer your research question. We will also discuss important planning issues, including differentiating facilitator and note taker roles, considerations before selecting a venue, and materials needed.

- Chapter 6 is about field research. Field research has a long history in a variety of disciplines; most notably anthropology but also sociology, labour studies, social or urban geography, organizational studies and social work. This chapter will outline strategies for conducting different non-participant and participant field research and writing high quality field notes.
- Chapter 7 is about unobtrusive methods. Materials produced by individuals, groups or institutions are valuable unobtrusive sources that can be used as standalone or complementary sources of qualitative data. After we describe the types of unobtrusive data that are available, we then turn to detailing various methods of collecting unobtrusive data, including covert and non-covert, systematic and non-systematic, and manifest and latent approaches.

Part III of this book provides you with the tools you will need to analyse your data and write up your research.

- Chapter 8 is about using coding to conduct data analysis. The first part of the chapter provides you with practical tools for preparing your data for analysis, including how to develop a codebook. The second part of the chapter details the practice of coding, including pre-coding, and First Cycle and Second Cycle coding techniques.
- Chapter 9 is about communicating qualitative research findings. In this chapter we systematically outline the expectations of different audiences (e.g., policy makers; multi-disciplinary versus single-disciplinary adjudication committees) and how researchers should approach writing a paper, a book proposal or grant application using qualitative data.

Now that we have outlined the spirit and intentions of our book, the next chapter takes you through the process of selecting a research topic and transforming that topic into a research problem. We specify data and theory driven sources of inspiration and guide you through the process of articulating your research problem.

2

HOW TO CONCEPTUALIZE RESEARCH:

GETTING STARTED AND ADVANCING ONGOING PROJECTS

---------------------------------- **Learning objectives** ----------------------------------

By the end of this chapter you will have the tools to:

- Identify and conceptualize a research topic
- Formulate a research problem
- Anticipate potential 'Who cares?' questions

---------------------------------- **Chapter summary** ----------------------------------

Conceptualization, the art and practice of discovery, is the first and some may argue the most difficult part of research. This chapter will provide researchers with strategies for conceptualizing qualitative projects, including how to use the literature effectively and how to formulate a research question.

INTRODUCTION

We tend to gloss over 'conceptualization'. Conceptualization is the process of not only selecting a topic, but formulating a defensible and researchable research problem; it is more than simply generating a list of interesting topics such as academic achievement gaps or homelessness. If you jump from a topic to data collection, you will likely end up with random bits of information that are of little use to the researcher or your intended audience. Such projects not only tend to lack analytical focus, but will be plagued by the challenges associated with the dreaded 'Who cares?'. Good conceptualization involves moving from a general topic to a clear research problem.

This chapter outlines concrete tools for conceptualization. We present them as steps, but fully acknowledge that in reality research happens in a non-linear fashion. We also note that some approaches are more exploratory, particularly at the beginning stages of a project. However, whether you start off with a perfectly good research question or not, you will eventually need to address each of the following:

1. **Select a Topic:** The first step of any project is to determine what you want to study.
2. **Establish the Problem:** You need to establish the problem that your project hopes to solve, including filling in a gap or extending the literature in a new and exciting direction.

SELECTING A TOPIC

> the common problem among students is the feeling that one has nothing to say ... you find the huge variety of things that *could* be said almost as overwhelming as the huge diversity of things that *have been* said. (Abbott, 2004: 85)

By design, researchers are deeply curious about the social world. If you are lucky, you may start a project with a topic that is inspired by your discipline, subfield, or event such as the Occupy Wall Street movement. You may even have some general questions in mind such as identifying the aspects of the Occupy Wall Street movement that were more or less successful, or whether it constituted a social movement in the first place. In such cases, you need the tools presented in this chapter to prevent you from relying on a particular lens simply out of habit. So if your tried and true method is to view such a movement through the eyes of the participants or as a Marxist, considering an alternative approach may help you forge an exciting and less travelled intellectual pathway (Abbott, 2004: 86).

Many budding researchers, however, are interested in many topics that may or may not be related, such as female body builders and cults, or a broad area, such as children's afterschool activities. Yet decisions (and sacrifices) have to be made in the interest of developing a coherent research design. Initially, pinning down a topic is useful for guiding researchers toward the literature and some preliminary sources of data. As we discuss below, some initial 'digging' can provide you with much needed background and inspiration. This part of conceptualization is an important *first*, but definitely not last, step toward developing an informative and interesting research project. This ground work not only saves time and cuts down on mistakes, it will undoubtedly come in handy time and time again, whether writing your literature review or defending your project at a proposal defence or to a journal reviewer.

In Table 2.1 we present a toolkit for generating ideas. You should not get too bogged down about which tool is better or whether you are executing any one of the options 'perfectly'; instead, see these exercises as brainstorming tools. You may also find some tools more or less useful than others depending on your approach.

We present five key sources for inspiration that are divided into two groups:

a)   Data and theory driven
b)   Researcher driven

Data and theory driven

Data driven conceptualization includes both secondary and primary sources. We discuss secondary sources first since they will likely be the most accessible option, particularly for more novice researchers. Secondary sources are generally one step removed from the original event or people and include published academic and professional articles, commonly referred to as 'the literature'. Primary sources include materials that are produced by, for, or about the people, group, organization or event under study by persons who have direct and intimate knowledge or experiences. We also discuss the possibility of conducting some preliminary data collection.

Table 2.1   What is my topic? Sources of inspiration

	Type	Example
a) Data and theory driven	1) Secondary sources	Journal articles
		Academic or professional books
		Research reports
	2) Primary sources	Online materials (e.g., blogs)
		Websites
		Government documents or public records
		Archival materials
		Brochures, reports, posters
		Diaries, letters
		Media (online, newspapers, magazines and TV)
		Pictures or videos
		Furniture, statues, clothing
		Music, poetry, art
		Maps
		Transcripts
		Academic and professional articles and reports that are used as primary sources of data
	3) Primary: Preliminary raw data that you collect or produce	Pilot project
b) Researcher driven	4) Mapping exercises	Mind map
		Concept map
		Literature map
	5) Abbott's (2004) 'Lists'	Aristotle's four causes

Secondary sources: The literature

The literature will be your first and arguably best friend in the development of a research project. The literature includes three main sources: a) academic journal articles; b) academic or professional books; and c) research reports. You will obviously need to use these sources to construct a literature review. However, in this section, we discuss how you can use the literature as a source of inspiration.

Academic journal articles

The first and most common source is published journal articles. These articles are peer reviewed and can be accessed through a variety of sources, including JSTOR and Scholars Portal. The term 'peer reviewed' means that the articles have been reviewed usually by two or three experts, and have likely been screened by the editor of the journal. While journals vary in terms of the degree to which articles are scrutinized, and in many cases rejected, the process provides a measure of quality control. If you are unsure where to start, ask experts in your field (e.g., your supervisor) or a librarian at your institution for the most appropriate sources. The journals supported by your discipline's professional association(s) are another great starting place. In sociology for example, the American Sociological Association, Canadian Sociological Association and the European Sociological Association all host a variety of high quality academic journals.

There are three main types of academic journal articles:

- **Research articles**: Research articles use primary (e.g., interviews conducted by the author) or secondary (e.g., archival materials) sources of data to advance a particular original idea, argument or theory.
- **Theoretical articles**: Rather than relying on primary or secondary data (though the author may refer to such data) theoretical articles attempt to advance or critique a particular theoretical concept or framework, or make an original theoretical contribution to the literature.
- **State of the field or review articles**: This type of article reviews a large body of research and theoretical articles. Review articles articulate key arguments, sources of data, theories and debates on a particular topic. They are a wonderful source, particularly for researchers who are newer to a particular area. Most disciplines also have journals that are specifically devoted to publishing review articles. *Annual Review of Sociology*, *Annual Review of Economics* and *Annual Review of Political Science* are a few examples.

 Quick tip: How to search for academic journal articles

Searching for articles on your topic is part art, part science. To 'strike gold', you will need to experiment with different terms and combinations. Some of these terms will be obvious (e.g., layperson terms), and others will be added once you become familiar with terms that are used in the literature. Below we present an example of searches from a project on school shootings. Start with the most obvious search terms (e.g., school shootings), then separate key terms on separate rows of the search engines (e.g., 'school' on row one and 'shooting' on row two). Use quotation marks to keep key works together (e.g., 'school violence'); if not some search engines will simultaneously search for these terms separately (e.g., you may end up with thousands of articles containing the word 'school' and thousands of articles containing the word 'violence' that have nothing to do with school shootings). In some cases you will be able to search on a key event, person or organization that is related to your topic (e.g., 'Sandy Hook' or 'Columbine', two famous school shootings). Once you are familiar with the literature, you may come across alternative terms related to your topic. In the case of school shootings some authors have referred to them as 'rampage shootings' or 'organizational deviance'. You may also add in other terms that according to the literature are related to school shootings (e.g., bullying), but recognize that these searches will likely yield many articles that have nothing to do with your core topic.

Example: Search terms

Key	Combination	Key events, people or organizations
'School shootings'	'School' AND 'shootings'	'Sandy Hook'
'School shooters'	'School' AND 'shooters'	'Columbine'
'School violence'	'School' AND 'violence'	

Academic or professional books

The literature also includes academic or professional books on your topic. Sources include, but are not limited to, academic presses.

There are four main types of books:

- **Academic or scholarly books**: Scholarly books include original research and 'state of the field' chapters that marshal a variety of data to frame a particular issue or make an original contribution. Most of these books are published by academic presses (e.g., NYU Press) or foundations that support scholarly work (e.g., Russell Sage Foundation).
- **Popular original works**: Popular original works target a wider audience, but may still be authored by experts. More novice researchers should tread a bit more carefully, since they will likely have fewer tools to evaluate the relative quality of the argument and any data that the author used. However, there are many wonderful examples of popular books that are both high quality and accessible. Venkatesh's (2008) *Gang Leader for a Day* is a perfect example. His book is popular in its own right, and is featured in the wildly successful *Freakonomics* (Levitt and Dubner, 2009). Yet, at the same time the book is grounded in years of rich field research.
- **Original or reprinted edited collections**: Edited collections can provide a different kind of breadth by marshalling chapters from a variety of authors and perspectives on a particular topic. Edited collections can include a series of original contributions such as previously unpublished data, concepts, frameworks or theories. They can also include reprinted material either in its entirety (e.g., one chapter that has been reprinted from a previously published book or article) or a summary of an original contribution.
- **Encyclopaedias**: Unlike a traditional encyclopaedia, scholarly encyclopaedias are typically produced for a particular discipline or sub-field (e.g., Health), or around a particular theme (e.g., Social Welfare). These sources will not provide you with a comprehensive examination of any one topic, but will provide you with a summary of hundreds of key terms, concepts, theories or methods, depending on the focus of the encyclopaedia. Such sources may help you formulate a handful of working definitions that you can use when discussing your key terms or concepts. Most also include cross-references and suggestions for further reading. *The SAGE Encyclopedia of Qualitative Research Methods* (Given, 2008), *The Encyclopedia of Social Networks* (Barnett, 2011) and *The Encyclopedia of Housing* (Carswell, 2012) are just a few examples.

Quick tip: So many books, so little time …

Despite the potential benefits, if you are on a tight timeline (e.g., a proposal deadline) you may need to initially limit the number of books you read since one book may take as much time as reading five or six articles on your topic. We are certainly not trying to discourage you from reading books on your topic, particularly classic, well-cited or award winning books! We are just noting that if you have a tight timeline, decisions will have to be made. To help you make such decisions, there are several sources to help you generate a list of 'must read' books:

- **Book reviews**: Read book reviews published in academic journals. There are also academic journals specifically devoted to book reviews. *Contemporary Sociology* is just one example. You should never take any one review as the 'final word' unless of course the reviewer is someone you trust. However, a good book review will provide you with a basic summary of the book and constructive criticism that is grounded within the larger literature.
- **Well-cited books**: Read the handful of books that seem to be continuously cited by known experts on your topic, including books that are controversial or that have received a lot of media attention. Reviewing the books (and journal articles for that matter) that are cited in the academic literature is a good place to start.
- **Recognized books**: Read books on your topic that have been recognized in some special way (e.g., an award by your discipline's professional association). You should also consider books on your topic that have been featured at recent conferences (e.g., author meets critic).

Professional reports

Professional reports include published research, theory, review and working papers. Most government agencies, think tanks, professional associations, advocacy groups or arms-length research consortiums produce professional reports that are widely available to the public online. Examples of such government bodies or organizations include UNESCO, WHO, the US Census Bureau, and the Ontario Ministry of Education. All of these agencies post online research articles, executive summaries or press releases that are chock full of original and secondary data, policy recommendations, and literature reviews.

Now what? How to use the literature to conceptualize

Key takeaways

- First identify key theories, terminologies, concepts, methods, data and interpretations presented in the literature.
- Second, identify what is not known, missing or problematic in the literature.
- Unless you are already very well versed in the literature, your initial review will require a lot of time.
- An ongoing 'small-c' critical examination of the literature is essential.

The literature, when used properly, can be a powerful conceptualization tool and can help you identify theories, terminologies or concepts, methods, or data (Maxwell, 2005: 55).

In Table 2.2 we present key questions to get you thinking about what is known in the literature (column one). Once you have identified the key questions, theories and concepts that dominate the literature on your topic, you can start to identify what is not known, problematic or missing (column two) in a manner that will not only aid in conceptualization, but is critical for developing an informed literature review. In short, these are questions you will need to answer at some point along your journey. Addressing these questions early on has additional benefits, most notably when you are ready to start your literature review. As Maxwell (2013: 40) cautions, a literature review is a 'dangerously misleading term'. Literature reviews that simply summarize or provide an overview of the existing literature tend to be descriptive or merely parrot what others have already said (e.g., repeating the limitations of a particular theory or method). This approach also tends to be only superficially connected to *your* project and research questions. By asking and answering the questions in Table 2.2, you will be in good shape to start to develop an original conceptual framework.

Steps

1. Search the literature on your topic (see sources above).
2. First identify key theories, terminologies, concepts, methods, data and interpretations presented in the literature. Second, identify what is not known, missing or problematic in the literature (see Table 2.2).
3. Verify that your rendering of the literature is correct. Speak to your supervisor and committee members. Return to your library search engines (e.g., JSTOR) and plug in key terms that relate to what you have identified as unknown, missing or problematic just to be sure that you have not missed an important article or stream of the literature.
4. Discussed in detail below, start to narrow in on the one or two 'holes' that you have identified to construct your research problem and research questions.

Table 2.2 How to use the literature to conceptualize

What is known?	What is not known, problematic or missing?
What questions have been asked about my topic?	• What questions have not been asked on my topic? • Is there a time, geography, or location dimension to these questions and if so, what would happen if I altered it? • What would happen if I turned dominant questions around? (e.g., rather than ask why there are so many high school drop-outs, ask why there are not more) • What if I turned positive questions into negative questions (or negative into positive)? (e.g., so rather than asking how drop-outs and graduates are different, ask how they are not different)

(Continued)

Table 2.2   (Continued)

What is known?	What is not known, problematic or missing?
What major theories have been used to examine my topic?	• Do these theories adequately capture the phenomenon under study? • Are there other possible theories that should be considered?
What major concepts have been used to examine my topic?	• Do these concepts adequately capture the phenomenon under study? • Are there other possible concepts that should be considered?
How have concepts been defined?	• Are there other possible definitions? • Are there problems with current definitions?
How have they been measured?	• Are there other possible ways concepts could have been measured? • Are there problems with how concepts have been measured?
What kinds of data have been used to examine my topic?	• Are there other possible sources of data? • Are there problems with the data that have been used?
What concepts, ideas or relationships tend to be in the foreground and background?	• Should a particular concept be given more or less weight? • What would happen if I switched the foreground and background?
What are the dominant interpretations or findings?	• Do the dominant interpretations make sense? • Is there a reasonable connection between the data and interpretations?
What relationships have been examined?	• Are there other relationships that could be examined? • Are the relationships currently under study still the most important, or should we consider new ones?
What has been the context?	• Is the context of my study the same? • Is the context of my study different? • Has the context changed?
What are the major debates on my topic?	• Have these debates limited the scholarship on my topic in a particular manner? • Does one side appear to have more credibility? • Do the debates focus on the data, theories, interpretations or some combination of the three?
How have others justified their study or its contributions?	• Can I use their rationales (with or without some tweaking) to justify my study and its contributions?
What do others have to say?	• Do their findings confirm or disconfirm research from my discipline? • What can I learn or take away from their concepts, data, or interpretations?
What frameworks, theories or data am I most comfortable using to study my topic?	• What alternative frameworks, theories or data are available on my topic? • How would critics of my approach, or scholars using alternative frameworks, theories or data examine my topic?

Some researchers may warn you about the dangers of 'ideological hegemony' generated from examining the existing literature too closely (Becker, 1986). And it is true, if you stick only to 'what is known' you may limit your ability to see your topic in a new light.

Importantly, if you cannot demonstrate how your study addresses an *unanswered* problem in the literature, then your study will be of little value to your target audience.

However, we argue that a comprehensive understanding and an *ongoing* 'small-c' critical examination of the existing literature will allow you to more confidently represent 'what is not known, problematic or missing' in a manner that *will* increase your chances of 'inspect[ing] competing ways of talking about the same subject matter' (Becker, 1986: 149). Equally important is that using the literature in the spirit of conceptualization does not marry a researcher to a particular approach since it is more a question of what or how you use the literature, rather than whether you should read the literature in the first place.

Primary: Using raw data

Key takeaways

- Examine raw data produced by, for or about the group, organization or event of interest.
- Consider how these data or presentation of the literature may be used as data in their own right.
- Consider conducting a small pilot project, even at very early stages of the project.

The use of primary sources of data is not limited to the 'data collection' phase of a project. There are two main sources of primary data that are worth considering for conceptualization purposes. The first source is raw data produced by, for or about the group, organization or event of interest. Data include online materials, including websites, textbooks, archival materials such as diaries or pictures, online videos, media reports and magazines. Beyond reviewing primary data for conceptualization purposes, you can also consider how these data may capture important dimensions of your topic and be used as data in their own right. Meyer et al. (2010), for example, mapped the growing presence of human rights issues in social science textbooks. Similarly, Wrigley (1989) conducted a content analysis of over 1,000 articles from popular literature targeted at parents to understand changing attitudes about children's development.

You may also want to consider using academic and professional reports as a primary source of data. Mizruchi and Fein (1999), for example, reviewed key journal articles to examine the social construction of knowledge. Similarly, Colquitt and Zapata-Phelan (2007) examined five decades of articles published in a highly influential journal, *The Academy of Management Journal*, to develop a taxonomy of the theoretical contributions to the field.

The second source of primary data is raw data that you collect or produce, sometimes referred to as a 'pilot project'. Some preliminary fieldwork, interviews or analysis of the materials is an excellent way to get your feet wet and to work out the direction and focus of your project. Pilot projects are not only incredibly important to work out key data collection instruments (e.g., an interview schedule) but can fundamentally shape the scope and direction of a project. You will need to consider this option with your institution's research ethics board in mind.

Researcher driven

Key takeaway

- Use brainstorming exercises at the early stages of conceptualization to articulate what is known about a topic, and to identify relationships, processes, concepts or missing information.

Researcher driven sources include a variety of brainstorming exercises that you develop to generate ideas. Below we present two such ideas, but there are certainly other strategies available.

Early mapping: Mind, concept and literature techniques

'Mapping' is routinely used in qualitative research, particularly at the beginning stages of data analysis. Mapping is a 'graphical tool for organizing and representing knowledge' (Wheeldon, 2010: 90). Such visual aids can serve as a powerful tool at many stages of a project by allowing (or forcing) researchers to classify and organize information in manageable chunks. Faced with mountains of data, including interview transcripts, field notes, documents or pictures and videos, researchers use this technique to sketch-out relationships, sense-making or organizational processes, and the linkage between data and concept or theoretical ideas. Importantly, mapping allows researchers to embed these understandings within a broader contextual framework. Mapping can also encourage researchers to take a 'reflexive approach to how we are classifying' (Hart, 1998: 143). Ideally, mapping requires researchers to think about their classification schemes, and the underlying logic that guides their decision-making.

For our purposes in this chapter, we articulate the benefits of what we refer to as 'early mapping' techniques for conceptualization. In particular, early mapping can also be used to develop a research project by allowing researchers to articulate what is known about the topic, and theorize possible or preliminary relationships, processes or concepts (Daley, 2004; Novak and Gowin, 1984; Novak and Cañas, 2006). Below, we present three kinds of mapping techniques: Mind Mapping and Concept Mapping and Literature Mapping (Table 2.3).

Mind and concept mapping

Though similar, researchers make a distinction between 'mind' and 'concept' mapping techniques. Mind maps are usually organized around one central idea, concept or theme, and tend to be more informal and flexible (Buzan and Buzan, 2000). Concept mapping by contrast is more structured, and often includes multiple ideas, concepts or themes as well as people, groups or organizations. Concept maps are developed with a good understanding of the context in which they will be used.

We caution against getting too bogged down about which method is better or whether you are doing either one 'perfectly' at the conceptualization stage. There are entire books written about doing both, and that detail various ways to get the job done (e.g., Kane and Trochim, 2007). We see it as an exercise in getting the pieces of the puzzle down on paper, developing a good grasp on the key dimensions related to your project, and thinking about possible puzzles that still need to be answered (Table 2.3). You will likely need to rework your mind or concept maps several times as your ideas develop.

Mind maps

Mind maps are perfect for researchers who are newer to a topic. Mind maps allow researchers to get a handle on the central characteristics, themes or concepts.

Mind maps have the following characteristics:

- Visual representation of key themes, concepts, ideas, organizations, people, units or theories.
- Built around one central idea or theme, as a flow chart or as a 'tree' diagram (Miles and Huberman, 1994).
- The use of simple lines to articulate connections.
- The potential to use different shapes to symbolize different components (e.g., using squares for organizations; circles for people) or different emphases (e.g., using squares for components directly related to the core; circles for components on the periphery).
- Flexible and less structured.

Concept maps

Concept maps are suitable for researchers who have a reasonable grasp of the literature or topic under study. Concept maps are more structured and multifaceted, and based on an understanding of the context that they will be used in (Novak and Cañas, 2006). Concept mapping includes structuring statements, words, and people, groups or organizations based on either what is known or theorized about the topic of interest. Concepts maps also include words, symbols and shapes to explain the nature or strength of relationships between two or more units. Rather than flowing from one concept or idea, concept maps represent multiple start points which may or may not be related to every other unit.

Concept maps have the following characteristics (Figure 2.1):

- A multi-hierarchical representation of information. Hierarchies may be based on relative importance, a process, or moving from the general to the specific.
- 'Information' may include not only key ideas, concepts, characteristics and people, groups or organizations, but also examples.
- The use of boxes, circles or other shapes to differentiate various kinds of information (e.g., circles to represent theories and boxes to represent concepts).
- The use of cross-links which include simple lines, directional arrows or circles to articulate a relationship between the various characteristics, outcomes and concepts/ideas or units.
- The use of linking words (e.g., more, less), shapes (e.g., squares for countries, circles for economic policies) or symbols (e.g., %, +) to explain or elaborate on a particular relationship.
- The structure of the concept map and the nature of the relationships are context dependent.

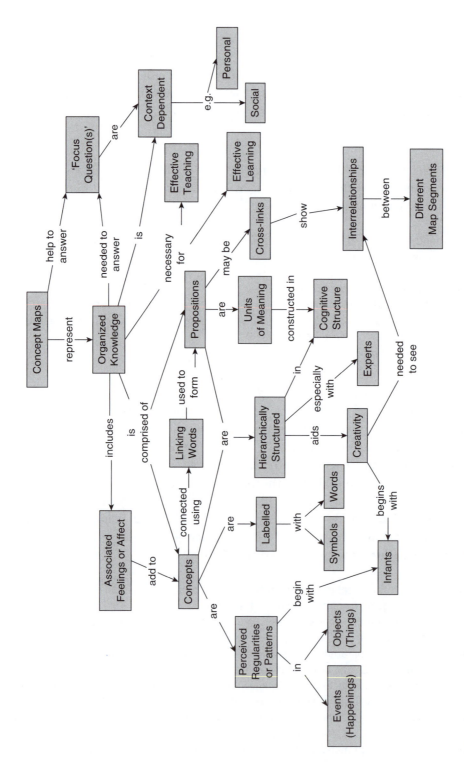

Figure 2.1 A concept map of concept maps

SOURCE: 'A Summary of the Literature Pertaining to the Use of Concept Mapping Techniques and Technologies for Education and Performance Support.' 2003. http://www.ihmc.us/users/acanas/Publications/ConceptMapLitReview/IHMC%20Literature%20Review%20on%20Concept%20Mapping.pdf

Table 2.3   General steps to mind mapping and concept mapping

Steps	Example
1 Start with a central theme Write down all of the characteristics, people, organizations and so forth associated with the central theme	You are interested in 'school readiness', a term used to describe children's literacy, numeracy and socio-emotional development just before they start school. The research that you have reviewed, documents the antecedents of school readiness, and its consequences to children's academic achievement You start to develop a list that you rework into several categories or chunks of information: *Antecedents of school readiness*: Family socioeconomic status – parent education; parent occupation Parent involvement/contact Parenting philosophy Social, family or other support/networks Neighbourhood conditions (e.g., housing, crime rates) Child's cognitive, physical or mental health Parents' cognitive, physical or mental health *Shorter term outcomes*: Transitions to schooling Pre-literacy and pre-numeracy skills Social skills Ability to concentrate or follow direction, routines *Shorter term interventions*: Targeted programmes (e.g., pre- and post-kindergarten school readiness, breakfast programmes) Social, financial and education support for parents *Longer term outcomes*: Grades Self-esteem School engagement Graduation or drop-out rates Postsecondary outcomes Labour market outcomes Physical or mental health Political/community engagement
2 Mind maps start with a central concept	Based on your literature review, start to think about all the characteristics, outcomes or concepts/ideas that help explain 'school readiness' and its consequences

(Continued)

Table 2.3   (Continued)

Steps	Example
Concept maps start off with several concepts, ideas and so forth	Based on your literature review, start to think *across the* spectrum of school readiness. If school readiness is an outcome of family and neighbourhood characteristics and social support for example, what other outcomes (beside school readiness) are associated with these conditions (e.g., children's mental and physical health)?
3 Draw the connections among the elements Mind maps build out from one master concept (e.g., school readiness)	Building out from school readiness, sketch out the various explanations and outcomes that are associated with it. Make connections between the various characteristics, outcomes or other concepts/ideas to demonstrate how they relate to one another (e.g., how school readiness is related to not only poor kindergarten outcomes but also post-secondary chances)
Concept maps have multiple key concepts, each of which is associated with a variety of related ideas or themes that may or may not be directly connected to one another	Start to build characteristics, ideas, people or organizations around each concept. Then draw lines to show how each concept is related to one another, and how ideas, people, organizations and so forth are related (or not) across concepts
	Consider whether using shapes to differentiate types of information or kinds of things represented on your concept map will help the conceptualization process (e.g., squares for people, ovals for organizations)
	Add layers to your concept map including words (e.g., more, less) or symbols about the strength or direction of relationships (e.g., arrows, + or - signs)
4 Now that you have a visual representation of the major elements and relationships associated with your central concept, you can review your map: What is not known, problematic or missing? Answering the 'What is not known, problematic or missing' question will help you not only formulate a research project, but will crystallize the research problem you hope to solve	Are school programmes aimed to address school readiness sufficiently developed? Have they been sufficiently evaluated, or promoted on the basis of limited support? Do the concepts and theories used to explain school readiness adequately capture the multi-dimensional nature of the problem? Or perhaps you find that the relationship between parent education and school readiness has been sufficiently researched, but few have looked at how fostering early home-school connections may ameliorate school readiness disparities

Literature mapping

Similar to mind and concept mapping, in literature mapping the intention is to generate a visual representation. Rather than focusing on key concepts, the point is to map out the literature by theory, methods and data, time period, context, interpretation or emphases, or geography. The goal is to identify similarities, connections, intersections, differences, and even holes in the literature (Table 2.4). These maps can be immensely useful for situating your study within the literature as well as highlighting one or two representative articles, books or reports (Creswell, 2003: 39). Beyond conceptualization, including a literature map (either in the body or as an appendix) in a thesis, article or book can be a very effective tool for all the reasons noted above.

Literature maps have the following characteristics:

- Organized around one central dimension of the literature, several dimensions of the literature or as a multi-hierarchical representation of the literature.
- Literature may be organized in a variety of ways, including by theory or time period.
- Literature may be represented in a manner similar to a mind or concept map or as a chart.
- Literature maps in the spirit of mind or concept maps can use boxes, circles or other shapes to differentiate various kinds of information.
- Literature maps in the spirit of mind or concept maps will use cross-links which include simple lines, directional arrows or circles to articulate a relationship between the various characteristics, outcomes and concepts/ideas or units.

In Figure 2.2 we present an example of a literature map. The example is a thematic literature map and represents a handful of themes in the literature related to the antecedents of school readiness. We could have just as easily organized it by how the literature has developed over time, theories, methods or data.

For the purpose of this exercise, we have kept the content of these examples very simple, but literature maps can become quite rich and complex as they develop over time. Each one of our categories, for example, could be easily decomposed into themes in their own right.

Major Theme	Description	Representative Literature*
Family Conditions	Parental education Parental occupation Parental income Parental mental or physical health Social support	Smith and Jones (2011) Collins (2008) Farhaz, Davis and Moral (2012) Fabb, Cooke and Jacobs (2010) Marion and Saab (2007)
Children	Cognitive and language development Emotional and social development	Lambert, Holland and Davies (2009) Sampson and Robert (2013)
Pre-school Experiences	Construction of time Formal learning opportunities (e.g., preschool) Informal learning opportunities (e.g., literacy enhancing activities at home)	Phillips (2007) Brint, Sutor and Chris (2013) Milne and Later (2005)
Neighbourhood Conditions	Social support Availability of resources Transportation conditions Housing conditions Crime	Parison and Axinn (2005) Xie and Lyndon (2011) *Fictional names

Figure 2.2 Thematic literature map: Antecedents of school readiness

Table 2.4   General steps to a literature map

1   Start to categorize the literature you have found around some broad organizing logic (e.g., by theory, method, time period, etc.)
2   Label each box or row based on your organizing logic (e.g., years 1850-1900)
3   Specify major publications. You may want to add a column that provides some kind of description or detail
4   Consider adding additional layers or rows/columns to include 'sub-sub-topics'
5   In the case of flow chart or 'tree' style literature maps, use lines to connect or signify a shortcoming, strength, or synergy between two or more groupings of the literature

Abbott's lists

In *Methods of Discovery* (2004), Abbott outlines several heuristics or ways to find a researchable topic in the social sciences. One of his suggestions includes using topical lists. We borrow from one of Abbott's lists, Aristotle's four causes, though you may certainly think of others, including the very simple '5 W' list – the who, what, why, where and when – on a particular topic. As Abbott notes, the point of this kind of exercise is to make these lists useful, not to quibble over whether the concept or list is exactly as the original author intended.

Aristotle's four causes

Fundamentally, Aristotle's four causes are about answering 'Why?' questions. Let's return to the Occupy Wall Street example. If you are interested in why the Occupy Wall Street movement failed to generate meaningful changes to the banking system you could play around with how material, formal or structural, effective or final causes contributed to the Occupy Wall Street movement (Table 2.5).

Table 2.5   Aristotle's four causes

Definition	Example: Occupy Wall Street
Material Causes refer to the social, physical or material matter that contributed to the final outcome	Who are the supporters and critics of the Occupy Wall Street movement? What qualities or kinds of people make up each group? Does the Occupy Movement attract a particular kind of person or persons?
Aristotle's examples of material causes include how bronze (the material) is the 'cause' of a statue	
Formal Causes are not about the kinds of people or substance of a particular thing, but rather its social structure or pattern	Does the Occupy Wall Street movement have a particular structural make-up? And was this structural make-up similar to or different from other kinds of social movements?
Effective Causes refer to the primary driver, reason or source of a particular change	How do members describe the early development of the Occupy Wall Street movement?
Final Causes refer to the ultimate goals or purpose for a particular thing	According to members, what are the goals of the Occupy Wall Street movement?

Applied to your own topic of interest, Aristotle's four causes can help researchers generate interesting topics. Perhaps most importantly for seasoned researchers, it can help break out of old habits or ways of thinking – many of which you are probably not aware of. Using this kind of list may help you identify your comfort zone, and push you to think of your topic in less conventional ways.

ESTABLISHING THE PROBLEM

——————————————————— **Key takeaways** ———————————————————

- Identify the intended audience and desired contribution.
- Articulate the foundation of your research problem and address the inherent limitations of that approach.

Before we identify what a research problem is, it is instructive to identify what it is not. The 'problem' we are referring to has nothing to do with the social justice dimension of your project. So simply stating that a financial crisis created a lot of heartache does not sufficiently justify your project. A research problem is also not the same as your research questions. Research questions are specific and focused inquiries that *derive* from the research problem, not the other way around.

Instead, the research problem articulates the gap in the literature or conceptual and analytical shortcoming that you plan on addressing in your project. Articulating the research problem will speak directly to how you will eventually craft your purpose statement since it similarly forces you to articulate 'why you want to do the study and what you intend to accomplish' (Locke et al., 2000). Take a look at most high quality books and articles on your topic. Most, if not all, of them will begin with a summary of the literature, including articulating what is missing or deficient. These articles then discuss how their research makes up for one or more of these limitations. Why? Put simply, if previous research sufficiently addresses the questions or issues you are interested in, then why on earth do we need another study? Fortunately for you, this is rarely the case.

What is my intention?

To answer the 'What is my problem?' question, researchers must first answer the 'What is my intention?' question. The nature of the problem formulation will be very much shaped by the kind of contribution you hope to make, a particular approach to research (e.g., more inductive) and your intended audience. You have to seriously evaluate whether your intended audience is really interested in what you eventually hope to 'sell'. Are you hoping to contribute to the academic or professional literature? Evaluate a policy or programme? Contribute to social reform? And what does your intended audience already know or want to know (Booth et al., 2008: 26)? Only you can answer these questions, but we have provided guidelines in Table 2.6 to start formulating your research intention.

Steps to using the 'What is my intention?' table:

1. Identify your target audience. Your initial target audience will determine the range of early problem formation strategies.
2. Based on your review of relevant literature and other resources, identify a research problem built on what your specific audience already knows and wants to know.
3. Articulate your specific research intention in a way that aligns with your target audience and research problem formation. Ask yourself: Does my research problem formation and potential contribution make sense given my target audience?

Table 2.6   What is my intention?

Possible audience(s)	Possible research problem formation	Possible contributions
• Academics • Professionals	Are interested in building ... • Theoretical frameworks • Concepts • Empirical data • Evaluation	That contributes to ... • Scholarly or professional literature • Programme evaluation • Policy reform • Social reform • Providing new factual information • Solving a practical problem
• Professionals • Policy makers • Group under study • Community group	Are interested in building ... • Concepts • Empirical data • Evaluation	That contributes to ... • Policy reform • Social reform • Providing new factual information • Solving a practical problem
• General public • Popular media	Are interested in building ... • Concepts • Empirical data • Evaluation	That contributes to ... • Policy reform • Social reform • Providing new factual information • Solving practical problems • Popular discourse (e.g., entertainment)

At the beginning stages of any project, it is hard to predict the potential impact of your work. If you are lucky, you may be pleasantly surprised when people beyond your initial target audience like your work, including researchers from other disciplines or the media. Additionally, as you become a more experienced researcher and writer, you will learn how to package your research in a variety of ways. So starting off with a clear target audience, at least in the interim, certainly does not limit a researcher from disseminating his/her findings more widely. However, if you are less experienced, articulating your intended audience and purpose will improve your chances of crafting a project that meets your more immediate research goals, and inform how you write up or present your research. If your primary intention is to affect a policy, then writing up your findings in a manner that relies too heavily on specialized terminology or complicated theories from your discipline will be of little use.

Quick tip: Ask yourself, are all three in alignment?

Use Table 2.6 to answer the following question by linking your audience, your initial problem formation, your intended contribution:

My project targets _____ (e.g., academics) and builds _____ (e.g., X theory). It contributes to the _____ (e.g., literature) by _____ (e.g., demonstrating that the theory may not apply to rural settings as previously thought).

Are all three in alignment? If, for example, your intended audience is a community group, then focusing your problem formation on some esoteric theoretical flaw makes little sense. As we note, as you become more experienced you will be able to repackage your research to reach a variety of audiences, but you should initially have a very clear understanding of your main target. Recognize that each audience has a limited capacity (or desire) for certain kinds of problem formations and contributions.

What is my research problem?

Once you have identified your intention and immediate target audience, the question of how you plan on connecting and contributing to that group looms large. We first discuss five common ways researchers can articulate their research problem. Strengthening your research problem rationale also forces you to orient your project and address gaps in the literature; it may also connect you to a potential research design. However, depending on the approach to qualitative research, the problem formation may be developed at different stages of the project. We do not seek to impose a specific timeline on when the research problem occurs, but rather stress the importance of evolving your research problem formation in a manner that speaks to your audience and to your approach.

The scholarship of me

Key takeaways ---

- The Scholarship of Me occurs when the author is emotionally invested in the topic based on his/her personal experience or identity.
- The key challenge is to communicate the wider significance of the topic. A personal problem is not the same as a research problem unless you are able to communicate its wider scholarly significance.

Many of us are inspired by personal circumstances or experiences such as a family member's occupation, a difficult illness or an event such as a divorce. We are also motivated by practical problems such as how we can prevent another Boston Marathon bombing (e.g., Booth et al., 2008). Yet a personal or practical problem is not the same as a researchable problem that will be of interest to your audience. *Instead, you must build on your inspiration and articulate the conceptual holes in the literature on that topic.* A question about why your parents divorced is completely uninteresting from a research standpoint. However, transforming that interest into a project that examines the antecedents of divorce has the potential to produce a stellar project. Inspired by her own breakup, Diane Vaughan (1986) for example, illustrated how the process of breaking up is a fairly standard and patterned process. She was able to transform the question of 'why did *my* relationship break down' into a question about how relationships 'uncouple' *more generally* (see also Khan, 2012).

To summarize, a personal problem is not the same as a *research problem* unless you are able to communicate its wider *scholarly significance* beyond your personal interests or experiences. In short, you must find a way to transform a 'scholarship of me' project into 'scholarship' in its own right.

The plus one

Key takeaways

- The Plus One approach adds a new case, group or variable.
- The key challenge is to demonstrate that the new addition makes a meaningful extension to the literature.

Most of us engage in what Kuhn (1962) referred to as 'normal science', an addition or extension to the existing literature. The plus one type of project adds a new case, group or variable to an established body of research, including a previously ignored sub-population or dimension of the topic, an emergent or changing population or sub-population, a different time frame, or an event that may have affected the group or organization of interest. In some instances, the emergence of new data or information has called into question previous approaches to your topic. These types of studies are perfectly reasonable and can make a very valuable contribution to the literature either by reinforcing or extending previous research in the area.

Yet adding a new case does not automatically make for an interesting research problem. If previous research on your topic has been largely conducted in the United States, simply adding a Canadian case study is not a good enough problem rationale. *You must first articulate why the new case is a meaningful extension to the literature, why the new case is a suitable addition or why it makes for an interesting point of similarity or comparison.*

To summarize, can you justify how your addition transforms our understanding of the topic through new data, conceptual framework or methodology? Can you convince your audience that the addition makes a significant contribution to the literature or addresses some wider policy or public concern beyond fooling yourself that 'more' or 'new' data must mean 'more' understanding?

Comparisons: Comparing like and unlike things

------------------------------ **Key takeaways** ------------------------------

- The Comparison approach compares like, unlike or deviant cases.
- The key challenge is to recognize the comparative dimensions and demonstrate that the comparison is appropriate. A comparative argument is not the same as a comparative research problem that is supported by a systematic comparative problem formation, research design and analysis.

For the purpose of this chapter, we consider two dimensions of comparative problem formation: i) recognizing the comparative dimension; and ii) demonstrating that the comparison is appropriate (for a similar discussion of representation as it relates to case selection, see Seawright and Gerring, 2008).

Recognizing the (potential) comparative dimensions of your project
Comparative arguments are common in qualitative research; however, the formation of comparative research problems (and design and analysis) are under-utilized. Specifically, when you construct your research problem with an implicit assumption of 'similarity', 'difference' or 'uniqueness', you must give equal weight to the other thing or group that you are implicitly comparing it to. In some cases, the comparative frame will emerge organically; however, in many cases potential comparison groups can be anticipated well in advance, either because it makes practical sense or based on prior knowledge.

Willis' (1977) *Learning to Labour: How Working Class Kids Get Working Class Jobs* is a famous example of a poorly designed 'comparative' argument. Willis followed a group of rowdy and defiant working class boys in an industrial part of England for about three years. Willis' central argument was that the working class students' ('the lads') resistance to school authority was more than teenage antics; it represented their insights into class reproduction. Their 'resistance' to school authority was an attempt to control their labour power, particularly given that working class kids were destined, as the subtitle suggests, for working class jobs. The lads' insights were held up against the radically different approach to that of the 'ear'oles' – the hardworking boys in the class who conformed to schooling authority.

Willis is sketchy on the methodological details, but his analysis suggests that most of his description of the ear'oles came from the lads (rather than from a direct examination of the ear'oles or their families). Most strikingly, had he by chance selected the 12 ear'oles who also hailed from similar working class families rather than the 12 lads for his study he could have arguably made the opposite argument: that working class kids have insights into the potential for human capital accumulation, meritocracy and class mobility. In short, *a comparative argument (or conclusion) is not the same as a comparative research problem that is supported by a systematic comparative problem formation, research design and analysis.*

Demonstrating that the comparison is appropriate

When considering the comparative dimensions of your research problem, you must be able to articulate (and defend) the appropriateness of your choices. We discuss two dimensions of this approach:

- Internally driven comparison.
- Method of agreement and difference.

Internally driven comparison

Internally driven comparisons demand that you demonstrate that the two or more units of interest (e.g., communities, organizations) are similar or different on the *key attribute of interest* or that the case represents a deviation from the norm on *the key attribute of interest.* Hochschild's (2012) famous study is a classic example of the former approach. She compared and contrasted bill collectors and flight attendants; not the most obvious choices! What they do share, however, is that both involve what Hochschild coined 'emotion work', labour that demands the management of feelings. While flight attendants must smile and work hard to inflate passengers' egos, bill collectors are expected to be nasty and deflate their clients' egos. Thus, while the organization of work is very different, in each setting workers must suppress what they really feel in order to elicit a particular response from their clientele.

Method of agreement and method of difference: Outcome driven

Method of agreement and method of difference approaches are similar to internally driven comparisons, but include examining several cases that had a particular outcome and working backwards (Mill, 1843). In the case of method of agreement, researchers isolate the conditions that may explain the generic conditions that led to that outcome in the first place. In the case of method of difference, researchers consider two cases that share many characteristics, but have had a different outcome (e.g., war versus peaceful negotiation). The missing antecedent is used to explain the divergent outcomes and in some cases make causal statements about the conditions that led to them (for discussions of this approach see, e.g., Goldthorpe, 1997; Mahoney, 2000).

Skocpol (1979), for example, famously used the method of agreement to argue that internal pressures and agrarian relations were sufficient causes of peasant revolts in China, France and Russia. She then used the method of difference to argue that countries that did not have these conditions (e.g., England, Prussia) also did not have peasant revolutions (for a discussion see Emigh, 1997; see also Skocpol and Somers, 1980). The countries that she selected varied immensely (e.g., language, culture) but they shared a common outcome, peasant revolt or no peasant revolt, that made them a suitable starting point for comparison (see also Ragin, 1987).

In summary, we stress the importance of considering key sources of similarity or difference, or key sources of deviation in the process of research problem formation.

Evolution

--------------------- **Key takeaways** ---------------------

- The Evolution approach examines a process or change.
- The key challenge is to demonstrate that the process or change makes a meaningful extension to the literature.

Questions that deal with what or how something occurred, how it was experienced, or how group members made sense of a particular event are routinely posed by qualitative researchers. These types of inquiry also span theoretical approaches – from grounded theory to more deductive process tracing (for a discussion see Bennett and Elman, 2006).

Like quantitative researchers, qualitative researchers can examine the process of a particular thing retrospectively; but unlike quantitative researchers, qualitative researchers can examine how something evolves or is experienced in real time. You may, for example, be interested in how patients experience a particular healthcare protocol or how school staff implement a new bullying prevention programme. But why should this be interesting to anyone? Similar to our Plus One discussion above, you must go beyond simply stating that you are going to show how something happened or how it works. In summary, *examining a process or change is only useful if you are able to clearly articulate how it makes a meaningful extension to the literature.*

The challenge: Empirical or theoretical

———————————————— **Key takeaways** ————————————————

- The Challenge approach articulates a conceptual, methodological or theoretical 'gap' or shortcoming.
- The key challenge is to articulate the shortcomings in a manner that is fair and accurate.

———

When articulating your research problem, we note the importance of outlining problems or omissions from the literature. However, *articulating a conceptual, methodological or theoretical gap is not the same as throwing a metaphorical hand grenade and ducking for cover.* Less experienced researchers will often feel like they have to 'pick a team' and demolish the literature with a scathing review or an assertion that 'no one has looked at X problem' before. Such proclamations are often wrong, are less sophisticated and quite frankly are usually not terribly interesting. This is not to say that this tactic is not used, and used quite effectively, but such arguments are usually advanced by someone after years of careful scholarship or *after* a major research discovery. As Firebaugh (2008: 8) notes 'the burden of proof rests with you to identify some shortcoming or flaw that is serious enough to raise questions about the reliability of earlier results. Personal anecdotes are not enough'. We wholeheartedly agree.

In summary, the relative weakness of the literature is more likely based on less than ideal data, substandard data analysis, a failure to capture a dimension of the problem at hand, or new evidence that casts some doubt on the original analysis. A less confrontational approach, such as 'the research on my topic has looked at X, but to date hasn't tended to look at Y dimension of the topic' is a much safer and likely more accurate rendition of the research problem at hand. If you take seriously the questions we pose above you will hopefully avoid this classic mistake by making an informed critique of the literature you hope to contribute to.

CONCLUSION

This chapter outlines concrete tools for conceptualization. To review, we first presented strategies for selecting a topic, including secondary and primary sources and various kinds of concept or literature mapping techniques. Next, we discussed how you can transform your topic into a research problem that is worthy of scholarly investigation. We articulated the importance of determining your audience and developing a clear understanding of the conceptual, theoretical or empirical gaps in the literature. Anticipating and preparing for these questions will improve your research design by forcing you to think about potential weaknesses and conceptual holes that could possibly weaken your project or contaminate the data collection process.

Now that you have the tools you need to select and justify a topic, the next chapter details the mechanics of research design. The chapter is designed to provide you with the tools you need to transform your topic to a researchable research question and project. By the end of the next chapter you will understand how to craft a researchable question, and how to marry this question with the best method for answering it.

KEY TERMS

Comparative Projects	Method of Agreement and Difference	Scholarship of Me Project
Empirical and Theoretical Challenge Projects	Mind and Concept Maps	Secondary Sources
Internally Driven Comparisons	Primary Sources	The Plus One Project
Literature Maps	Research Intention	
Literature Review	Research Problem	

HOW TO DESIGN A QUALITATIVE PROJECT AND CREATE A RESEARCH QUESTION:
SELECTING THE RIGHT TOOLS FOR THE JOB

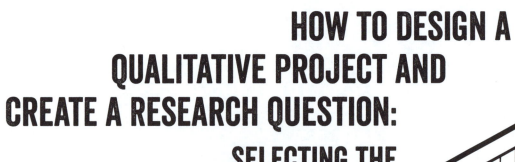

──────────────── **Learning objectives** ────────────────

By the end of this chapter you will have the tools to:

- Design a qualitative research project that spells out the goals of conducting research, articulates the functions of the research questions, and enumerates the methods that connect to your research objective
- Connect your research questions to the structure of your project
- Decide on a sampling strategy
- Write a successful research proposal

──────────────── **Chapter summary** ────────────────

A good research design is one in which all the components work harmoniously together. In contrast, a poor design can end in unfocused research and questionable findings. While it is necessary to plan ahead, qualitative research requires revisiting and modifying your design throughout the research process in response to new developments or problems that arise. We offer a step-by-step guide on how to design your project, but we want to emphasize that we are not offering a formula. You must design a project that takes into account the particularities of the research problem you will address.

INTRODUCTION

> Research is formalized curiosity. It is poking and prying with a purpose. (Hurston, 1942: 143)

Zora Neale Hurston's eloquent turn of phrase captures the heart of conducting qualitative research. While being a good researcher requires openness and curiosity, it also requires a thoughtful and precise plan. In this chapter, we give you a step-by-step guide to designing your study and writing your research proposal.

Once you have conceptualized and mapped out your topic, you are ready to design your research project. That said, we are aware that these two stages are often intermingled. A research design includes decisions about conceptualization, theoretical and methodological considerations, and finally identification of the contribution your research will make to the development of knowledge in a particular area (Cheek, 2008).

In this chapter, we will walk you through the important questions to ask yourself and considerations to take in designing your research project:

Develop a Research Question: Based on the work you've done conceptualizing your research problem, you will need to design a question.

Connect Methods and Question: Mapping out your methodology and connecting them to your research questions ensures you are choosing the right method to answer the question.

Collecting Data: Identifying the strategy you will use is key to ensuring the validity of the data collection plan.

Writing a Proposal: We provide tips on how to write a competitive and competent research proposal to fund your project.

Collaborations With Non-Academic Groups: Collaborations with community and other non-academic groups can offer many benefits and challenges. Here we outline some of the important considerations to avoid collaborations going wrong.

DEVELOPING A RESEARCH QUESTION

If a writer asks no specific *question* worth asking, he can offer no specific *answer* worth supporting it. (Booth et al., 2008: 41)

─────────────────── **Key takeaways** ───────────────────

- Pose only one or two master research questions.
- Limit yourself to three or four sub-questions that are intimately tied to your master question(s).
- Craft neutral questions that avoid imposing assumptions about the nature of the phenomenon under study.
- Make an informed decision to use or not use language that invokes causation (see discussion below).
- The questions should reflect your theoretical approach to qualitative research.
- Your questions must be *researchable*.

In this section we examine the formulation of research questions in qualitative research. We link these questions to several qualitative approaches. We then offer guidelines for evaluating the merits of your research question.

Guidelines for crafting qualitative research questions

Instead of posing closed questions (e.g., Does X cause Y?), qualitative researchers *typically* develop questions that allow for more inductive intellectual inquiry (Creswell, 2003: 105; Maxwell, 2013). We say 'typically' because there are traditions that do examine a qualitative version of causation which we discuss below. This does not mean that 'anything goes'; in fact the questions should align with the topic (obviously) and may also speak to a research problem that you may have already identified (perhaps less obviously).

We present four parameters for crafting qualitative research questions:

a) Number of questions.
b) Degree of openness and neutrality.

c) Theoretical approach.
d) Evaluating your research questions.

Number of questions
Required: One or two master questions
The master question orients the project in a manner that is consistent with the project's methodological (qualitative, quantitative or mixed-methods) and theoretical or paradigmatic approach. Like others (Creswell, 2003; Miles and Huberman, 1994), we recommend articulating only one or two 'master' questions to guide your inquiry. Unlike quantitative research, your master question(s) may evolve or change completely; however, these questions will guide your initial research design. The nature of your questions and the degree of flexibility will be determined in part by your theoretical approach discussed below.

Optional: Up to three or four sub-questions per master question
Though not required, each master question may be followed up with three or four sub-questions that are *intimately* tied to it and the subsequent data collection strategy. While master questions tend to be more open and broad, sub-questions are meant to flag specific dimensions of the master question. In short, sub-questions are not the place where you get to articulate every single question you ever had about the project. When developing sub-questions, you must continually integrate them: Do they meaningfully extend the original master question? Or do they potentially take the project into a different direction?

Others (e.g., Creswell, 2003; Miles and Hubeman, 1994) allow for more sub-questions; however, we suggest no more than three or four to enhance the likelihood that the project stays focused and on-track, a task which in our experience is particularly challenging for novice researchers. Well-read and experienced researchers are positioned to add more sub-questions in line with more generous recommendations.

Degree of openness and neutrality
Qualitative researchers usually have to strike a balance between crafting a research question that focuses the project on a specific phenomenon while at the same time allowing for more inductive inquiry. Openness often also relates to crafting 'neutral' questions, though there are exceptions to this position as we discuss below. For the purpose of qualitative research, neutrality has two dimensions: a) assumptions about the nature of phenomenon under study; and b) causation.

Avoid building in assumptions about the nature of the phenomenon under study
The first and most obvious point is to ensure that your question does not impose a particular set of assumptions on the topic you are interested in studying, including its *nature*

(e.g., good or evil), *conditions* (e.g., happy or sad) or its relative *quality* (e.g., better or worse). Equally important is to avoid language that implies direction (e.g., affect) or hierarchical ordering (e.g., more than).

Example 1: Assumptions about nature, condition or quality

Question: 'How do cohabiting couples cope with the stigma associated with living together?'
    The question assumes that cohabiting couples:

*   experience stigma;
*   have or require coping strategies;
*   experience stigma or have or require coping strategies that are unique to cohabiting couples.

A better question would still allow you to explore these possibilities (e.g., stigma), while still remaining open to a variety of experiences, meanings or outcomes for participants, such as 'How do couples conceptualize and experience cohabitation?'.

Example 2: Assumptions about direction or hierarchical ordering

Question: Do cohabitating non-married couples face greater financial troubles than cohabitating married couples?
    The question assumes:

*   that non-married and married couples have financial troubles in the first place;
*   that 'marriage status' defines the group (since you may find that other characteristics such as education or religion are more important to defining a group and how they relate to money).

Although you may find some or all of it to be true *after* you collect your data, your question should not prematurely impose assumptions about the group or thing under study. In fact, qualitative researchers routinely use language that implies direction, hierarchical ordering and process causality at *later* stages of the data collection and analysis (e.g., statements about how a particular event mattered more than others or fundamentally shaped an outcome). However, we recommend that researchers should avoid building these assumptions into their research questions. A better question such as 'How do cohabiting and married couples understand their financial wellbeing?' would still allow you to explore whether cohabiting couples have more (or less) financial troubles than married couples; however, it would allow you to remain open to the possibility that both groups are more similar than you originally thought, that married couples may experience more financial troubles than non-married cohabiters, or that other characteristics (e.g., education) are more important to how couples organize their finances or perceive financial 'trouble'.

    There are some exceptions to this rule, including when a statement is not merely an assumption, but backed by a substantial body of research. However, you still have to be careful about the historical, contextual, geographical or other nature of this research and the very real danger of limiting your scope of inquiry. If researchers in the area of cohabitation had continued to rest on previous research, they might have failed to see *declining* stigma associated with cohabitation or that non-married *and* married cohabitating couples experience many of the same challenges.

Becker's (1953) study on marijuana smoking is a classic example. Rather than assuming that some people are predisposed to marijuana use based on some collection of established demographic or individual characteristics, Becker found that whether an individual uses marijuana or derives pleasure from it is largely a function of learning to smoke it in a manner that produces a pleasurable effect that is seen to be linked to the drug. In so doing, Becker was able to see that motivation and ability to get high on marijuana were acquired through a process of social interaction with other users.

Make an informed decision: 'Causation'

Qualitative researchers vary on whether questions should invoke causation. Delving into the nuances of this debate is beyond the scope of this chapter. Instead, we present them as two options that serve different purposes and speak to different approaches to qualitative research. Option 1 comes from the school of thought that research questions and research more generally should avoid any notion of causation. Option 2 invokes a *qualitative* notion of 'causation' that differs greatly from traditional positivist definitions. This approach is captured by 'process' or 'realist' theories and approaches to qualitative research. We spend more time on this discussion as a way to introduce and inform our readers, especially given the dominance of Option 1 in the literature and the fact that many qualitative researchers invoke process or realist approaches without even realizing it, either from the outset or in their conclusions.

Option 1: Avoid language of causation

Creswell (2003: 107) and others advance the position that qualitative researchers should avoid using terms such as 'why', 'affect', 'determine' or 'relate' that imply causation. This option typically avoids direct reference to theory or the literature. In some cases it is about retooling your questions in a manner that still speaks to this topic and to a particular theoretical approach.

Example

Original question: What effect does divorce have on children?

Retooled question: How do children experience divorce?

Option 2: Process theory – build in (qualitative) notions of causation

'Causation' has been particularly controversial, and rejected based on the assumption that it violates most qualitative research paradigms. Yet, when qualitative researchers invoke the term 'cause' or 'causation' they are referring to a 'process' or 'realist', not a positivist, notion of causation. Process theory (also referred to as 'realist' and 'generative' theory) sees the value in asking research questions that orient the project toward identifying the unique situations, historical events, sequences and even values, intentions and meaning-making that led to a particular outcome or condition (Maxwell, 2012: 656; see also the discussion of method of agreement and method of difference in Chapter 2). Process approaches to causation are grounded in thick description and an in-depth examination of meaning, contexts, and social, cultural and institutional mechanisms (Maxwell, 2012). The context shapes not only whether a particular causal process or mechanism matters or not (e.g., whether adding or subtracting a variable matters), but fundamentally shapes the nature of the process or mechanism itself (see also Anderson and Scott, 2012; Maxwell, 2004a).

Below we provide an example to further emphasize the difference between variant-theory and process-theory. While the variant-theory question focuses on measuring differences and explanatory variables between younger and older PhD graduates, the process-theory question seeks to understand the process by which a particular decision was made. The difference is subtle, but important. And like Option 1 above, we also suggest avoiding language such as 'effect', 'affect' or 'relate' at the outset since it implies a quantitative rather than a qualitative notion of causation.

Example

Variant-theory question: Do older PhD graduates select non-academic career options more so than younger PhD graduates, and if so, what explains this?

Process-theory question: How do PhD candidates make decisions about whether they enter non-academic or academic career paths? Do older and younger students differ in how they make decisions?

Process questions, as you can see from above, are commonly generated when we ask 'what?' and 'how?' types of questions in qualitative research. And our conclusions, in the spirit of qualitative (not positivistic) sense of the term causation often invoke a particular sequencing (or direction) or hierarchical ordering of events to explain how and even why something occurred according to how our participants come to understand, act and interact according to their definitions. This approach is very much in line with qualitative ontologies and epistemologies (Maxwell, 2012).

Variance-theory versus process-theory

Researchers in this tradition make a clear distinction between variance-theory and process-theory. Variance-theory 'deals with variables and the correlations among them found in experimental, survey or other quantitative research designs' (Maxwell, 2004a: 4; see also Mohr, 1982). This is the traditional or positivistic understanding of examining correlation or causation, whether one (independent) variable makes a change in the other (dependent) variable. For qualitative researchers, this definition is rightly like fitting a square peg into a round hole (Maxwell, 2012).

In contrast, process-theory is something supporters such as Miles and Huberman (1994: 147) argue that qualitative methods are uniquely positioned to do; qualitative methods 'with its close-up look, can identify *mechanisms*, going beyond sheer associations. It is unrelentingly *local*, and deals well with the *complex* network of events and processes in a situation'. In other words, causal mechanism and a particular effect are not static, but rather highly context dependent. As illustrated by Anderson and Scott (2012: 679), rethinking causality as a process rather than as relationships between variables allows us to think about *indirect* causality:

> For instance, we know that social class correlates highly with academic achievement. Academic achievement rises as family incomes rise (not necessarily the other way around). Does this mean that poverty 'causes' school failure for poor children? Most researchers would say no. However, although poverty does not directly cause low achievement, its effects do. In other words, there is often a series of chains of effects that result in low academic achievement (e.g., poor neighborhoods are saddled with toxic waste, causing more asthma among poor children, causing students to miss more days of school, causing lower achievement for poor children). Moreover, poor neighborhoods experience higher rates of violent crime, HIV infection and death, percentage of population incarcerated or with felony convictions preventing their ability to vote or secure reliable employment, and homelessness. Like a trail of breadcrumbs, a chain of causes and effects lead from low achievement back to poverty, and ultimately, to structural inequality.

The method of agreement and method of difference discussed in Chapter **2** is a clear example of process-theory. This approach is designed to identify the necessary or sufficient conditions that led to (or caused) a particular outcome (Mahoney, 2000). Similarly, as Mahoney (2000) points out, research like Skocpol's relies on 'ordinal comparisons' – the process of ranking of conditions, things or categories based on their pervasiveness or presence. However, qualitative researchers develop 'propositions' rather than hypotheses. Propositions are provisional statements about the workings or connections that are developed *after* rather than before data collection and analysis is well under way (Miles and Huberman, 1994: 75).

Theoretical approach: The nature of inquiry

Qualitative research ranges from approaches that examine the mechanisms that underlie a particular theory (see process-theory above) to those that avoid at least the appearance of anything beyond being 'theoretically sensitive'. The nature of your questions is related to the theoretical approach (see discussion below).

Evaluating your questions: Knowing the good, the bad and the ugly

> The connection between research question and philosophy is the match between what the researcher wants to understand and what exists and can be known. (Trede and Higgs, 2009: 17)

What constitutes a good question will be determined by one or more factors, including the project's purpose, your disciplinary aims and your theoretical approach. A normative question such as whether it is good or bad to allow a terminally ill patient to end her life is perfectly reasonable within a discipline such as philosophy that ponders what is desirable or optimal. However, we expect social scientists, regardless of their theoretical approach, to ask 'researchable' questions that can be answered through the collection and analysis of one or more sources of data. So rather than pondering whether euthanasia is good or bad, qualitative researchers might instead ask questions about why some groups support it in the first place. Good researchable research questions orient the project, inform appropriate data and methods, and provide the researcher with some parameters.

When determining whether a question is 'researchable', social scientists should ask themselves whether their proposed study is feasible, interesting and has the potential to make a contribution. Questions of worth address the fundamental contribution of the research study. Questions of quality or appropriateness on the other hand attack the merits of the research design, working definitions and data analysis. These questions are not only critical for determining the viability of any project, but versions of them are standard fare at most thesis proposals and thesis defences (Table 3.1).

Table 3.1   Checklist for determining a researchable question

Feasibility

1   Can I answer my question? Or are there aspects of my question that are virtually impossible to answer?
2   What kind of data will I need to answer my question? Are there appropriate data available? And will I have access to those data?
3   Do I have the resources (time and money) to gather the data I need in order to answer my research questions?
4   Are my research questions or data required to answer my research questions ethical?
5   Does my question make sense? Is my question too narrow or complicated? Is my question based on an empirical, theoretical or policy problem?

Interest, contribution and potential criticisms

6   Will my research questions accommodate (possibly inconvenient) surprises?
7   Will my research questions allow me to accommodate findings that challenge conventional wisdom?
8   Has my question already been asked before, and if so what will I add to the literature?
9   Do established people in the field think my research question is interesting?
10   What are the potential criticisms or potential flaws with the kind of question I am considering asking (e.g., focusing too much on consumers and not enough on sellers)?

Feasibility: Questions 1–5

The first five questions have to do with the basic feasibility of your study. These questions address whether the question has inherently unknowable qualities (e.g., whether dogs go to heaven), is limited by the knowledge that is currently available (e.g., whether condom use will decline once there is a cure for HIV), or by the kind of access to the population or data that you need to answer your question. You must be realistic as to whether you have the money, time, skills or credentials to carry out your project to the end. A study on the Spanish Revolution that requires you to travel to Spain and dig through mountains of archival material makes little sense if you do not have the resources to spend an extended period of time living in Spain, nor the language proficiency to read and interpret documents (for a discussion see Firebaugh, 2008).

Equally important for qualitative researchers is whether your population or organization of interest is willing to participate in your study. It makes no sense to build an entire project around a particular group if that group flat-out denies you access to its members or other materials that you need to answer your research question. A preliminary literature review and pilot project will go a long way in helping you determine whether the study is doable given the scope, access and resources required to execute the project (see Chapter 2). Some research has to be ruled out simply because it is unethical. A study that requires similar methods to Laud Humphrey's (1970) famous *Tearoom Trade* (e.g., participant observation of sex acts in public bathrooms) will be rejected on ethical grounds not only because of the potential harm to participants, but also to protect the researcher.

Finally, you need to consider whether your question makes sense. Is it too narrow or complicated? A narrow question that examines the perceptions of texting while dining out with friends may generate too few types of responses (e.g., rude, not rude or indifferent) to generate a meaningful analysis (Creswell, 2003: 105). Similarly, a complicated question suffers from the opposite problem, and muddies the project by confusing your audience (and often the researcher) about the central aims of the project. You also have to consider whether it generates a 'straw person', a logical fallacy based on the misreading, misinterpretation or generation of an empirical, theoretical or policy issue. In other words, is your question based on something that actually exists?

Here is an example of a research question sent by a student at the beginning stages of a research project. What he initially asked was: 'Is being physically active the only way to stay fit and does being unfit really constitute a learning deficiency?' The first part of the question implies that there is another way to be 'fit' other than through physical activity (unless of course he was referring to another kind of 'fit', such as being emotionally or cognitively fit, which he was not). The second part of the question implies that the literature and/or policies define being unfit as a learning deficiency, which it does not. This kind of question is un-researchable simply because the question formulation is so poor, both in terms of pitting two things that are essentially the same (being fit and physical fitness) and another thing that does not exist (defining poor physical fitness as a learning disability). After much discussion, we formulated the question he *really* intended to ask all along which was: 'Does poor physical fitness affect young children's learning?' Unlike the first question, this question has a clear focus and is researchable. And for his purposes (a second year research paper), the question oriented the paper toward a mountain of literature on the relationship between physical fitness and academic achievement.

Interest, contribution and potential criticisms: Questions 6–10

Four of the last five questions have to do with whether your research questions will help you advance a project that is interesting and that makes a contribution. In particular, unless your aim is to advance a very particular cause, social science research questions should be designed to accommodate unconventional findings. For qualitative researchers, the potential for surprises is often hardwired into their research questions to allow for inductive inquiry (see the Robert Wood Johnson Foundation (2014) website). 'Surprises' can come in many forms, including inconvenient, weaker or stronger findings than you would have otherwise expected (Firebaugh, 2008). You may also be hit with findings that assault your personal experiences, beliefs or morals.

Based on your own experience, for example, you may be convinced that contrary to popular belief, children of divorce do not fare worse than children who grow up in intact families (e.g., self-esteem, academic outcomes). You may also have the benefit of drawing on more recent quantitative research that seems to suggest that you are right. Yet, when you're setting up your project, you have to be cognizant of framing your research questions in a manner that allows for a variety of outcomes, including the possibility that your assumptions are wrong or highly contextually dependent (e.g., material conditions in the home).

The last question has to do with considering how others will perceive your research questions. If you are asking a well-established question in the literature (e.g., What is the connection between academic achievement and social class?), you must articulate your research questions in a manner that demonstrates that you are making a meaningful extension to this question whether it be through novel data or data collection methods, examining a different dimension of the problem and so forth, since your research question will ultimately orient your entire project, including your research design. Answering this question is not so clear cut. When posing potential research questions to experts in your field you will undoubtedly receive a range of responses.

CONNECTING YOUR METHODS AND RESEARCH QUESTION

————————————————— Key takeaways —————————————————

- A coherent research design requires connecting research questions to methods, and ensuring that the different methods fit together.
- Determining and justifying your sample depends on the objectives of your research and how they connect to existing theory. Sampling relies on a 'purposeful' design.

Your research design needs to be clearly defined to articulate coherence between research questions and methods. It is important to be cognizant of the fact that the methods you use to collect your data are not necessarily a 'logical deduction' from your research questions (Maxwell, 2013). Instead, think about how your methods will enable you to answer your research questions. You will need to decide what types of data you will gather, the structure of your research design, and the population(s) and/or texts your sample will include. We outline considerations for each of these decisions in this section.

Types of data

In the following chapters, we give you detailed information about how to gather different types of qualitative data. Here we offer a brief overview of considerations you need to think about in connecting your research question(s) and design.

In-depth interviews

Key to the commonly employed method of in-depth interviews is its focus on the individual. Research questions that seek to understand people's feelings and experiences, including perspectives on family, work and social life, are a good match for this method. In-depth interviews allow you to explore a wide range of activities, 'from illegal border crossing to becoming a paid assassin' (Rubin and Rubin, 2012: 3). They are the only method for collecting data when you are seeking to understand the perspectives of individuals contextualized within their own history and/or experiences. In-depth interviews facilitate the comprehensive exploration of multifaceted issues, allowing you to connect these to personal circumstances (Ritchie and Lewis, 2003). This method frequently takes the form of semi-structured interviews: the researcher directs the content to be discussed while allowing participants to shift ideas in new but related directions. The goal is to identify themes and higher-order patterns – relationships among themes – and to explain and theorize them.

Example

Elliot Weininger and Annette Lareau (2014) conducted 87 in-depth interviews with parents of young children from a large Northeastern US city and its surrounding suburbs. Their research question asked about the decision-making processes of families from different backgrounds in choosing particular neighbourhoods in which to live. Interviews allowed Weininger and Lareau to uncover the importance of networks in this decision-making process.

Focus groups

Focus group research has become more common as a social scientific methodology in recent decades. It involves a small group of people with common characteristics and/or experiences who participate in discussions about a topic, guided by a moderator. Group discussion relies profoundly on interactions and conversations between participants, distinguishing it from individual in-depth interviews that focus solely on individual meanings and perspectives. This method is especially useful in settings and situations where a 'one-shot collection' is necessary, the research topic is culturally sensitive, or research participants come from marginalized backgrounds (Berg and Lune, 2012). Group discussion allows participants to refine their thoughts, and it provides data that is created through conversations with others (Ritchie and Lewis, 2003). Focus groups are especially suited to attitudinal research where the group can discuss or debate the nuances and differences of their perspectives, providing a forum where these differences can be explicitly addressed. This contextual backdrop facilitates reflection and allows participants to better articulate their reasoning and beliefs. Interactional group discussions can spur creative thinking, and facilitate the identification of solutions.

Example

Verta Taylor and Leila Rupp (2003) set out to study how drag-queen performances in Key West, Florida, are political in their ability to contest conventional thinking about gender and sexuality. To answer this question, one important component was to understand how audience members, both heterosexuals and non-heterosexuals, understood the drag-queen performances. They conducted 12 focus groups with 40 audience members who had attended the show. Half were women and half men, and 70% identified as lesbian, gay or bisexual. These groups' discussions allowed them to assess how audience members viewed the performances as a challenge to conventional thinking.

Field research

Field research, also referred to as ethnography and participant observation, is the methodology of choice for projects in which the research question focuses on processes, events and relationships. It requires immersion in and systematic observation of the social life of a group or culture for a prolonged period of time, and writing extensive notes based on these observations and experiences (Hammersley and Atkinson, 1995). Observation enables researchers to gain knowledge of perspectives, behaviours and cultural diversity, of meaning-making systems, and of the changes to social worlds and cultures over time. Collecting observational data can vary from a more open-ended approach that seeks to find patterns to a more closed tactic that seeks confirmation of patterns. Field research can be participatory, where the researcher becomes an accepted member of the community, or non-participatory, where the researcher remains an outsider who observes systematically without interacting with participants.

Example

Melanie Heath (2012) conducted research on the social consequences of marriage promotion policies in the United States. The idea of promoting marriage as a solution to intergenerational poverty among poor, single mothers has been highly contested in the United States, but at the time of her research there had been no in-depth research on what was happening on the ground. Heath conducted extensive field research for 11 months to discover many unintended consequences, including the fact that the services were not targeting poor women, and, that when they did reach the target population, these efforts often had a negative impact.

Unobtrusive methods

Unobtrusive methods allow you to answer research questions that address how societies log or record information concerning social behaviour. This method involves no direct contact with the study participants, and tends to be combined with other methods in social scientific research. Data can include print and non-print materials (Baker, 2008). Print materials comprise current and archival documents, such as historical pamphlets, diaries, letters, newspapers, government documents and census data, among others. Researchers might analyse photographs, paintings, graffiti and sheet music. Textbooks could be another data source. Non-print data includes various forms of technology-generated communications, such as tweets, chat rooms, listservs and blogs. Audiotapes, films, television and videos can also provide interesting data for understanding behaviour and social and cultural patterns. The lack of face-to-face contact that unobtrusive methods allow can provide more reliable information, especially when you are studying a sensitive topic.

Example

Laurel Westbrook and Kristen Schilt set out to study how social and cultural beliefs determine gender in various social spaces and to develop the idea of 'gender determination', using reactions to transgender rights legislation (2014: 38). To analyse these social behaviours, they determined that a content analysis of media articles would contribute to the literature by theorizing gender determination 'beyond face-to-face interactions through an analysis of policy and law debates and imagined interactions, situations that often display a call for explicit criteria for deciding who counts as a man or as a woman' (2014: 38).

What is the structure of my research design?

Decisions about the research design flow from the research questions and help to determine the structure of the research project. In considering the structure of your project, you must decide on the role of case studies and of comparisons. You must also consider whether your study will be longitudinal and whether you will use a mixed methodology. We outline these four components below.

Case study

A case study approaches one or a few instances of a phenomenon to study them in depth. While there is much disagreement about exactly what constitutes a case study, we offer the definition of Jane Ritchie and Jane Lewis, who argue that the primary defining features are

> multiplicity of perspectives which are rooted in a specific context (or in a number of specific contexts if the study involves more than one case). Those multiple perspectives may come from multiple data collection methods, but they may also derive from multiple accounts - collected using a single method from people with different perspectives on what is being observed. (2003: 52)

Case studies are structured around context rather than individuals, as would be the focus of an in-depth interview project. You might design a case study based on a process (e.g., the phenomenon of cyberbullying, with the case involving perpetrators, victims and parents), or an organization/institutional context (e.g., the child sexual abuse crisis in the Catholic church, with the case involving the Vatican (such as statements), bishops, priests and victims).

One of the main strengths of the case study approach is its ability to capture multiple perspectives and to build a more in-depth understanding of a phenomenon or phenomena. The definition of case study overlaps with ethnography, field research and participant observation. Karen O'Reilly (2008) argues that the key difference is methodology: the defining feature of ethnography or field research is its incorporation of participant or non-participant observation (among other methods, such as in-depth interviews), whereas a case study can include a mixed-methods approach which can also involve quantitative and statistical elements (see below for our discussion of mixed methods).

In designing a case study project, the first important step is to determine the social context(s) of your research to help select your case or cases. Again, your research question(s) are key in guiding these decisions. There may be differences in the populations you will study in each case, and you will need to choose how consistent the selection of groups of people and/or organizations will be. Too many cases can lead to a very large sample size. You must ask yourself: How feasible is a project with multiple cases or that includes multiple populations? Can you complete the project in a timely manner? Do you have the funding to be successful? What are the compromises you need to make in attaining breadth over depth to answer your research question and design a feasible research project? (See our discussion below on 'What will your sample consist of?')

Example

Suzanne Staggenborg (2001) studied the relationship between culture and politics in the women's movement. Her research design offered a case study of feminist action in Bloomington, Indiana, from the 1960s to the 1990s. She outlined how her choice of site influenced her findings concerning the processes in which women's movements evolve and endure. In particular, the local movement in Bloomington encompassed a 'political field' (Ray, 1999), shaped by Indiana University, a university town of about 90,000 residents. Staggenborg noted that, while Indiana is a conservative state, the presence of the university in Bloomington provided a liberalizing effect on local movements. Thus, Bloomington as a case would shed light on the advantages and disadvantages for mobilizing that would affect the possible kinds of activism. She concluded, 'The site is a good place to examine the effects of culture-building on the larger women's movement' (2001: 511).

Comparative research

Comparison is central to empirical social science and involves evaluating the associations and differences between phenomena. Most qualitative research incorporates some form of comparative research. For example, comparisons are often made in ethnographic studies of core categories or themes. Comparative research is frequently built into the research design, such as case study comparisons, comparative political research, historical comparative research, and comparisons based on content and discourse analysis (unobtrusive measures). Comparisons may also emerge inductively between groups during the analytical process.

The fundamental goal of comparative research is to uncover correspondence and variance between the elements being compared. Qualitative approaches to comparative research focus on understanding similarity and difference, whereas quantitative methodical approaches place emphasis on measuring differences. The advantage of designing a comparative study is summed up by Melinda Mills: 'Comparisons not only uncover differences between social entities but also reveal unique aspects of a particular entity that would be virtually impossible to detect otherwise' (2008: 101).

Quick tip: Considerations for designing comparative research (Ritchie and Lewis, 2003)

A comparative research design is the right match if your goal is to:

- Isolate the presence or absence of an entity among different cases.
- Identify whether and how phenomena vary between groups.
- Compare social processes across times and places.
- Explain how the presence or social consequences of an entity vary between groups.
- Compare the variations and interactions of phenomena in different social contexts.

Deciding on the cases or sample is an important component of comparative research (Ebbinghaus, 2005). Generally speaking, the selection of cases should be theory driven (e.g., theorizing multiculturalism through a comparative study of policies in Canada, Australia, the United States and the United Kingdom). Charles Ragin (2006) notes that many social scientists choose their populations for comparative research based on taken-for-granted categories. These 'given' populations, such as research comparing registered voters in New York and Los Angeles, are beneficial when conducting descriptive research, but he calls for giving greater attention to theoretically driven understandings of populations. Constructing understandings of populations can offer a more nuanced and innovative research design, such as comparative research on anti-colonial movements in the 20th century, which requires theoretical articulation to advance meaningful categories.

The comparative method can be an important tool that enables qualitative researchers to make causal inferences. Comparison can allow you to test the 'counterfactual' of what would have happened if the presence of the presumed cause were absent (Maxwell, 2004b: 253). Causal relationships are also important in comparative historical research, a method that analyses historical events to build explanations beyond a particular time and place, either through direct comparison to other historical/recent events or by building theory. This method focuses on historical sequences and their causes across a set of similar cases.

While comparative research offers many benefits to a research design, it also presents challenges. For example, deciding on the scale of your project presents a conundrum. Choosing a small sample size can, on the one hand, allow for descriptive depth, but, on the other, can mean too many comparative factors that get in the way of identifying competing causal models or explanations. A larger sample size (e.g., countries, cases) that only allows for more general comparative characteristics risks superficial findings (Mills, 2008). Again, designing your research is a continuous process that must be negotiated throughout the data collection and analysis phases. You must remain flexible to change your design if your sample proves to be too small or too large (see below for a detailed discussion of choosing your sample).

No matter what method or combination of methods you decide on for your project, you will want to consider carefully how comparative research might strengthen your research design. Comparison provides an entry point to numerous topics that allow you to incorporate multiple types of qualitative methods.

Example

Michèle Lamont (1992) set out to study how middle class men in France and the United States differentiate between people who they believe have greater or lesser worth. She employed the comparative method to uncover differences within the national samples on the basis of region (New York and Indianapolis in the United States, and Paris and Clermont-Ferrand in France), occupation (profit and public sectors) and mobility (first and third generation upper middle class). Her comparative model allowed her to illuminate national differences. It also provided evidence of similar patterns in the two countries based on the increasing importance of socioeconomic boundaries.

Single episode or longitudinal research?

Another factor to consider in designing your project is whether data will need to capture changes over time and/or a sequence of events. One solution for research that will be collected in a single episode is to rely on retrospective accounts. Retrospective interviews offer participants the opportunity to tell their stories about some event from beginning to end and can help identify processes and sequencing. You might consider using specifically designed calendars or diaries for participants to record their thoughts and reactions to a series of questions over time.

There are shortcomings, however, to this strategy. The quality of the data may be compromised by 'problems with recall, distortion and post-event rationalisation' (Ritchie and Lewis, 2003: 53). If the evolution of events or the processes being recorded are a central component of your research, and the data represents complex sequencing or long time-spans, a single episode of data collection may not be sufficient.

Longitudinal studies can be an answer to this problem by including more than one episode of data collection. Longitudinal designs are prevalent in quantitative research, but are becoming more common among qualitative research as investigators acknowledge the importance of understanding changes in people's lives. There are two general forms of longitudinal research. First, panel studies are built on the idea of interviewing the same participants more than once. Second, repeat cross-sectional studies interview successive samples of new respondents (Ritchie and Lewis, 2003).

Qualitative panel studies shed light on micro-level variation among individuals (Ritchie and Lewis, 2003). For example, they can investigate individual biographies over time, such as orientations and action strategies of participants. The fundamental idea is to capture participants' reactions and thoughts as they arise after a period of reflection. Mostly, panel studies seek to capture change over a long timespan to illuminate particular outcomes and social consequences that are difficult to uncover in a single episode of interviews or focus groups. The goal is not to measure change, which is the objective of panel studies in survey research. A qualitative panel design allows you 'to describe the different types of changes that take place or the different outcomes that result, to account for them by showing how they arise, and to explain how and why there are differences between sample members' (Ritchie and Lewis, 2003: 54).

Cross-sectional studies focus on macro-level change and the broader social context in which these evolutions take place (Ritchie and Lewis, 2003). You might use a cross-sectional design to study what shapes attitudes about immigration, for example. A longitudinal panel study would allow you to specify changing attitudes, how they have developed, and the social consequences.

Qualitative longitudinal research has many benefits, including creating a more nuanced understanding of change and greater narrative depth over time. There are also challenges. It is difficult to anticipate the obstacles to conducting second or more interventions when qualitative research tends to demand more time and commitment on the part of participants than survey research. Multiple interventions may also be more difficult to fund. Still, the potential of this method to obtain rich, dynamic and contextualized accounts of people's experiences over time cannot be discounted.

Example

Virginia Morrow and Gina Crivello (2015) worked with a team of researchers who gathered data on 'Young Lives', a longitudinal study investigating childhood poverty in Ethiopia, Peru, India and Vietnam over 15 years. The goal was to uncover the causes and consequences of childhood poverty and the role of policies in improving children's life chances. Data were gathered quantitatively and qualitatively from two cohorts of children in each country. The qualitative component has to date four waves and involves 200 children, their caregivers and other key figures. These researchers consider factors influencing households moving into and out of poverty, and the consequences for children. Data collected allowed the researchers to map out aspects of children's lives in ways not possible in cross-sectional research, including how the dynamics of poverty influence children's lives over time.

Quick tip: Considerations for longitudinal research (Ritchie and Lewis, 2003)

A good longitudinal design will include consideration of the following:

- **Number of interventions and timing.**
  - o   These are guided by your research questions and objective.
- **Initial sample size.**
  - o   For panel studies, you will need to address the possibility of attrition.
- **The right methods for a longitudinal design.**
  - o   In-depth interviews with their individual focus are better suited to panel studies.
  - o   Focus groups are better attuned to gathering contextual and group information.
- **Selecting the follow-up sample.**
  - o   Whether to include the entire first-stage sample in subsequent interventions.
  - o   Whether to use a purposive sample (see the section below on sampling) to study particular issues or groups of people.
- **Analysis of all stages of data collection.**
  - o   Planning ahead how you will integrate later stages of data to facilitate comparisons and analyse evolutions.

Using multiple methods

Qualitative researchers frequently collect data using multiple methods. The term 'mixed methods' can refer to the incorporation of qualitative and quantitative approaches in a single study, but the term can also be applied to mixing different qualitative methods to carry out an investigation that draws on the strengths of each. We highlight three purposes for mixing methods and discuss the challenges that a mixed-method research design presents.

First, *triangulation* – the incorporation of multi-methods to reduce deficiencies of a one-method approach – can be a strategy to strengthen your research design. This approach also allows for a deeper understanding of the issues you are studying. You might combine different sources of data (e.g., official documents, interview data, field notes), and different methods of collecting data (e.g., formal and informal interviews, participant observation, anonymous questionnaires). You can also triangulate data collection by gathering accounts from different participants in a prearranged setting, from different phases of activities in a singular setting, and from different sites of the setting. In this sense, triangulation involves cross-checking the consistency of data across settings, participants and at different times. We discuss in depth the importance of triangulation as a way to ensure validity below in 'Step 3. "What is the nature of the data I will collect?"'.

Second, you might choose to incorporate multiple methods to broaden the range of data you collect rather than as just a way to strengthen your conclusions. For example, observation is often combined with interviews to shine light on how events or behaviours naturally occur and how they are constructed through individual understandings of behaviour. Thus, while interviewing provides an efficient way to learn about people's perspectives, conducting observation can allow you to draw inferences on these perspectives that would not be possible if you were to rely solely on interview data (Maxwell, 2013). Employing a mixed-methods approach can help uncover tacit meanings and elicit data that respondents might be reluctant to divulge in a more structured interview setting.

Finally, combining qualitative and quantitative methods (a specific kind of triangulation) builds on the strengths of both approaches to address specific research problems. Employing quantitative and qualitative research can bridge the macro–micro gulf. Quantitative research addresses the structural features of social life and can illuminate what happens 'if' X occurs. Qualitative research is more adept at uncovering processes and answering the question of 'how' or 'why' X occurred. There are numerous reasons to consider employing quantitative/qualitative mixed methods, including the incorporation of quantitative evidence to help generalizability. Quantitative research can also fill gaps in a qualitative study to include more structural elements. Many research questions require measurement of some kind, *as well as* better understanding of the nature or origins of an issue, and each approach offers a distinctive kind of evidence.

John Creswell (2013: 15) presents three primary models for designing a mixed-methods project. First is the 'convergent parallel mixed methods' model, which merges qualitative and quantitative data to provide a more comprehensive explanation of a phenomenon. This design generally means collecting the two forms of data simultaneously and integrating it into the interpretation of the results, facilitating a deeper discussion of contradictions or incongruent findings. The second model is 'explanatory sequential mixed methods'. Beginning with quantitative research on a topic, analysing it, and using it to enhance your qualitative research represents a sequential approach that strengthens the quantitative findings. This approach presents a challenge of favouring a quantitative design, making it difficult to deal with the very different sample sizes of the two methods and what this means for finding conclusions. Finally, 'exploratory sequential mixed methods' begins with the qualitative and uses these data to construct the quantitative component. The qualitative data may help you to build an instrument to better test a hypothesis using quantitative methods. Or you may be able to identify important variables to include in survey research by analysing the in-depth qualitative data. The challenge in this method is determining which aspects of the qualitative data to analyse that can contribute to a quantitative project.

Example

Simon Roberts et al. (2004) conducted research to understand how employers and service providers responded to provisions of the Disability Discrimination Act in the United Kingdom. They used an explanatory sequential mixed-methods model, first conducting

2,000 telephone survey interviews, and using these interviews to perform case studies with 38 employers and service providers. They noted that the quantitative component led them to focus qualitative interviews on the workplace rather than the overall organization, allowing them to talk to line managers who could share with them actual practices beyond scripted responses of top management.

Table 3.2 provides examples of different options for connecting your research objectives to the structure of your data collection and methods.

Table 3.2 Connecting research to structure

Research question	Some design options	Example
What is happening? How and why does it happen?	Case Study: An in-depth examination of a wider phenomenon	Shifman and Katz (2005) provide a case study of humour created in the course of immigrant assimilation (the wider phenomenon), regarding jokes ($n = 150$) told by Eastern European old-timers at the expense of well-bred German Jews who migrated to Palestine/Israel beginning in the mid-1930s
What is the process? Has there been a change? What are the long-term consequences?	Longitudinal Qualitative Research: The goal is to investigate and interpret change over time, exploring the processes involved while taking account of the social context	Thomson et al. (2012) employ a longitudinal study of new mothering, using observational data to explore interactions between researcher, mother and child relating to food
How are A and B different and similar? What explains similarities and differences? What are some possible consequences?	Comparative Research: This method emphasizes the holistic nature of cases, the interaction of attributes, and multiple paths to an outcome	Cress and Snow (2000) use qualitative comparative analysis to chart the different pathways to various outcomes for homeless social movement organizations
How are A and B different and similar over time? What are the consequences? How 'X' influences A (or A and B similarly/differently)	Multi-Method Longitudinal Comparison: This approach allows for sophisticated 'macro-qualitative' comparative research designs, emphasizing the relationships among methods	Bagnall et al. (2013) conducted a 12-month longitudinal-matched comparison study incorporating three sets of data: psychometric scores and other data from structured questionnaires; routinely collected data on use of healthcare services; and self-care beliefs and behaviour from qualitative interviews

What will your sample consist of?

Sample selection is an essential feature of your research design, whether your research is qualitative, quantitative or a mix of the two. Research involving small populations or single case studies must attend to who will be studied and in what settings, in a similar manner to large projects that encompass extensive ethnographic data sets or comparative designs (Hammersley and Atkinson, 1995). Deciding on a sample includes two related elements for both qualitative and quantitative research: First, you need to define the full data set or what is generally called the population. Second, you need to select a subgroup from that population.

In most cases, qualitative research relies on nonprobability sampling techniques for selecting a study population. This means purposely selecting a population to reflect particular features of a group(s), event(s) or activity(ies). Unlike quantitative methods, sampling in qualitative research does not seek statistical representativeness, referring to samples where the chances of selection for each element are unknown. Qualitative researchers link their research question(s) to the characteristics of a population in determining selection of the sample. This purposeful strategy is important to small-scale, in-depth studies. Thus, a good sample will be one that attends to homogeneity along some dimensions and heterogeneity along others in a study population. The more common types of nonprobability sampling techniques are convenience sampling, which has no rationale except availability, and purposive sampling, which includes multiple options. Below, we summarize these approaches.

Convenience sampling

A convenience sample selects research participants based on their ease of availability, and lacks any clear sampling strategy. The selection process relies on including those who are the most eager and able to participate in the study. A small convenience sample may be useful to test the appropriateness of a research design or interview questions before delving into a more intensive and larger project. However, due to concerns about the validity of the data and their interpretation given the lack of sampling strategy, we do not recommend this type of sample except for very preliminary research. Patton (2015) makes a distinction between convenience and opportunistic sampling, the latter focusing on the need for a researcher to take advantage of unforeseen opportunities as they arise during the course of fieldwork. This kind of flexible approach can be very important in fieldwork where unexpected events are likely to unfold.

Purposive sampling

Some characterize purposive sampling as more or less synonymous with qualitative research. From this perspective, purposive sampling, which requires a number of strategic choices about where, how and with whom you will conduct your research, is the backbone of a qualitative research design. Sampling is fundamentally tied to a project's objectives and research questions, signifying some form of purpose. The diversity of objectives and research questions entails multiple possibilities for purposive sampling. Michael Patton (2015: 266–72), for example, provides an overview of 40 purposive sampling options to aid in the selection of information-rich cases. We review here the approaches we believe to be the most salient in qualitative research design.

Snowball sample

Snowball sampling, also referred to as referral chains, is a common strategy for obtaining a sample in qualitative methods. It relies on asking people who you have already interviewed to name others who fit the selection criteria. This strategy can be helpful when your research involves populations that are dispersed or hard to reach. This is particularly true for populations that have been historically marginalized, such as lesbians and gay men of colour. It can also be a useful strategy when you are studying populations that practise some kind of deviant or illegal activity. Another strength of this sampling technique is its ability to build a sample of 'natural interactional units' of people who relate to one another on a regular basis (Biernacki and Waldorf, 1981).

Snowball samples also have limitations. For example, it can be challenging to find the right respondent(s) to create referral chains of participants who complement your research objective. You might also compromise the heterogeneity of the sample if all new participants are generated through existing ones, resulting in a sample that is too homogeneous. This can be mitigated to a certain extent by identifying characteristics that will ensure diversity and asking respondents to suggest other participants based on these characteristics. You will also want to avoid automatically including family members or close friends in your sample. Another possibility might be to refrain from interviewing the new contacts identified by your existing sample, and instead ask these individuals to identify others who meet your criteria. This has the advantage of creating some distance between sample members, but can be cumbersome as a method. As a rule of thumb, we recommend that you only interview two to three people from any one chain/source, and, rather than relying solely on snowballing, use it to supplement other methods of generating a sample frame.

Maximum variation and homogeneous sampling

Maximum variation sampling seeks to locate cases or individuals in order to include a wide spectrum of attitudes and perspectives on a phenomenon. When dealing with small sample sizes, too much heterogeneity can present problems when individual cases differ substantially from each other. Sampling based on maximum variation transforms this perceived limitation into a strength by identifying core experiences and central patterns in heterogeneous populations or phenomena. A statewide initiative, for example, may have programmes aimed at several different populations. Your sampling strategy might seek to include at least one programme from each population to provide variation among the programmes studied.

In contrast, homogeneous samples are sometimes deliberately chosen to give a detailed account of a particular phenomenon. A homogeneous sample might limit its breadth to a subculture or a group that presents many of the same characteristics. The advantage of this approach is to facilitate in-depth investigation of social processes in a specific social context. Elijah Anderson's *Code of the Street* (1999) offers an ethnographic account of street violence in a disadvantaged African American community of Philadelphia. He conducted fieldwork on this population to uncover the emergence of a subculture regulated by 'the code of the street', that combines elements of respect, loyalty and honour to regulate social interactions in the impoverished neighbourhood where his project was conducted.

Typical case, disconfirming and extreme sampling

Another strategy for sampling is to select a case or cases that you identify as 'normal' or 'average' to study mainstream aspects of society. In other words, cases might be of interest simply because they are ordinary. Howard Becker (1970) wanted to understand how medical students were socialized into their profession. He conducted his research at the University of Kansas Medical School because the school was seen as typical of the medical school experience (Palys, 2008). This strategy demands some prior knowledge of the population or phenomenon to identify it as 'typical.' You might gain this knowledge through your literature review or by conducting an exploratory study.

Another strategy for sampling is to seek cases that might disconfirm a theory or a finding that you have identified through exploratory research or in your literature review. Seeking to disconfirm a theory may be a way to strengthen your argument to support a competing theory. Ted Palys (2008: 698) sums up this general principle as, 'If you think your results are not generalizable or the existence of a particular kind of case will undermine all that you "know" to be true about a phenomenon, then look for that kind of case'.

Finally, in contrast to the typical case sampling strategy that seeks the ordinary, extreme sampling searches cases because they are extraordinary or special in some way that can shed light on a topic. Studying extremes or exceptions can illuminate a topic by uncovering the importance of outliers in creating what is considered normal. Ethnomethodologists, for example, often choose deviant sampling to expose implicit assumptions and norms (Palys, 2008).

Purposeful random sampling

While nonprobability sampling assumes a non-random sample, a purposeful random sample can be a strategy to increase the credibility of your methods. Patton (2015) describes his collaborative research with a programme that conducts in-depth interviews on the 'war stories' about their clients' successes and struggles. These researchers decided to enhance the credibility of these narratives by systematically determining what would be included in the case histories, and then setting up a procedure to randomly select clients. These stories, though not generalizable, were randomly selected before knowing the outcomes of who experienced success or failure in the programme, adding credibility to their findings. It is thus important to keep in mind that a purposeful random sample is not representative. Rather, its purpose is to reduce suspicion about why certain cases were selected for study.

Stratified purposeful sampling

A stratified purposeful sampling strategy incorporates a hybrid tactic to bridge homo- and heterogeneity (i.e., maximum variation and homogeneous sampling strategies). The objective is to select groups that offer variety in regard to a particular phenomenon, but each of which is fairly homogeneous, allowing the comparison of subgroups. Another strategy is to combine a typical case sample with others, stratifying the cases around an average. The purpose is to clarify variation 'rather than to identify a common core, although the latter may also emerge in the analysis' (Patton, 2015: 305). Thus, the strata would offer a predominantly uniform sample, while differences would exist between the strata. For example, you might use this sampling strategy to study different models of implementing online learning in lower and higher socioeconomic classrooms.

Criterion sampling

This sampling strategy seeks to incorporate cases or individuals who meet a predetermined criterion of importance, such as a shared characteristic or experience. In general, employing this technique requires carefully designating inclusion/exclusion criteria. For example, married men who have been clients of sex workers might be the criterion from which you build your sample. Implicit to this sampling strategy is the idea that the criterion is contrasted to cases that are external to it. Thus, unmarried men who have been clients of sex workers would be a good comparison case.

Theory-guided (emergent) sampling

A more deductive or theory-testing approach to research design would seek to include individuals or cases specifically on the basis of their potential contribution to theory. This approach is mainly associated with grounded theory – a systematic method of conducting inductive qualitative inquiry aimed toward theory construction. A theoretical sample moves between sample selection, fieldwork and analysis: a preliminary sample is selected, fieldwork carried out and data analysed; this process is repeated to refine emergent categories or theories until no new insights are generated.

Sample size

Determining the size of your sample relates to a number of factors that link to your research objectives, questions and sampling strategy. If you are conducting comparative or longitudinal research, your sample size is likely to be larger than if your research is a case study. On the one hand, a sample that is too large can lead to a point of diminishing returns where very little new evidence is obtained (in fieldwork, this is called the point of saturation; see Chapter 6). Since a qualitative project does not involve the need to measure, or establish incidence/prevalence in the ways that statistical inference requires, you will want your sample to be small enough to yield rich information. On the other hand, if your sample is too small, it may fail to include key players or lack diversity to study variation and the influence of different factors on the population/topic you are studying. Thus, a good purposive sampling strategy is key to ensuring that your sample will be rich in terms of constituencies and variability (Ritchie and Lewis, 2003). The sample size for a project that relies on in-depth interviews will likely include no more than 50 participants, but again, you will need to consider the kinds of comparisons your project will make (how many sub-populations are included in the sample) and how you will combine different methods (in-depth interviews and fieldwork) to ensure you can answer your research questions.

Quick tip: Considerations for determining your sample size (Ritchie and Lewis, 2003)

- *The heterogeneity of the population*: A diverse population will likely increase the required sample size, whereas a more homogeneous population will allow a smaller sample.
- *The number of selection criteria*: The criteria you identify in designing the sample will influence its size. The more you identify, the larger the sample.
- *Groups of special interest that require intensive study*: If your project includes groups that require intensive study, you will need to include them with sufficient representation and diversity, requiring a larger overall sample.
- *Multiple samples within one study*: If your research design includes more than one sample for reasons of comparison or control, your sample size will increase based on the number of cases that need to be included for each sample population.
- *Type of data collection methods*: The sample size will increase depending on your methods of data collection, whether single interviews, paired interviews, small or average size group discussions, or multiple methods.
- *The budget and resources available*: The more complex your research design and sampling method, the more intensive resources are necessary for data collection and analysis.

Ethical considerations

Ethics in qualitative research speak to the relationship between researchers and those they study. They are a central aspect of research design and all decision-making processes throughout the project. Research designs are expected to be ethical, meaning that researchers must treat the participants in their research with humane consideration, and the presentation of results must observe the principled conventions. One central concern of research ethics is the integrity of the research activity, where honest revelation of a study's strengths and limitations mark its integrity. Some social scientists consider any type of covert research, for whatever purposes, to lack integrity because it can mislead the people being studied and does not facilitate the process of peer review. Such has been the critique of Laud Humphrey's (1970) participant observation of sex acts in public bathrooms. Ethical issues have particular importance in qualitative research due to the fact that the methods involve in-depth study and anticipated events.

Generally, issues arise because qualitative researchers work with participants face-to-face, over long periods of time, and possibly in intimate circumstances. There can be a fine line between building relationships that are caring and not exploiting participants. Reporting the findings also presents ethical challenges, as most participants have access to what is published or presented about them. Ethics in this case has to do with the effects that research reports will have on participants.

Informed consent

Researchers must obtain informed consent from participants, providing them with information about the study's purpose, funding, the research team, how data will be used, and what will be required of them. Informed consent also means specifying that participation is voluntary, and how participants will be identified in reports from the study. Providing too much information in the recruitment stage may deter participation or ultimately alter participants' responses. On the other hand, not providing enough information can lead to problems later on when the participant is surprised by questions being asked or by other aspects of the study.

Anonymity and confidentiality

How you will deal with anonymity and confidentiality needs to be carefully planned and communicated to participants. Anonymity refers to the protection of identity for those taking part in the study. Some participants may want to be identified, while others will want to remain anonymous, and you can give them a choice, such as selecting their own pseudonym if they desire. When participation is arranged by or through a third party – such as an employer – anonymity may be compromised. In this case, you will need to inform participants that you cannot absolutely guarantee anonymity. Confidentiality refers to ensuring that the attribution of comments in your reports or presentations does not identify participants.

Protecting participants from harm

You will need to consider if taking part in the research project will have any harmful effects for members, and, if so, take curative action. Research that deals with sensitive topics is likely to uncover painful experiences, perhaps which have not been previously shared. You will need to give participants enough information so that they have a clear understanding of what will be required of them before taking part in the study.

Protecting researchers from harm

Conducting fieldwork can also place you at risk, and arrangements should be made at the beginning of the study to minimize these. You should consider the kinds of risks that may arise in public places, such as arrangements for getting to your research site, and in private, such as conducting interviews in participants' homes.

DATA COLLECTION AND VALIDITY CONCERNS

-- **Key takeaways** --

- Ensuring the validity of your findings is a key component of a good research design.
- Validity threats in qualitative research include researcher bias and reactivity.
- There are a number of ways to test the credibility of your conclusions: length of time conducting research, the richness of your data, obtaining feedback from participants, triangulation, among others.
- While differing radically from quantitative methods, it is possible to generalize qualitative findings.

Validity in qualitative research broadly refers to whether a study is 'well grounded' (Ritchie and Lewis, 2003: 270). It is a key component of your research design and your research proposal (see the next section on how to write your research proposal), but it is a difficult component to account for. There is no easy guarantee that your study will be valid, or that the results will reflect reality. Moreover, no method can absolutely confirm that you have captured the actual phenomena that you claim to describe. Maxwell (2013) points to the fact that validity is relative, meaning that it must be evaluated according to the context and objectives of the project. One's evidence, and not simply the chosen methods, establishes the validity of the research.

Accounting for validity involves the ability to test claims against the real world to show that your account is not wrong. A key concept in conceptualizing validity is *validity threat*, or the ways that you might be wrong. These threats include alternative explanations or other ways of understanding your data not accounted for – 'for example, that the people you interviewed are not presenting their actual views, or that you have ignored the data that don't fit your interpretation, or that there is a different theoretical way of making sense of your data' (Maxwell, 2013: 123). Your research design needs to conceptualize these threats and how you will deal with them. In this section, we outline specific ways to understand validity threats and steps to deal with them. We conclude with a discussion of generalizability and an example of a conceptual map to articulate the interactions of the research design.

Validity threats

Strategies to deal with validity threats differ markedly between quantitative and qualitative methods. For quantitative or experimental designs, controls are generally built into the design to deal with expected and unexpected threats to validity. Qualitative researchers, in contrast, do not have statistical means to 'control for' probable threats, and these threats are often dealt with once data collection has begun. This means considering factors that might present as threats before beginning the research process and attending to their evolution or to new threats. There are two broad types of threats to validity that you confront: research bias and reactivity (Maxwell, 2013).

Research bias

Research bias refers to the tendency that researchers have to collect, interpret or present data that support their own prejudgments, theories or goals. This concept has to do with the subjectivity of the researcher, a term that is often favoured over the term bias within qualitative research. The need to deal with issues of subjective bias can arise from multiple sources and at numerous stages within the research process, including during research design, sample selection, data collection, analysis or writing. Rather than seeking to eliminate bias – it is not possible to jettison your own perspectives, experiences or beliefs – dealing with research bias means understanding how your viewpoints can influence conducting qualitative research. Identifying possible impacts of your predispositions on your research project will allow you to retain the positive effects and avoid the negative ones. For example, you might be inclined to devise methodological strategies that could favour particular findings. In this case, it is important to think about alternative strategies and the consequences of these for your research design.

Reactivity

Reactivity, or observer effect, occurs when the process of conducting research alters the behaviour of the participants, challenging the validity of the data. There are several types of reactivity. One is the Hawthorne effect, which links changes in behaviour to study participation. Experiments conducted by Elton Mayo at a plant in Hawthorne, Illinois, during the 1920s and 1930s found that, when changes in working conditions were introduced, such as better lighting, productivity increased. Mayo hypothesized that workers were actually responding to the attention they were receiving as research participants rather than to better working conditions. Another type of reactivity is the novelty effect, which occurs when individuals modify their behaviour after the introduction of something new, such as the presence of the researcher. This effect is usually short-lived. Reactivity may also result when participants act in a certain way to please the researcher. Characteristics of the observer, such as race, gender or age, can result in reactivity, especially when there are substantial differences between the investigator and the participant(s) (McKechnie, 2008).

In qualitative research, reactivity can apply to both the researcher and participants. The goal is not to remove the influence of the researcher on the research process (again, an impossible objective), but to ensure that reactivity is identified and channelled in a positive way. When conducting research with participants, it is important to keep reflexive notes to document how your own behaviour and understandings may affect the research process. Next, we present a series of validity tests proposed by Joseph Maxwell (2013) to increase the credibility of your conclusions.

Validity tests

Methodological approaches cannot guarantee valid findings, but a good research design can help bolster the credibility of your conclusions. Maxwell (2013: 125) argues that it is important to 'test' the validity of your conclusions rather than to verify them. Testing involves searching for evidence that calls into question your findings. We provide a number of strategies below for testing the validity of your findings, but keep in mind that not all strategies work for all studies. Your research objectives and questions can guide you in deciding which threats are important to address, and how to test for validity.

Intensive, long-term involvement

Long-term participant observation can be a good method to test the validity of your findings. It allows you to gather a diversity of data, and you have the time to check and confirm your observations and understandings. Conducting interviews and observations in tandem over time can help to 'rule out spurious associations and premature theories' (Maxwell, 2013: 126). You can also test alternative theories or postulates. Howard Becker (1970) conducted long-term participant observation of medical students, allowing him to dig deeper under the cynical surface that the students maintained to uncover the idealism with which they approached their profession.

Rich data

Long-term observations and intensive interviewing produce rich data that can aid in testing the validity of your conclusions. Verbatim transcripts of interviews and detailed field notes can give you a broad picture of the circumstances and contradictions that take place in social life. According to Howard Becker, rich data can

> counter the twin dangers of respondent duplicity and observer bias by making it difficult for respondents to produce data that uniformly support a mistaken conclusion, just as they make it difficult for the observer to restrict his observations so that he sees only what supports his prejudices and expectations. (1970: 53)

Respondent validation

Obtaining feedback from respondents can be an important strategy to test your interpretations against those of your respondents. You might solicit this feedback throughout the research process or wait until you have written up your results. Judith Stacey (1990), for example, elicited feedback from the two key informants of the two families she studied at the end of her research. She included these responses in an appendix to reflect on differences between her views and those of her respondents. In the end, this information offered *evidence* of the validity of her conclusions (i.e., the responses were not more inherently valid than the interviews and fieldwork she conducted).

Intervention

Qualitative researchers unavoidably intervene in the social world they study. This fact can create challenges to ensuring valid conclusions but can also represent an opportunity to test the validity of your findings, using intervention as a way to test your interpretations. Maxwell (2013) gives the example of Goldenberg (1992) who studied the effects of a teacher's expectations and behaviour on students' reading progress. Goldenberg shared with the teacher his theory about why a student was unable to meet the teacher's expectations, which resulted in a change in the teacher's behaviour towards the student and improved the student's reading abilities. Thus, Goldenberg was able to successfully test his claim that the teacher's behaviour toward the student rather than her expectations was the primary cause of the student's lack of progress.

Searching for discrepant evidence and negative cases

If you find evidence that cannot be accounted for in your interpretations or explanations of a phenomenon, this is a good sign that you need to rethink the validity of your conclusions.

If you find yourself in this situation, you will need to decide whether the discrepancy is based on just one aspect of the evidence you have gathered and can be ignored, or whether you need to revisit your conclusions to ensure that this piece of evidence disconfirms them. You might ask others to consider your evidence and the discrepant evidence to ensure that you are not relying too much on your own perspectives in making conclusions. You might also decide to report the discrepant evidence in your write-up and allow your audience to draw their own conclusions.

Triangulation

Triangulation, as discussed above in our section on mixed methods, decreases the chance of systematic bias due to relying only on one specific method. Norman Denzin (1989b) theorized four basic types of triangulation that can strengthen the validity of your findings. The first is *triangulation of methods of data collection*, which means combining methods such as interviewing, surveys and observation across various times and places to offer multiple perspectives. For example, focus groups might be conducted initially as a way to explore themes that will then be addressed through in-depth interviews. The second is *investigator triangulation*, which can strengthen the trustworthiness of findings by including more than one investigator in the collection and analysis of data. Multiple investigators can offer insights and can shed light on assumptions that may be missed if there were only one person collecting and analysing data. A third possibility is *triangulating data sources*. Drawing on evidence from a variety of data sources can also increase the credibility of research findings. Evidence gathered from interviews, participant observation, archival and historical documents, and public records will yield different kinds of evidence and elucidate different understandings of the phenomena under study. Finally, *theory triangulation* approaches research findings from different theoretical lenses to guard against wearing ideological blinders that favour only one theoretical approach. This kind of triangulation does not permit integration of results (making it less useful for confirming validity of findings), but it can be helpful in explaining dissonant data or negative cases. This approach might also yield new insights into aspects of the research problem.

Numbers

Maxwell notes that many of the conclusions that result from qualitative research have 'an implicit quantitative component' (2013: 128). Claims concerning prevalence or typicality of a phenomenon, or how common a theme or behaviour is, require some quantitative support. Incorporating an appropriate use of numbers to assess the amount of evidence you have is a good way to increase the credibility of your conclusions. Maxwell (2010) offers a comprehensive assessment of the importance of numbers in qualitative research.

Comparison

We have discussed the importance of comparison in linking your methodology to your research questions. Comparisons are also an important way to address validity threats. Comparative research can address an important weakness in qualitative research – its 'inability to explicitly address the "counterfactual" of what would have happened *without* the presence of the presumed cause' (Maxwell, 2013: 129). Comparisons help to draw out regularities and specify the underlying social mechanisms and processes that generate these regularities, thereby strengthening the validity of your conclusions.

Generalizing from qualitative research

Generalization refers to extending findings from a study based on a sample of particular individuals, settings, times or institutions as relevant beyond that sample. In both quantitative and qualitative research, researchers propose two main types of generalization: *empirical* and *theoretical* (Hammersley, 2008; other terms have also been employed to capture the broader idea of two types of generalization, see Maxwell, 2013). Empirical generalization concerns applying findings from qualitative research to populations or settings beyond the particular sample of the study. Some argue that a better term to capture this idea is 'transferability', involving a transfer of knowledge from a study to a new situation (Ritchie and Lewis, 2003). The second context of generalization is theory building, which refers to the formation of theoretical concepts that have a wider, more general, application. Conclusions from a case study or other types of qualitative methods are typically used in developing wider theory.

We embrace the view that the findings of qualitative research can be generalized, albeit in a manner that differs substantially from how generalizability occurs in quantitative research. The distinction made by Maxwell (2013) offers a particularly useful approach to generalizing your findings:" *internal generalizability* and *external generalizability*. Internal generalizability allows you to generalize within the organization, setting or case, to others (e.g., to a different part of an organization), that were not directly observed or interviewed in the data collected. External generalizability moves beyond the case or cases specifically studied to other institutions, people or settings.

Internal generalization

Internal generalizability refers to the representativeness of the data and conclusions for the phenomena or people you are studying. This means that it relies primarily on empirical rather than theoretical generalization. In particular, this form of generalization is important to the validity of your results. It involves sufficiently representing the variation in the setting or group of people you are studying. Being able to generalize internally is intimately tied to your sampling strategy. If you are conducting participant observation, you cannot observe all the factors of the setting, and it is thus important to account for the kinds of diversity that can exist in a particular location or social context. What have you missed, and how does this affect your overall findings? In analysing your data, you should pay attention to data that do not fit prior expectations, and make sure to retain the important differences you have built into your design. For example, are you imposing an artificial coherence on the data?

External generalization

External generalizability in qualitative research concerns theoretical generalization or the transferability of particular results to other cases. It attends more to a logic of replication than to a sampling logic, which is the focus of quantitative generalization: it seeks to make theoretical extensions and not provide statistical representativeness (Maxwell, 2013). In fact, external generalizability in qualitative research often depends more on its lack of statistical generalizability, in that it seeks to illuminate an ideal type or an extreme case. Judith Stacey (1990), for example, studied two 'unrepresentative' families made up of devout Christians who mix feminism and fundamentalism to understand changes that are occurring in family life. Thus, generalizing in qualitative research is based on the development of a theory about the processes being studied that might operate in other cases but that may also end in different outcomes in different circumstances (Maxwell, 2013). The analysis strategies relating to internal generalization are also relevant for external generalization, in this case through theory development. For example, you may need to test a theory to search for discrepant data. It may also be important to develop alternative theories and search for evidence to indicate which theory(ies) best explain your data.

Modelling your research design

A good research design is able to identify the key components of the project in a concise and clear manner. Maxwell (2013) suggests creating an interactive model to help you think about the ways that your research components connect. In Figure 3.1, we offer an example of a conceptual map from the dissertation research of Jessica Braimoh based on these principles. For her PhD dissertation, Jessica Braimoh (2015) was interested in examining how geography shapes the organization of social services for marginalized youth. She conducted a case study of a single youth organization that works across rural and urban settings. The diagram that Braimoh created puts the research questions at the centre. She has one central question: 'What is the relationship between geography and the standardized provision of social services to marginalized youth?', and three sub-questions. She uses arrows to show that these questions are the 'hub' that connects all the other components in the design. The upper part of the diagram concerns the conceptual components. Her research questions are clearly and directly connected to her research problem (how does geography affect a 'one-stop shop' model of social services), conceptual model (neighbourhood effects, social capital, etc.), and her analytical framework (comparative). The lower portions are the operational half of the design, specifying how she will collect data and ensure the validity of her results. The broken lines represent the fact that the research design will need to evolve over time. The research questions will remain the hub, and as these are modified, so too will the other components.

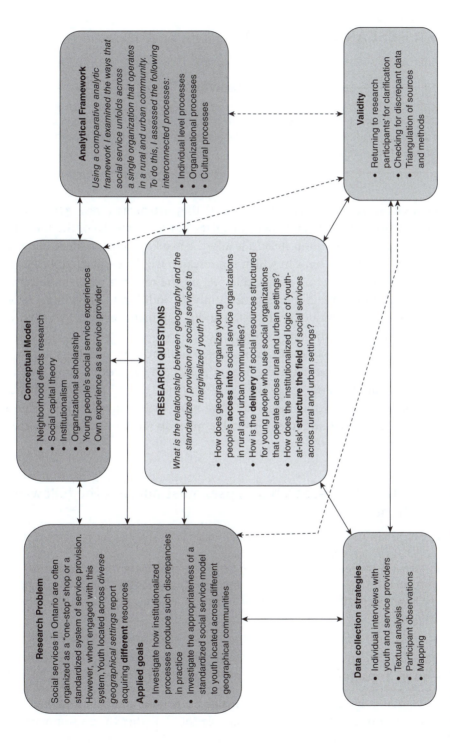

Figure 3.1 A design map of Jessica Braimoh's dissertation research

WRITING A RESEARCH PROPOSAL

─────────────────────── Key takeaways ───────────────────────

- Research proposals articulate a research plan and convince others of the soundness of that plan.
- A research proposal is fundamentally about making a good argument to explain and justify the reasons to conduct the research you are planning.

───

Research proposals serve two primary purposes: 1) they articulate a research plan; and 2) they seek to convince others (an audience of experts and non-experts) of the soundness of your plan. The goal is to communicate and justify the need to study an identified research problem and to articulate the steps in which the research will be conducted. Research proposals offer an extensive literature review that sets up the research problem and provides evidence for the need to conduct the proposed study. In addition to providing a rationale, a proposal describes the methodology in detail and a statement on anticipated outcomes and/or benefits derived from the study's completion.

You should write your proposal for a non-expert audience. An interdisciplinary panel is often assigned to review competitive grant proposals, and successful proposals are the ones that can communicate and justify the research plan to a non-specialist audience. For dissertation proposals, faculty members may have more or less specific knowledge about your area of interest, so the same rule-of-thumb applies about writing for a non-specialist audience.

 Quick tip: Your research proposal must address the following questions

- What will your research accomplish? Explain in clear terms the research problem and what you are proposing.
- What is the reason for conducting this research? This is where you justify what you plan to do. Specifically, your proposal needs to answer the 'So what?' question.
- How are you going to do it? Provide a convincing argument that what you propose is doable.

Making a good argument

A research proposal is fundamentally about making a good argument to explain and justify the reasons to conduct the research you are planning. Rather than a summary or pure description, a proposal provides the logic behind a research plan. Each part of the proposal should link to the overall argument. Joseph Maxwell (2013) points out that a good argument is a coherent one. He names two types of coherence that are essential. 1) The proposal itself has to cohere – each point must flow from one to the other and make sense as a whole. To make a convincing argument, you need to understand what you will do and why, demonstrating the connections between different components of your research design. 2) The argument itself has to be coherent, that is it needs to make sense to a general audience. The writing should be clear and precise, and it should avoid unnecessary verbiage and jargon.

Parts of a research proposal

There are typically several standard parts of a research proposal. One key component is justifying the research, which addresses its purpose and answers the 'So what?' question. This is where you make the case as convincingly as possible for your research plan, explaining both short- and long-term interest and value. Here, we build on Joseph Maxwell's (2013) structural model for writing your proposal (see his Chapter 7 on research proposals for useful outlines and examples).

Abstract

The abstract offers a roadmap of the study and the arguments you will make in your proposal. The abstract is a good place to begin and end. Your first draft can begin to articulate the arguments that will follow in the proposal. Once you have filled in all the elements of the proposal, you can return to the abstract to revise it into a concise and abbreviated summary of the research plan.

Introduction

The introduction sets the stage for the research in one to three paragraphs that succinctly answer the following four questions: 1) What is the central research problem? 2) What is the topic of study related to that problem? 3) What methods should be used to analyse this problem? 4) Why is this research important, and why should someone reading the proposal care about the outcomes from the study? Your research questions can be presented in full after you have articulated the conceptual framework. The end of the introduction should also provide an overview of the structure of the rest of the proposal.

Conceptual framework

This section of your proposal is often called the literature review. Reviewing the literature and existing theory offers an overview of what research has already been done on your topic to date and how your research will contribute to the overall state of knowledge in this area. It provides a justification for the need to conduct further research; that is, for the particular piece of research being proposed. This section also introduces the theoretical framework that informs your study.

The keyword for writing a good literature review is *relevance* (Maxwell, 2013). Each piece of literature or theoretical approach should be relevant to your proposed research. Your proposal should explain how the literature and theories you are using are relevant. How do they inform your research plan and what are the implications for your study? Thus, you will want to incorporate only research and literature that specifically relates to your topic and builds a coherent argument concerning the 'why' of the research. If you have conducted a pilot study, this is the place to describe it and explain its implications for your research.

Research questions

Statement of your research questions is central to the proposal (just as it acts as the hub in a map of the research design, see Figure 3.1). While the research problem is presented in the introduction, the research questions might be better articulated at the end of the conceptual framework work or in a separate section that follows. This is due to the fact that the justification for your research questions may not be clear until after you have mapped out the gaps in the literature and theoretical approach to your research problem. In stating your research questions, you should articulate how they relate to prior research and theory and to the goals of the research. You should also make clear how these questions relate as a whole. Are there one or two central questions? How do the sub-questions relate to the master question(s)?

Research methods

Your methods section should not seek to justify the use of qualitative research methods in general. Rather than going into lengthy discussions about debates over conducting qualitative research, you should focus on and justify the methodological decisions you have made. In this section, explain specific data collection strategies, including addressing the questions of what, where, when, how and about whom data will be collected. Describing the setting or social context is a good strategy to justify your choice of research questions and methods. If you are writing a grant proposal, you will also need to explain what funding you have already received.

Important elements to discuss in your methods sections are as follows. 1) What kind of study is this? Are you conducting a qualitative interview study, a case study, a comparative study? 2) How will you establish your research relationships? This is particularly important to articulate if your research encompasses ethical or methodological challenges. 3) What is the setting? Will people be involved as research participants? If so, how will principles of ethical research be upheld? 4) How will you collect the data you need to answer your research questions? Here, you should describe specifically the kinds of observations, interviews or focus groups you will conduct and provide justifications for their use. Maxwell (2013) points out that there are always practical reasons for choosing certain methods, and that you should be candid about this in your methods section. 5) How will you analyse the data you collect? Make sure to articulate in this section how data analysis will help you to answer your research questions. Finally, you should discuss formal ethics approval, and when and how it will be obtained.

Validity

A section specifically dealing with validity can signal that you are taking this issue seriously. Outline the known limitations and parameters of the study. You should also address how you will ensure trustworthiness (e.g., triangulation of methods, member checking), and how will you deal with competing explanations and discrepant data.

Preliminary results

If you have already started collecting data, you can discuss in a separate section some of your preliminary results. This can be a useful way to justify the feasibility of the research and to clarify your methods.

Conclusion

Here is the place to summarize the objectives of the research and pull together the main arguments concerning all of the elements you address in the proposal. Summarize the research goals, the contribution, and the study's relevance to broader fields. The conclusion is also a good place to rearticulate the answer to the 'So what?' question.

References

This section should only give references that were actually cited in the proposal (unless otherwise instructed).

Appendices

The appendices may include: a timetable for the research; ethics forms and letters of introduction; interview guides or other instruments; a schedule of observations; a description of analysis techniques and software.

Quick tip: Anticipating and overcoming criticisms

Be ready to answer general questions about **worth**:

- Why is A worth studying?
- How does your question, data or method improve our understanding of A?
- Others have been studying A for many years in X country. How does replicating this study in Y country add to the literature?

Be ready to answer general questions about **appropriateness**:

- Others have used Y method or data for studying A. Why did you select X method or data?
- Others have used Y theory to study A. Why did you select X theory to examine A?
- Researchers define X differently.
- There are other factors that contribute to X.
- Why didn't you consider A or B?

COLLABORATIONS WITH NON-ACADEMIC GROUPS

———————————————————— Key takeaways ————————————————————

- Partnerships come in all shapes and sizes, ranging from a small community group to multiple groups and institutions.
- The objectives of this arrangement include practical, contractual, responsive and paradigmatic partnerships.
- Potential challenges, including difficult gatekeepers, knowledge asymmetry and intellectual property issues, can be mitigated through careful planning, negotiation and formal agreements.

Qualitative research is often portrayed (and experienced) as a 'lone wolf' activity. However, research collaborations are not only available to qualitative researchers but are sometimes strongly advocated by funding agencies and research communities. There are now separate funding envelopes, prizes, awards and international conferences that are dedicated toward three varieties of research partnerships. The first includes collaborating with academics from other departments, countries and different disciplines. Interdisciplinary research is a term frequently used to describe this type of partnership. The second includes Industry and University Research Partnerships (or IURPs), including those with pharmaceutical or high-tech firms. The third, which we concentrate on in this section, is work conducted with non-academics, including community groups (e.g., parent groups), institutions (e.g., schools) and complex organizations (e.g., school boards). Partnerships with non-academic groups come in a variety of forms that vary in their complexity and intentions. Partnerships also span from the partner group providing some 'input' all the way to their full and active involvement throughout the research process (e.g., Participatory Action Research or PAR). In this section, we outline how partnerships with non-academics can be organized and how researchers can anticipate and minimize potential sources of conflict.

Why partner? Key objectives

Partnerships come in all shapes and sizes. A research partnership may consist of one researcher and a small community group, or a dynamic cast of characters, including researchers from several universities, a variety of government agencies (e.g., state education department, child welfare, police), dozens of partner organizations (e.g., school boards) and thousands of potential participants (e.g., students). The range of potential partners available to researchers is equally broad. Partnerships can include highly complex institutions such as government agencies, hospitals and corporations all the way to a local community or advocacy group. Groups and organizations may hail from the state, for-profit or non-profit and philanthropic sectors and vary in size, target audience, complexity and mission.

Practical partnerships

In some cases formal partnership are necessary to make contact with a group or organization. Partnerships may be required to gain access to documents, records or key informants. They may also generate mutual benefits – you benefit in the form of data for your project or thesis, and they benefit from the generation of usable information or a pre-agreed-upon report.

Contractual partnerships

A research contract may be initiated from outside academe. A group or organization may contact a researcher and contract him to conduct a particular project (e.g., evaluate a programme).

Responsive partnerships

The development of a partnership may be in response to a particular group or organizational need. The partnership may be sought out by the group or organization, initiated by an outside party, or known to the researcher. Partnerships may be seen as the optimal method for addressing social, economic, practical or other problems.

Paradigmatic partnership

Partnerships may be built on a desire to help facilitate social change or provide participants with a stake or voice in the process. Terms to describe this approach include Participatory Action Research (PAR), Community-based Participatory Research (CBPR), and Action-oriented Research. All share the belief that partnerships generate research that is more responsive to the issues faced by the group of interest (Small and Uttal, 2005). These approaches subscribe to the belief that ideally the research topic comes from the community or group and is based on the community or group's understandings of what the problem or issue is. These approaches subscribe to a strong social justice ethic aimed at changing or improving a particular condition with, rather than for, the group of interest.

Anticipating challenges

There are several considerations that should be anticipated and negotiated before and during the research process. Most of these considerations are generic to research collaborations while others tend to be more endemic to projects that include partnerships with larger organizations and community groups (see Table 3.3 for a summary of the challenges).

Table 3.3   Key challenges and questions

Gatekeepers	What is the role, positive or negative, of gatekeepers?
Knowledge asymmetry	How do you balance what constitutes 'good' research with the knowledge and methods preferred by the group or community?
Time asymmetry	How does time affect the participation of potential research collaborators?
Decision-making, roles and responsibilities	What is the process of decision-making? Who has right to the intellectual property generated by the research collaboration? How and by whom is the research disseminated?
Professional and cultural norms	What role do professional and cultural norms play?
Intellectual property	Who has rights to the intellectual property or by-products generated by the research project? How will the intellectual property be used?

Gatekeepers

We will discuss the importance of gatekeepers – key people and informants – in Chapter **6**. They can provide access as well as much needed legitimacy with other group members. They may also potentially block access or contain the research process. You may also find yourself with a gatekeeper who offers access, but does so minimally. The gatekeeper may not share your enthusiasm or sense of urgency and may find ways to circumvent your access to information, events or people.

Knowledge and time asymmetry

The fundamental goal of research partnerships of any sort is to bring together a diversity of perspectives, knowledge and skill-sets. Knowledge asymmetry, however, can generate tensions between researchers and the group. Researchers and non-academics each bring with them a different skill-set. Researchers bring with them knowledge of the literature and a methodological toolkit that is informed by their discipline's standard of 'best practices' or 'good science'. Non-academic members bring with them knowledge of the group's condition that is grounded in their intimate contact with the people and issue at hand. These two skill-sets – one grounded in formal or academic knowledge and the other in local knowledge – are not always aligned.

Time asymmetry may also be an issue. Qualitative projects tend to be very labour intensive. Research partnerships magnify this challenge since it often requires the non-academics involved in the research project to devote some if not all of their time. A project may also require a substantial commitment to participating in training or information sessions in addition to some or all of the research protocol.

Decision-making, roles and responsibilities

Outlining the authority or decision-making structure of the partnership, the roles each of the partners will play and the type of responsibilities that are tied to each role are critically important. You cannot assume by virtue of the structure of the partnership (e.g., full partnership) that roles and responsibilities will be obvious to everyone involved, including you. Who designs the project, and what does that role look like? Who handles the 'dog work', such as bookkeeping or scheduling, handling the project's finances and getting supplies? Who is assigned blame if something goes wrong? These are important questions to address before entering a partnership.

Intellectual property

We often think of intellectual property in the context of high-tech, medical or other hard science disciplines. Yet survey data, field notes, interview transcripts and information generated through consultation with or by group members are also a form of tangible 'goods'. A key ingredient of a successful partnership will also include determining access to and uses of the intellectual property generated in the context of the research project.

Professional and cultural norms

Once you are 'in', you will start to learn about the professional and cultural norms of the group. As scholars who study organizational behaviour know well, all organizations tend to have a 'formal' and 'informal' structure. You will likely learn about the formal structure before you enter the group or organization; it includes all the codified systems, policies and rules. However, all groups or organizations have an 'informal' structure which includes the norms, behavioural patterns and politics of the group; it includes the unspoken rules about who has status and power in the group, how communication actually works, and notions about how things should get done. These rules may be based on emotions, attitudes, professional socialization and even the history of the organization.

All potential challenges, including difficult gatekeepers, knowledge asymmetry and intellectual property issues, can be mitigated through careful planning, negotiation and formal agreements. It is important to enter partnerships with your eyes open, and to seek open communications and agreements to ensure that problems do not arise that could cause significant delays or difficulties in completing your project.

CONCLUSION

To design a qualitative study, you cannot simply apply a set of rules or a logical structure and implement them faithfully. Throughout the research process, you will need to design and redesign your strategies for your qualitative project. You must continually move between the different components of the design to assess their interactions and implications. You must continually consider how your design influences and is influenced by the social context in which you are conducting your research. Remaining flexible to change is key to designing a good qualitative project.

KEY TERMS

Case Study	Homogenous Sample	Reactivity
Comparative Research	Informed Consent	Research Question
Convenience Sample	Longitudinal Research	Researcher Bias
Criterion Sample	Maximum Variation Sample	Snowball Sample
Degree of Openness	Multiple Methods	Stratified Purposeful Sample
Disconfirming Sample	Negative Cases	Theory-Guided Sample
Discrepant Evidence	Purposeful Random Sample	Triangulation
Extreme Sample	Purposive Sample	Typical Case Sample
		Validity
		Validity Threats

PART II

THE INS AND OUTS OF COLLECTING QUALITATIVE DATA

4

HOW TO DO INTERVIEWS:
MAKING WHAT PEOPLE SAY MATTER

———————————————— **Learning objectives** ————————————————

By the end of this chapter you will have the tools to:

- Access the different types of interviews
- Access methods of interviewing, including face-to-face and photo interviewing
- Access hardware, software and service options
- Prepare for the interview
- Develop an interview schedule
- Develop supplementary data collection tools for interview studies
- Conduct an interview
- Make transcription decisions
- Manage interview data

———————————————— **Chapter summary** ————————————————

This chapter will first outline potential benefits and challenges associated with various types of interviews, including face-to-face and online options. We then provide you with concrete strategies for getting prepared and creating your data collection tools. This section of the chapter will take you through the process of crafting interview questions, preparing transition statements and probes, and organizing your interview schedule in a logical manner. Next, we outline standard practices for contacting potential interviewees, when to follow-up, how to 'close the deal', and what to consider when recruiting interviewees. We then focus on specific interview techniques, including body language, effective listening and the use of silence. Finally, the chapter will outline approaches to transcription and data management.

INTRODUCTION

Interviewing is one of the main qualitative data techniques used by students, researchers, and public and private firms. Interview studies are empirically and intuitively appealing. As a research tool, they can provide you with an instrument to probe more deeply into the thoughts, experiences or perceptions of their participants. Interviews can be used as a main or complementary source of data. Interviews are also personally appealing to qualitative researchers. They afford you the flexibility to craft questions that can be reworked or expanded as the project develops. They also may provide you with the feeling of having some control over what often feels like a murky and chaotic process.

This chapter is suitable if you are interested in approaches that focus on participants' experiences and sense-making all the way to interviews that are used to hone quantitative survey questions. Our aim is to help you prepare for an interview study, structure an interview schedule and manage your data. Our guidelines can be easily expanded on or modified to suit various kinds of interview studies (e.g., telephone), qualitative approaches (e.g., phenomenological) or research designs (e.g., longitudinal).

This chapter starts off at the point that you have decided to conduct interviews and have selected their potential pool of interviewees. These decisions are discussed in great detail in Chapter 3. To outline the tools needed to conduct an interview study, this chapter presents the following sections:

Structure of Interviews: We will review types of interviews that are available, including conversational and semi-structured approaches.

Method of Interviewing: We will review various methods of interviewing, including face-to-face and internet options.

Getting Prepared: This section will outline practical tools you will need to conduct an interview, including hardware and software options and organizing an interview bag.

Data Collection Tools: Next we will show you how to construct an interview schedule and supporting data collection tools.

Closing the Deal: We outline practices for contacting potential interviewees, when to follow-up, how to 'close the deal', and what to consider when recruiting interviewees.

Interviewing Techniques: We then outline interview techniques, including body language, effective listening, probing techniques and the use of silence.

Transcription Decisions: This section describes de-naturalist and naturalist approaches to transcription.

Managing Interview Data: Finally, we discuss options for managing recruitment and participant information.

STRUCTURE OF INTERVIEWS

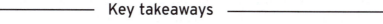 **Key takeaways**

- There are five basic structures of interviews: Conversational, Narrative, Guiding, Semi-Structured and Fixed-Response.
- The structure of the interview depends on a number of factors, including the research question and disciplinary standards.

There are five basic structures of interviews that range from a 'friendly conversation' model (Spradley, 1979; see also Bauer, 1996; Gall et al., 2003) all the way to more closed, fixed-response interviews (Table 4.1). Studies can contain more than one type of interview, so for example a project that begins with standardized, open-response interviews may also benefit from informal conversations that spontaneously develop in the field.

Table 4.1 Four basic structures of interviews

Structure	Description	Benefits/challenges	Examples
Conversational	Informal and spontaneous interactions and conversations with participants	Allows for the spontaneous generation of questions Lack of comparability between responses	Interviews during fieldwork
Guiding interview	Includes a set of general guiding questions that are asked of every interviewee	Also allows for some spontaneity, and can provide a measure of comparability	Life story or biographic interviews Narrative interviews
Semi-structured	Standardized, but open-ended interview schedule. All interviewees are asked the same set of questions, but they are free to approach the question and answer it in any manner they choose	Also allows for some 'spontaneity', while providing a fair degree of comparison between participants and more systematic data analysis. Adds another data point, by allowing researchers to analyze *how* participants respond to questions	Phenomenological and ethnographic interviews
Fixed-response	Standardized, closed-ended interview schedule. Interviewees are asked the same questions in the same manner, and responses are selected from a pre-set range of options	High degree of comparison between participants and straightforward data analysis Does not allow for responses that deviate from the schedule	Clinical Large-scale or multi-researcher interview studies

The structure selected is based on a number of factors, including the research question, the research design, disciplinary standards, and the interviewer's experience and comfort with qualitative methods. Some research questions, problems and populations also direct the structure and type of interviewing. If you are interested in a particular online community, for example, it may make perfect sense to conduct an online interview using a conversational or guided interview schedule. Rather than repeat material already covered in Chapters 2 and 3, we will simply ask you to consider: What is your research question? And what is the best method for answering it?

METHOD OF INTERVIEWING

─────────────────────────── Key takeaways ───────────────────────────

- Interview methods come in four basic varieties: Face-to-Face, Photo or Video, Telephone and Internet interviews.
- The benefits and challenges of any method of interviewing are highly contingent on factors such as the skill of the interviewer.

Interview methods come in four basic varieties (Table 4.2). We have organized the four varieties of interview methods into two categories: In-Person and Remote interviews. We have made this distinction simply to capture the geographic proximity between you and your participants since each category of interviewing shares many of the same *potential* benefits and challenges. We stress the word potential to signal that many of the benefits and challenges of any method are highly contingent. Factors such as the quality of the interview schedule, skill of the interviewer, extenuating circumstances and the relative fit between the method and the research question all contribute to the outcome of an interview study.

Table 4.2 Methods of interviewing

	Potential benefits	Potential challenges
In-person interviews		
Face-to-face	• Stronger rapport with participants • Ability to see non-verbal communication	• Interviewer effect • Cost • Time • Convenience and flexibility • Lower representation of difficult to reach populations
Photo or video	• Stronger rapport with participants • Ability to see non-verbal communication • May improve communication with vulnerable populations (e.g., children) • Richer responses • Participant participation	
Remote interviews		
Telephone	• Cost • Convenience and flexibility • May be more appropriate or desirable for sensitive, painful or embarrassing topics • Improve representation of difficult to reach populations • Safety	• Weaker rapport with participants • Inability to see non-verbal communication • Time • Lower representation of less technology savvy participants (internet only)
Internet	• Cost • Convenience and flexibility • May be more appropriate or desirable for sensitive, painful or embarrassing topics • Improve representation of difficult to reach populations • Safety • Transcribed data	

In-person interviews: Description

Face-to-face interviewing

Face-to-face (or in-person) interviews are a mainstay and often preferred method in qualitative research and involve the researcher and one or more participants. Face-to-face interviews occur in real time, and there is no time delay between questions and the responses.

Photo or video interviewing

Photo or video interviews can be a powerful extension to traditional face-to-face interviews. There are two main approaches: *Photo or Video Elicitation Interview Studies* use photos or videos throughout the interview. You can also use a variety of other materials, including newspaper clippings, maps, paintings, YouTube clips and Facebook pages. These resources may be taken from the participants' personal collection or provided by you. *Auto-driven Photo and Video Driven Interview Studies* are considered a form of 'collaborative seeing' (Luttrell et al., 2012) that includes participants in some or all aspects of data collection and analysis. Also referred to as 'photovoice', photos and videos are taken by the participants. Typically, you provide participants with a few themes or guiding questions, but generally participants have complete control over the content and representation of the images.

Two sources of data are generated from this approach. First, after the photos or videos are taken, participants are usually asked to participate in an interview in which they are asked to reflect on the data. The photos and videos are used to guide the discussion, and are especially useful when engaging with populations that are unable to fully communicate because of age, language barriers, education or other circumstances. Second, you can also analyse the content of the photos or videos independently.

Example: Children framing childhoods

Wendy Luttrell's (2010) research on children living in a working class urban centre is an exemplary example of interview studies using photos and videos. Luttrell and her colleagues were interested in children's perspectives about gender, race and immigrant status.

Thirty-four grade five students were given a disposable camera with 27 frames. Over four days they were asked to photograph their family, school and community lives. To encourage the children to photograph their surroundings from their own point of view, Luttrell gave the children minimal direction. Children were given a handful of prompts, including asking them to take photos that represent what makes them proud, places where they feel respected or a sense of belonging, and pictures of what learning is like at the school.

The research team met with each child shortly after and asked them to talk about their pictures, what they wanted to communicate through their pictures, and to share any images that they wanted to take but did not. The children met in small groups shortly after the interview and were asked to share their favourite photos with their peers.

In a follow-up study, Luttrell was able to contact 26 of the original participants. Now in high school, the students were asked to reflect on their original photos and consider how their lives had changed. Most of these students agreed to take new photos; later they were invited to make a short video of their lives using these images as well as adding others, music and sound. This research has documented not just how these children lived, but importantly how they perceived their social worlds (Luttrell, 2010; Luttrell et al., 2012; see also Photovoice, n.d.).

In-person interviews: Benefits and challenges

Potential benefits

There are many potential benefits to sharing the same physical space as your participants. You may be able to build a stronger rapport and trust with participants, particularly if the contact is for an extended period of time or over multiple interactions. The ability to hear *and* see participants also allows you to witness conscious and unconscious forms of non-verbal communication, including a participant's physical and emotional response to your questions.

Photo or video interviewing may generate additional benefits. In the case of elicitation, the use of photos or videos can be a powerful tool to guide an interview or probe deeper into an issue. Elicitation may also be used to generate memories, particularly if the topic under consideration occurred in the distant past or if the participant has trouble remembering. Collier (1957), who coined the term 'photo elicitation', compared and contrasted the responses from interviews with and without the use of photos. Collier and his team concluded that the response generated using photos 'was precise and at times even encyclopedic' (1957: 856). The photos not only generated richer and longer responses, but also increased the participants' understanding of questions asked by the researchers. Interviews with very young children or persons whose first language is different from the researcher may also benefit from the use of visual aids.

Auto-driven photo or video interviews are commonly associated with Participatory or Community-based Action Research (or PAR and CBPR). Including participants in the research process is seen to give a 'voice' to populations who are considered vulnerable (e.g., children), marginalized (e.g., people living with HIV/AIDS) or disenfranchised from policy or other kinds of decision-making processes. The interpretation of visuals or other sources of unobtrusive data is highly subjective. Photos and videos that are taken by participants not only allow them to control the message, but the interviews that typically follow may allow you to learn about the multiple meanings that participants associate with those pictures or videos.

Potential challenges

Despite the potential benefits, you should also be aware of the potential problems associated with this kind of interview study. Most notable is the potential for interviewer bias, a term used to describe the influence interviewers have on participants' responses. Researchers have noted how researcher and participant characteristics such as gender, age and social status can affect the quality and quantity of responses. These characteristics can also lead to participants underreporting or over-reporting behaviours that are considered more or less socially desirable. In the case of structured interviews, you may inadvertently influence participants' responses.

The time and costs of travelling to and from the interview site and, in some cases, of childcare must be factored in (see Quick tip: Time budget considerations below). You will often have to work around the participants' schedule and location preferences which may or may not be the most ideal from a convenience, safety, interview quality or recording quality standpoint.

In-person interviews may also prevent some people from participating. Time, money, childcare and the physical ability to travel to and from an interview site are factors that may prevent participation. Some interviewees may not want family, friends or co-workers to know that they are participating in an interview, especially if the topic is particularly sensitive, embarrassing or contains some elements about the participant that is unknown to their associates. These challenges may result in a much lower representation of particular segments of the population.

Example: Student researcher profile

For her MA thesis, Lisa Touesnard (2008) was interested in examining marriages that had experienced infidelity. The challenge for Lisa was to find participants. Infidelity is usually relatively hidden, and most people do not advertise that they or their spouse have had an affair. Interestingly too, the literature seemed to suggest that infidelity is not necessarily the product of an unhappy marriage, so searching for participants at various marriage support groups was also not a good option, since it would only capture a segment of Lisa's target group, in addition to generating other methodological and ethical problems.

To generate a sample, Lisa decided to use newspaper and online advertisements. She placed a $3\frac{1}{2}''\times 2''$ ad in three newspapers over five consecutive Saturdays. She also placed ads on kijiji.ca. Given her recruitment methods and the nature of the topic, Lisa did the following to enhance her safety:

- Lisa added two study lines to her home-phone line, one for Kitchener–Waterloo and one for Hamilton, Ontario. Each phone line was tied to a unique phone number that could not be traced back to Lisa's personal residence. The city-specific phone lines also ensured that participants did not incur any long distance charges. The lines were disconnected at the completion of the study.
- Lisa created a unique university email address that did not include her name or other identifiers.
- All recruitment advertisements only included Lisa's first name.
- All personal interviews were conducted in public spaces.

Photo and video interviews, particularly with auto-driven research, may also magnify other kinds of problems, particularly for student researchers. The most basic challenge is cost. Unless participants have access to a smartphone that has picture and video capabilities, you will need to have a budget for equipment. Pioneers of this approach used disposable cameras; while this is a relatively inexpensive option, additional steps are required if you want to scan the photos onto a computer. Other options such as digital and video cameras are relatively expensive options, and you will have to build in time and money for possible equipment failure, breakage and theft. Time and convenience is also a factor (e.g., briefing participants, printing or uploading photos, follow-up interviews).

Quick tip: Time budget considerations

Practically speaking, in-person interviews are very labour intensive. You will need to build in time for recruitment, travel to and from interviews, conducting the interview, transcribing the interview and coding the interview. Recruitment includes time to mail out introductory letters, scheduling phone calls and the occasional 'no show'. Estimates will vary, but here is a reasonable time breakdown.

Activity	Time estimate per interview (hours)	Time estimate for 50 interviews (hours)
Recruitment	0.5	25
Travel	1	50
Interview	2	100
Transcription	8	400
Coding	4	200
Total	**15.5**	**775**

If you plan to conduct 50 interviews, you will need to budget approximately 775 hours. After you get over the initial shock, you may rationalize that it constitutes a little more than one academic term to collect 'all' of your thesis data. More experienced researchers, however, will recognize that most interview studies take much longer, largely due to scheduling and quality issues. Few studies afford researchers the luxury of scheduling interviews back-to-back. And such a model may compromise the quality of the interviews, especially given the mental and emotional energy that many interview studies demand. In many cases, interviews are spread out over many months to accommodate the time commitments of the participants and to allow researchers time to reflect on their interviews.

Remote interviews: Description

Telephone interviewing

Telephone interviews allow you to collect your data in real time, and may provide you with the opportunity to access a wider range of participants. Telephone interviews are used as a stand-alone approach or in tandem with other methods such as face-to-face and online options.

Internet interviewing

The internet has long been a source of data for researchers, including analysis of online communities, blogs and websites. The focus of our discussion below will be on using the internet for interview studies. Referred to as internet-mediated research (IMR), the internet interview is used as primary source of data, rather than viewing materials online after-the-fact (Salmons, 2014). Online interviews may be conducted one-on-one, between one participant and one researcher, or in larger group formats that are more akin to a focus group. Some formats will allow you to send or post materials, including audio and video files, photographs and charts. Participants may also be able to generate responses that include these materials and share personal artefacts (e.g., photographs). Online interviews may be supplemented with other forms of online data, including a web-based question-naire. It is usually possible to save the communication; this feature provides you with an instant transcript of the exchange and will save hundreds of hours of transcription work.

There are two main types of internet interviews: Synchronous and Asynchronous. 'Synchronous' interviews occur in real time and use technologies that are afforded by vari-ous instant messaging programs such as Facebook Chat, Twitter, Mobile Instant Messaging or Skype. Several options offer video-calling, multi-channel and web-conference features that will allow you to communicate with more than one participant and stream text, voice and videos in real time (see Salmons, 2014).

'Asynchronous' interviews do not occur in real time. There are a variety of text-based asynchronous tools, including email, blogs, social media sites, wikis and various chat forums that allow researchers to send or post questions. Some multi-channel options also allow you to send or post audio and video files, including video clips and photographs.

Remote interviews: Benefits and challenges

Potential benefits

Telephone and online interviews have numerous benefits. Practically speaking, they are low cost and convenient. Unlike face-to-face interviews, neither method requires travel, book-ing time off or special childcare arrangements. They may provide both parties with more flexibility (e.g., scheduling an interviewer later at night or during a lunch break) and often allow you to take notes without distracting the participant.

Telephone and online interviews may also allow you to reach reluctant, relatively hidden or difficult-to-reach segments of your sample. Fathers, for example (hardly a group living in the shadows of society), are notably under-represented in research. As a consequence the perceptions and experiences of fathers are absent, communicated by the mother or the child, or assumed to be the same as those of the mother. Davis Kirsch and Brandt (2002) found that the telephone option was appealing to fathers since it allowed them to schedule interviews early in the morning or later in the evening (or before and after work). We have personally found that a telephone interview is an excellent 'plan b' option, particularly when a potential interviewee balks at the thought of a face-to-face interview.

Telephone and online interviews may provide you with a measure of safety, particularly if the study includes people who engage in deviant or illegal activities, or if the research setting presents some danger (e.g., see Ferrell and Hamm, 1998). In some research settings, participants may not want others to know that they are participating in an interview (Sturges and Hanrahan, 2004). Telephone and online interviews afford a respondent a measure of privacy, and allow the person to participate without fear that reputation, job security or safety will be compromised. Participants may also prefer the relative anonymity afforded by telephone and online interviews, particularly if the focus of the interview includes sensitive, painful or embarrassing topics.

Potential challenges

Telephone and online methods will not provide you with the opportunity to see participants' non-verbal communication, including body language, physical surroundings or other social artefacts. As a consequence, some researchers argue that these methods may compromise the quality of interview data and should only be used when the researcher does not have access to the participants, when the participants or research setting pose serious risk to the researcher (see Creswell, 2009), or when the nature of the research demands a telephone or online approach (e.g., researching an online community).

Research suggests that such concerns may be overstated. Researchers who have systematically compared telephone interviews with face-to-face interviews have found no significant differences in the quality of the interviews. Sturges and Hanrahan (2004), for example, found no differences when they were forced to switch from face-to-face to telephone interviews half-way through their study. Comparing transcripts from the interviews conducted in person and by phone, they found that the interviews were similar in terms of length, number of responses per question, and importantly the depth and nature of the responses. Others have also argued that responses can use a variety of non-verbal forms of communication. You can also consider the pace and timing of the response, the length of silence between responses, and the volume or pitch of the respondent's voice over the telephone.

Text-based and video-conference options, whether synchronous or asynchronous, also have features that allow you to capture dimensions of participants' emotions, feelings and physical responses. Respondents can use a range of fairly universal emoticons and acronyms to express themselves (e.g., LOL, ☺). While not sharing the same physical space, video-conferencing allows you to see participants' conscious or unconscious non-verbal communication. While you will have to be aware of potential culturally-based meanings associated with certain text or physical responses, there are a variety of strategies for overcoming at least some of the criticism associated with telephone and online interviewing (Opdenakker, 2006).

Aspects of online research that cannot be easily fixed are the length of time it takes to collect data and the amount of data that is collected. Jowett et al. (2011) found that a typical one hour interview conducted face-to-face took them three hours to complete online. More troubling is that the three-hour online interview generated about half the material of the face-to-face interview, or 6,000 compared to 12,000 words. Although it is arguable that quality matters more than quantity, the concern for qualitative researchers considering this option is whether online research generates the same breadth and depth of responses. The added time may also deter people who would be otherwise willing to participate in a research study.

Some online studies also demand a level of technical competence and familiarity with instant message, video-conferencing or other programs. Although the digital divide has certainly shrunk considerably, the level of technological literacy of the target population should be seriously considered before embarking on a project that includes technology.

GETTING PREPARED

--- **Key takeaways** ---

- Hardware options include digital recording devices and foot pedals.
- Software options include voice recognition and qualitative analysis software.
- Synchronous internet interviews use text-based, video-conferencing and multi-channel Information and Communication Technologies such as Skype.
- Asynchronous internet interviews use text-based, picture and video Information and Communication Technologies such as email and social media.
- You should also prepare an interview bag that contains everything you need to conduct an interview, including your interview schedule and consent forms.

This section will outline practical tools needed to conduct an interview, including hardware and software options and organizing an interview bag.

Hardware and software considerations

The most low-tech option is to rely on your memory or note-taking abilities to record the interview. You may decide on this option to limit distractions or barriers to developing a good connection with the interviewee, particularly if they are self-conscious or hyper-aware of the recording device. For various reasons, including comfort level or the sensitivity of the topic, your interviewee may also ask you not to use a recording device.

The problems with this option should also be considered, including your ability to accurately and completely capture what the interviewee has told you, how you asked a particular question and additional probes that you used to encourage your interviewee to engage in a broader conversation about a particular topic or issue. Unless you are a master of shorthand, both options will require you to retrospectively recreate the interview after the fact. Consequently, your 'transcript' may unwittingly contain inaccuracies, omissions or misrepresentations.

While many researchers use note taking throughout their data collection process, most projects also rely on variety of hardware and software options (Table 4.3). We present some general hardware and software options; however, the type and aims of the interview will indicate the tools that are most appropriate for your study.

Table 4.3 Hardware and software considerations

	Hardware options	Software options	Examples
Face-to-face	Digital recorder	Voice recognition software	Dragon Naturally Speaking
	Video recorder	File-sharing	VEC foot pedal yousendit
	Smartphone for voice, photo, and video recording	Qualitative data analysis software	NVivo, Atlas.ti, MAXQDA
	Foot pedal		
Photo or video interview	Camera		
	Video recorder		
	Digital recorder		
	Smartphone for photo, and video recording		
	Foot pedal		
Telephone interview	Telephone		
	Digital recorder		
	Call recorder adaptor		
	Foot pedal		

	Information and Communication Technologies (ICTs)	Examples
Synchronous internet interview	Text-based	Facebook Chat
	Video-conferencing	Twitter
	Multi-channel	Mobile Instant Messaging
		Skype
Asynchronous internet interview	Text-based	Email
	Pictures	Blogs
	Videos	Social media
		wikis
		Chat forums

The interview bag

You will need to create an interview bag of sorts that contains everything you will need to conduct an interview. The method of the interviews (e.g., face-to-face or online options) as well as a variety of other considerations (e.g., whether you are driving or taking public transit) will factor into what you actually need to include in your interview bag (Table 4.4). Having an interview bag will keep you organized and prepared to conduct an interview at a moment's notice.

Table 4.4   Interview bag checklist

Interview schedule

- 2 hard copies
- 1 emailed copy

Other materials

- Any visual aids or other materials

Consent forms

- At least 10 hard copies
- 1 emailed copy

Recording

- Digital recorder
- Pad of paper, clipboard, pens

Participant information

- Date and location of the interview
- Cell number or email address

Interview location

- Programmed into cell phone or GPS or hard copy of map
- Parking information
- Local bus information
- Numbers of local cab companies in case you get stuck somewhere

Supplies

- Extra batteries for digital recorder
- Extra pens
- Cell phone charger
- Good assortment of change for parking

DATA COLLECTION TOOLS

Interviewer studies can include a range of data collection tools, but more commonly include the interview schedule, a demographic survey and memos. An interview schedule includes all the questions you plan to ask and the probes that you may need to elicit a response or more detail. A demographic survey is an efficient way to create a snapshot of participants, and will save you a lot of time compiling the information from the transcripts after the fact. Lastly, memos that you create will force you to reflect on your data throughout the collection process.

The interview schedule

The rigidity of an interview schedule varies. At one end of the continuum, researchers may only rely on a handful of guiding questions. At the other end of the continuum are fixed-response interviews that demand the researcher read the questions verbatim and in the same order every single time in order to compare and contrast responses between participants. In this section, we have provided you with a template for creating one of the most common types of interview schedules in the social sciences – a 'semi-structured' interview schedule (Table 4.5). However, many of the same rules apply to less and more rigid interview types.

A semi-structured interview schedule has three main parts: Introductory Remarks, Body and Closing Remarks. Introductory remarks set the stage and include any administrative details such as recording procedures and ethics forms. The body contains the questions reflecting the central aims of the research project; it may also include the most sensitive or difficult questions. Closing remarks should reflect a concerted effort to provide the interviewee and interviewer with some closure. In addition to these main sections, interview schedules often include transition statements and probes.

Table 4.5   Generic interview template

	Template	
	Question	**Probes**
	Section One: Introductory Remarks	
A1		
A2		
	Transition Statement	
	Section Two: The Body	
B1	Warm-up	
B2	Warm-up	
B3	Warm-up	
	Transition Statement	
C1	Central	
C2	Central	
C3	Central	
	Transition Statement	
D1	Cool-down	
D2	Cool-down	
D3	Cool-down	
	Transition Statement	
	Section Three: Closing Remarks	
E1		
E2		
E3		

The content of an interview schedule: Part 1

--- **Key takeaways** ---

- Interview schedules have three main parts: Introductory Remarks, Body and Closing Remarks.
- The body of the interview schedule contains your key questions. The most sensitive or difficult questions are usually placed somewhere in the middle of the body to allow for sufficient time to build rapport.
- Transition statements allow you to move from one section of the interview schedule to the next.
- Verbal and visual probes are used to clarify or generate a more elaborate response.

With the generic interview template in mind, we now turn to the actual content of the interview schedule. We have divided this discussion into two parts. In Part 1, we provide the broad strokes, and outline the basic contents of each section of an interview schedule. We first answer the questions: What do you want to ask? When will you ask it? How will you ask it? We also discuss the utility and content of transition statements and probes. In Part 2, we provide detail as to the question types, organization of questions and the wording of questions.

Section one: Introductory remarks (Table 4.6)

Introductory remarks serve to establish rapport with the interviewee and to provide the interviewee with some context. Embedded in a formal interview schedule, it also serves to remind you to review important administrative tasks.

Table 4.6   Section one: Introductory remarks

Section one	
Introductory remarks	**Example**
1 Introduce yourself and provide information that may be relevant to the interviewee	'My name is John. I am a PhD student. For the past few years I have been working with Dr Zap on a project about summer literacy programmes offered by the school board'
2 Thank the interviewee for their participation	
3 Provide a brief description of the project	
4 Establish the project's purpose	'I am interested in learning about the potential benefits of the programmes'
5 Establish how you will use the information	'The interviews portion of the study helps us understand the needs of families and children attending the programme. I plan to share the broad findings with the school board'

Section one

Introductory remarks	Example
6 Handle administrative details including: • How long the interview will take • Review and sign ethics forms • If applicable ask for permission to record the interview and for how you will use the recording 7 Ask the interviewee if they have any questions or concerns before the interview begins	

Section two: The body (Table 4.7)

The body of the interview contains your central, or the most pressing, questions. The body is usually organized like a story arc or a 'workout'. It includes three parts: warm-up, central and cool-down questions. Warm-up questions continue to build rapport with participants. Central questions tackle the main issues or themes and can include participants' experiences, perceptions or emotional responses. The most personal or sensitive questions should be situated somewhere in the middle after a degree of rapport has been established and to provide the

Table 4.7   Section two: The body

Section two

Warm-up questions	Example
1 Set the stage for the main themes or issues explored in the interview including: • Biographic questions • Background questions • Baseline perception or attitudinal questions	How long have you lived in this community? Before enrolling in X programme, what did you know about it?

Central questions

2 Cover all the main issues, themes or concepts of the study. It includes the most difficult or sensitive questions • See Part 2 for organization and wording guidelines	

Cool-down questions

3 Wrap-up questions • May be future oriented	What do you think are the next steps for X programme?
Other options include questions that serve as a form of member-checking	Thank you for speaking to me about X programme. My impression is that you feel x and y about X programme for a and b reasons. Am I on the right track?

interviewer with sufficient time to cool-down the emotional intensity of the discussion. Such cool-down questions may also include more future-oriented types of questions, and member-checking to ensure that you have sufficiently understood what the participant has told you.

Section three: Closing remarks (Table 4.8)

The end of the interview should provide the interviewee with a sense of closure. After a participant has taken time out of their schedule to talk to you and in some cases discuss personal or painful experiences, it is important to communicate the value of their time and how this discussion has contributed to your understanding and stock of knowledge about the issue at hand. It may also be an opportunity to build on a referral chain and to think of new questions that could be incorporated into the interview schedule. Additionally, it is important to remind the interviewee that you are an email or phone call away should they have questions or concerns at a later time.

Table 4.8   Section three: Closing remarks

Section three	
	Example
Establish that the interview is coming to an end	
Provide the interviewee with a specific example of how their insights have made a contribution	'Thank you for agreeing to speak to me today. I had not thought about how staff hiring affects programme decisions'
Unless you are conducting a fixed-response interview, ask the participant if there are additional questions that should be asked or issues that should be examined	'What questions should I be asking to really get at staffing issues?'
Try to build new referral chains	'Can you recommend any other people I should speak to?'
	'If you think of anyone else I should speak to about X programme, please pass on my name and contact information'
Remind the interviewee of potential follow-up with the researcher or research team	'If you have any other questions or comments, please feel free to contact me. My information is on your copy of the consent form'
Thank the interviewee again	

Between section tools: Transition statements

Transition statements are usually two or three sentences that serve as a bridge from one section of the interview schedule to another. It is worthwhile to plan the movement between sections to maintain the flow of the interview and to avoid awkward or abrupt movement between topics. In other words, constructing a seemingly natural conversation with an interviewee may require some planning ahead!

- The length of a transition statement will vary. If the next section builds on the previous one, the transition statement can be short.

Example 1: Shorter transition statement.

Now that we have talked about how you found out about the summer camp, I'd like to ask you some questions about your child's experience attending the camp.

- A longer transition statement is often needed if the next section constitutes a new topic or if the researcher needs to set the context.

Example 2: Longer transition statement

Now that we have talked about your child's school performance, I would like to ask you some questions about your relationship with her teacher and the school principal. We're really interested in learning more about connections between home and school.

Ongoing tools: Probes

Probes serve to clarify questions or generate a more elaborate response by the interviewee. Sometimes interviewees do not understand a question as it is originally worded, they fail to provide sufficient detail or their statements are vague. Probes are useful to plan in advance to ensure that any additional visuals, questioning or comments on the behalf of the interviewer remain neutral and communicate the intended meaning and tone that is desired by the interviewer. They also serve as a good reminder to the interviewer to dig deeper beyond surface level responses and to push for further clarification.

Probes come in two basic varieties: Verbal and Visual.

Verbal probes (Table 4.9)

Verbal probes are pre-prepared follow-up questions that encourage the participant to expand on his responses. In the example below, a clarification probe is used to encourage the participant to describe what is meant by the term supportive.

Researcher (*main question*):	What does the term parent engagement mean to you?
Participant:	That's hard to say. It can mean a lot of things. I think for me, it's about being supportive. You know, being there for your child.
Researcher (*probe*):	Can you tell me a bit more about what it means to be supportive? What concrete actions or examples would you associate with the term supportive?

Verbal probes generally encourage the participant to provide more detail, to elaborate or to clarify what the participant wants to communicate.

Table 4.9   Verbal probes

Verbal probe type	Examples
Who, when, what and how questions	Who else was with you?
	When did X happen?
	Where did X happen?
	What was your role?
	What was the outcome?
	How did you feel about that?
	How did you find out about X?
	How would you explain the outcome?
Elaboration questions	Can you tell me a bit more about that?
	Are you able to provide a few more examples?
Clarification questions	What do you mean by that term?
	How do you define X?
	Can you explain the process a bit more?
	How would you classify X?
	How would you identify X?
	Do others define X differently?
Comparison or relational	What characteristics would distinguish that from X?
	How does X compare with Y?
	How does X relate to Y?
	How would you prioritize X in relation to Y?
Imaginative questions	What would you propose?
	What is the ideal X?
	How would you change X?
	If you could start over, what would you do differently? What aspects of X would remain the same?
Verbal cues	Oh, I see
	Uh-huh

Visual probes (Table 4.10)

Visual probes are also used to encourage participants to expand on their responses, but involve the use of visual aids and using appropriately timed visual (and verbal) cues. As we discussed above, the use of visual aids can also be a powerful tool to generate memories or enhanced communication between the researcher and the participant.

Table 4.10   Visual probes

Visual probe type	Examples
Visual aids	Photos, videos, maps, diagrams, flyers
Visual cues	Nodding, smiling, maintaining eye-contact, positive body language (e.g., avoid crossing arms)

The content of an interview schedule: Part 2

Key takeaways

- Good interview questions share many of the same properties: They are clear, not double-barrelled, organized in a logical fashion, non-leading, value-neutral and open-ended.
- Descriptive questions are used more inductively, often to examine localized understandings. They cover everything from basic experiences all the way to interviewees' understandings of a particular condition or outcome.
- Theoretical questions take a more deductive approach and start with a theory or concept, and develop questions that allow you to explore its micro-foundations.

This section largely refers to Section Two of your interview schedule, or the 'central' questions. Once you have established the basic structure and content of your interview schedule, it is time to do the heavy lifting of the interview and construct questions that will allow you to answer your research questions. We outline three key considerations: The Wording of Questions, The Nature of Questions and The Organization of Questions.

The wording of questions (Table 4.11)

Qualitative researchers spend a lot of time writing, re-writing and reflecting on their questions. Below we present some general rules that apply to many interview studies. However, some of these rules will vary depending on the nature of the research. For example, interviews with professionals or experts may contain specialist language or insider jargon, evaluation studies may contain questions that are more value-laden and structured interviews may also quite appropriately contain several closed-ended questions.

The nature of questions

What kinds of questions do you need to ask in order to answer your research questions? Interview questions come in two basic varieties: Descriptive and Theoretical. There is

Table 4.11 Wording questions well

Good questions usually	Phase 1: Original question	Phase 2: Re-written question
Are clear and avoid using jargon, specialist language or acronyms	What publics does the CHP serve?	What groups participate in the community housing programme?
Ask one thing at a time	What programmes are offered for seniors and young families?	What programmes are offered for seniors? What programmes are offered for young families?
Are organized in logical order or sequence	When did you exit the programme? Can you tell me about how you found out about the programme?	Can you tell me about how you found out about the programme? When did you exit the programme?
Are non-leading	Did the programme make you feel better?	How did the programme make you feel?
Are value-neutral	Do you really think that the programme benefits participants?	How do you think the programme affects its participants?
Are open-ended rather than closed-ended	Do you know about the community housing services?	Can you describe the services offered by the community housing programme?

often substantial overlap between the two. Certainly descriptive questions help us answer theoretical questions, and theoretical questions are often descriptive in nature. Interview schedules often contain both kinds of questions and are used at different times for different purposes depending on what you need the information for. We use that distinction simply as a way to categorize the initial starting point for interview questions (for a review of how this relates to coding, see Saldana (2013)).

Descriptive questions (Table 4.12)

Descriptive questions are used more inductively, often to examine localized understandings. They cover everything from basic experiences all the way to interviewees' understandings of a particular condition or outcome. While it may seem obvious, more novice researchers sometimes fail to ask the very questions that may best answer their main research questions. Hoping to derive interviewees' feelings about a particular event or process is not necessarily the same thing as simply asking them directly!

When considering these types of questions, you have to seriously reflect on crafting questions that get at the heart of your research questions. Are you attempting to understand participants' experiences, perceptions or emotions? Are you trying to understand a particular process? Or why or how a particular condition, event or process happened?

Table 4.12 Types of descriptive questions

Starting point	Description	Examples
Knowledge	Questions that examine who, what, why, where and how	Who developed the programme?
		When did the programme start?
		Where did you meet to discuss the programme?
		How did the programme develop?
Experiences and behaviours	Questions that examine participants' involvement, knowledge or history	Can you describe your involvement with the programme?
Experiential	Questions that examine how participants' experience that involvement, knowledge or history	Can you walk me through a typical day?
Interpretation	Questions that examine participants' comprehension	How would you explain X event?
Perceptions	Questions that examine participants' insights or interpretations	What did you learn from that experience?
		How would you describe parents' commitment to the programme?
		How do you think X person would understand that?
Comparison or relational	Questions that examine how participants understand one thing in relation to another	What characteristics would distinguish that from X?
		How does that compare with X?
		How does that relate to X?
		How are things different now compared with 3 years ago?
		How would you prioritize that?
Emotions	Questions that examine participants' feelings, reactions or sentiments.	How did the programme make you feel?
Imaginative	Questions that examine how participants would create, change or revise a particular event or thing	What would you propose?
		What is the ideal programme?
		How would you change the programme?
		If you could start over, what would you do?
Past or future oriented	Questions that examine perceptions or understandings of what was or what will be	How was the programme organized before?
		What do you think the programme will look like in five years?
Values	Questions that examine participants' morals, standards or beliefs	How do you think the programme affects the community?
Evaluative	Questions that examine participants' assessments, estimations or valuations	What impact does the programme have on the community?
		How did you decide to do that?

(Continued)

Table 4.12 (Continued)

Starting point	Description	Examples
Frequency	Questions that examine participants' understandings about duration, regularity or commonality	How often do you attend the programme?
Outsider	Questions that examine how participants would explain something to an outsider or someone with limited knowledge Questions that examine how participants understand their critics	How would you explain the programme to someone who had never heard of it before? What do critics have to say about this programme?
Local causation	Questions that examine how participants understand why something occurred	Why do you think the programme was started?

Adaption and expansion of ideas found in: Saldana, J. 2013. *The Coding Manual for Qualitative Researchers*. Sage Publications, Inc. Saldana's book is one of the best coding manuals on the market

Theoretical questions (Table 4.13)

Theoretical questions take a more deductive approach, and build questions around a theoretical proposition. This approach starts with a theory or concept that you want to explore, and develops questions that allow you to explore its micro-foundations. As we discuss above, often the distinction between descriptive and theoretical questions is more about the *intention* or purpose of the question rather than the nature of the question itself.

Table 4.13 Example of theoretically driven questions

Starting point	Main question ideas	Sample questions
Parents and cultural capital	Alignment with schools Philosophy of parenting Non-school time Parenting practices	How would you describe your relationship with your child's teacher? What role should parents play in their children's learning? Can you describe what your child does on a typical school night?

The organization of questions

You have probably heard the term 'timing is everything'. This statement is particularly true in interview studies. We have already noted the importance of situating the most sensitive or difficult questions within the body of the interview schedule, after introductory remarks and warm-up questions have paved the way.

The main rules still apply (e.g., leaving sensitive questions to the middle); however, there are other organizational considerations. So what timing is right for you, or more specifically, for your research project? Some interviews may demand chronological question ordering. Other interview studies may demand structuring questions in a manner that outlines a particular process or development. Also common is bundling questions by issue, concepts or theories. Bundles can be organized around a particular descriptive account (e.g., local causality), thematically (e.g., patient advocacy) or theoretically driven. Building in such blocks of questions is a useful way to ensure that issues related to that concept are sufficiently addressed, rather than hoping to make connections backwards to a particular theme or theory from a collection of disparate statements made by the participants. It may also facilitate data analysis.

Table 4.14 gives an example of how a researcher could start to theoretically bundle interview questions around three types of 'capital' that have been associated with school success. Starting with the main chunks, the researcher constructs question ideas (and eventually main or sub-interview questions) that address each kind of resource. We have only provided a few examples in each column for illustration purposes, but if this were a real project columns 2, 3 and 4 would include many more categories and questions.

Table 4.14   Example of theoretical bundling of central questions

Step 1	Step 2	Step 3	Step 4
Main bundles	Focus	Sample categories	Sample questions
Cultural capital	Parents	Philosophy of parenting	What role should parents play in their children's schooling?
		Frames of reference	
		Development of pre-literacy and pre-numeracy skills	Can you describe what your child does on a typical school night?
		Non-school time	
		Parent education, occupation	
		Alignment with schools	
Social capital	Networks	Connections to schools	How would you describe your relationship with your child's teacher?
		Information flows	
		Support system	
Economic capital	Resources	Preschool	What was your childcare arrangement before school started?
		RESP	
		Tutoring or other supports	

The demographic survey

Key takeaway

- Asking your respondents to fill out a demographic survey will allow you to efficiently collect information about your participants, including their age, education, occupation and income.

The second source of data is a demographic survey. A demographic survey allows researchers to efficiently collect a variety of key demographic features such as the age, gender, education, occupation and income of their respondents. Many qualitative journal articles and books contain a summary chart containing the key characteristics of the interviewees. The survey is usually filled out by the interviewees, typically at the end of the interview.

Template: Qualitative interview demographic survey

Sex: _____

Age: _____

Ethnicity: _____

Highest level of education: _____

Occupation: _____

Marital status: _____

Residence: Own or Rent or Other: _____

How many children live in the home full-time? _____ Ages? _____

What is your best estimate of your total household income, received by all household members, from all sources, before taxes and deductions?

> Please check off which category best fits you:

____ $0-$29,999

____ $30,000-$69,999

____ $70,000-$99,999

____ $100,000 or more

Summative, theoretical, methodological and personal memos

──────────────────── **Key takeaways** ────────────────────

- There are four categories of memos: Summative, Theoretical, Methodological and Personal.
- Memos include your ongoing reflections, experiences, interpretations and challenges.

The third source of data is the creation of memos. Memos are used to memorialize your ongoing reflections, experiences, interpretations and challenges. Some memos serve as an early form of data analysis, while others point to areas that you need to work on. Memos are your personal notes, and you should not censor yourself.

Just like writing good field notes, we suggest separating your memos into four basic categories (see Table 4.15).

Table 4.15   Summative, theoretical, methodological and personal memos

Type of memo	Description
Summative memos	A summary memo is your 'check sheet' and includes a short description of the interviewee and the broad strokes of the interview
Theoretical memos	Summarize theoretical or conceptual ideas that emerged during the interview Reflect on the connections between theories and concepts that are central to your project and your interviews
Methodological memos	Summarize the methodological issues that emerged during the interview, including events that could affect the quality of the interview, problematic questions, and any new questions that should be added to the interview schedule
Personal memos	Personal memos summarize how you felt during the interview or any personal issues that may have affected the quality of the interview (e.g., you were not feeling well)

CLOSING THE DEAL

————————————————— Key takeaways —————————————————

- The recruitment process includes three key steps: Initial Contact, Follow-up and Scheduling.
- The initial contact usually includes presenting or mailing a potential participant an information letter or flyer.
- Recruitment materials should be staggered in a manner that can accommodate a manageable pool of interviewees at any given time.
- You will often need to follow-up after the participant receives a letter of introduction. If you are *mailing* the introductory letters, each batch should be sent out one week and followed-up approximately 5-7 days later. If you are *emailing* the introductory letter, follow-up times are much shorter, within 48 hours.
- We recommend trying to contact potential participants *no more* than two or three times by phone or email.
- Once you have successfully landed an interview, try to schedule the interview as soon as possible.

If you are fortunate, interviewees are pre-selected and organized in advance. Most interview studies, however, require researchers to actively recruit people who are essentially strangers. Most people are inundated with various kinds of requests by advertisers, businesses, charities and quasi-legitimate research outfits, making recruiting participants for qualitative research increasingly challenging.

So how does one close the deal, particularly when one is trying to engage strangers? At many universities and government agencies, recruitment guidelines are often specified by the research ethics office. These guidelines include recruitment scripts, letters of introduction and other formal consent procedures. However, we can provide you with a set of general guidelines and tips for increasing your recruitment success.

The recruitment process includes three key steps: Initial Contact, Follow-up and Scheduling.

Initial contact

The initial manner by which you contact people will vary depending on whether you have access to the sites or people. However, many research ethics boards also demand some type of formalized introduction. Typically, participants are first mailed or emailed the letter of introduction before being contacted by telephone or email. Other times an information letter or flyer is given to participants at the time of recruitment. The introduction letter, email or flyer usually includes a brief description of the project, the type and duration of participation that is being requested, contact information, and usually a formal request for participation. It can also specify suitability for the study. If applicable, it will also include statements produced by your institution's research ethics office.

Sample: Introduction letter

Dear Parents,

My name is David Smith. I am a researcher at the University, Department of Sociology. I am conducting a study on after-school activities (e.g., ballet, tutoring).

My goal is to generate a sample of families who have *all* of the following characteristics:

- At least one parent who has received at least an undergraduate university degree.
- At least one parent who has been or is employed in a professional, managerial or business related field (e.g., teacher, doctor, financial advisor).
- Currently has at least one child under the age of 14.

I will be calling you shortly. If your family has all three of these characteristics, I will be asking you to participate in an interview. Interviews will take approximately one hour, and will be conducted at a time and location that is most convenient for you.

My project is currently funded by the Government Agency (Grant number: OO-2345). The project has received full ethics clearance by the University (Certificate number: 2013-01-09).

Sincerely,

David Smith
Email: david.smith@university.com
Home: 617-666-7777 Cell: 617-333-5555

Timing

Recruitment materials should be staggered in a manner that can accommodate a manageable pool of interviewees at any given time (Table 4.16). If you are the sole researcher on the project, then it makes no sense to mail out 150 introductory letters all at once. All 150 candidates must be contacted and could theoretically agree to participate – an impossible task to accommodate even by the most seasoned researcher. Estimates will vary depending on the willingness of people to participate and how many interviews can be accommodated in any one week. If you are contacting strangers, it is reasonable to plan for a 10–20% rate of participation, so adjust the pace of your initial contact accordingly.

Table 4.16   Timing of mailed introductory letter

Week	Introductory letters mailed	Follow-up phone-call using recruitment script	Scheduled interviews
1	1-25		
2	26-50	1-25	2
3	51-75	26-50	2
4	76-100	51-75	1
5	101-125	76-100	3
6	126-150	101-125	2
7		126-150	3
8			2
	Total	150 letters	15 interviews

Follow-up

If you are fortunate enough to have access to the potential interviewee's phone number or email, you have the opportunity to follow-up and provide more detail about the study, answer questions and importantly secure an interview. If the interviewee is a stranger, then additional factors should be taken into consideration.

Recruitment script

A recruitment script is commonly used for telephone or email recruitment. It is often used to follow-up after a letter of introduction has been given to potential interviewees.[1] It may be especially important when people other than the researcher are handling recruitment since the person will essentially be representing the project, even if it is only for a few minutes.

---

[1]It may also be used as a primary form of initial contact, though consult with your institution's research ethics board.

However, even if the researcher is handling the recruitment, it is a good idea to work through how the project should be communicated and represented to potential participants and to ensure that they receive all the necessary information they need to make an informed decision. While it may seem redundant, researchers should not assume that the potential interviewee has actually received the introductory letter or email or, even more likely, read it carefully. Similar to the letter of introduction, a recruitment script includes a brief description of the project, the type and duration of participation that is being requested, and usually a formal request for participation.

Example: Sample recruitment script

P = Potential participant; I = Interviewer

I – May I please speak to the owner or manager of the business?

P – I'm the owner, Bob. How may I help you?

I – My name is Chris Jones and I am a PhD student in the Department of Education at the University. I am working on a project about the private tutoring industry. My supervisor and I are conducting interviews with business owners. The questions include your background, the history of your business, and the characteristics and tutoring habits of your students. You should have received an information letter about this project approximately one week ago. Did you receive this information?

P – Yes, I received the letter last week.

I – Wonderful. Would you be willing to participate in an interview? The interview would last about one hour, and would be arranged for a time convenient to your schedule.

Timing

The timing of contact is important. If you are *mailing* the introductory letters, each batch should be sent out one week and followed-up approximately 5–7 days later. If you are *emailing* the introductory letter, then follow-up times are much shorter, within 48 hours if the recipient has not already contacted you. It is best to schedule the interview soon after the interviewee agrees to participate in order to maintain enthusiasm and reduce the chance that they will forget or change their mind. See Table 4.16 above.

Other timing contingencies matter for recruiting. Think carefully about the population under study and whether things like the day of the week, time of day, weather or time of year matter. A Monday evening follow-up phone call may seem perfectly reasonable to a retiree, but may be a source of irritation for a parent struggling to put young children to bed. Similarly, day-time follow-up calls may be suitable if you are intending to contact stay-at-home moms, but not sensible if you are interested in mid-career professionals. And as strange as it sounds, you should be aware of other contingencies such as the weather. Phoning people who have struggled to make it home after a severe snow-fall will not put you in participants' 'good books'.

Contact attempts

After sending the letter, we recommend trying to contact potential participants *no more* than two or three times by phone or email. After two or three unsuccessful attempts to reach someone, you can reasonably assume that the person is not interested in participating.

Personality

Recruiting strangers is a very challenging task. It requires a degree of sales(wo)manship! You have to consider whether you have the right personality to entice potential interviewees. If you are very uncomfortable or awkward recruiting interviewees, it may be worthwhile having someone who has more confidence or charisma to follow-up and close the deal on your behalf.

Scheduling

Once you have successfully landed an interview, try to schedule the interview as soon as possible. Long delays between your initial contact and the interview may increase the likelihood a participant will cancel or lose interest or forget about the interview. The day before the scheduled interview, you should phone or email the participant to remind them of the interview, and confirm its location and time.

As a rule of thumb, you should be prepared to conduct the interview at a moment's notice. In some cases, your newly recruited participant may want to conduct the interview right then and there. Unless there is some methodological reason for begging off the request, have your interview schedule and recording devices (e.g., digital recorder, call recorder adapter) ready to go – this is when you will be especially thankful to have an interview bag ready to go!

INTERVIEWING TECHNIQUES

───────────────────────── **Key takeaways** ─────────────────────────

- Before conducting a face-to-face, photo or video or video-conference interview, you should know your interview schedule inside and out.
- In most cases, you will be interviewing virtual strangers. It is important that you make your participant feel comfortable and build a rapport.
- During the interview, you have to engage in active listening and seeing. Active listening and seeing involves more than sitting quietly and politely; it involves being highly attuned to not only what your interviewee has to say, but also what is communicated through body language.
- Good interviewers stay in control and manage their physical and verbal reactions to participants' responses.

At first glance, it seems strange that many books and articles about interview studies have lots to say about gaining access and ethics, but provide little detail in terms of how one actually conducts an interview. How come? Well, part of the reason is that unlike other methodological issues, many aspects of conducting interviews defy standardization. The structure of the interview, the topic of the study, and the characteristics of the interviewer and the participants shape how an interview is actually conducted. This does not mean that anything goes, however. There are some general rules that transcend all forms of interview studies and personalities.

Know thy interview schedule

Before conducting a face-to-face, photo or video or video-conference interview, you should know your interview schedule inside and out.

- First, memorizing the interview schedule will allow you to quickly move back and forth between sections. In the context of a guided or semi-structured interview, your participant may jump around from one part of your interview schedule to another and you have to be prepared to go with the flow, return to questions that are still unanswered and stop yourself from re-asking a question that the participant has technically already answered out of sequence.
- Second, reading from an interview schedule not only makes you look unprepared, it will limit your ability to build a rapport. How can you put your interviewee at ease and make eye contact if you are constantly looking down at a piece of paper, or flipping wildly through your interview schedule? Periodic and discrete glances at the interview schedule are fine, but should be done only as a quick reminder.
- Third, in the case of remote interviews, the interviewee may not be able to see you, but they will be able to hear you. Reading from the interview schedule will make you sound robotic and unnatural. Similar to other types of interviews (e.g., face-to-face) you will have difficultly managing exchanges that are fast-paced or that jump back and forth between topics unless you can easily move seamlessly from one question to another.

Build a rapport

In most cases, you will be interviewing virtual strangers. It is important that you make your participant feel comfortable.

- First, identify yourself and thank them for participating. If the interview is in person, shake the person's hand, make eye contact, and smile warmly (however, you must be aware of cultural or religious practices that discourage physical contact). Even if you are nervous, you should exude a degree of confidence.
- Second, if it is appropriate, try to connect with the participant on a personal level in some way. In most cases, any personal exchanges should be about positive and non-controversial topics (e.g., not the results of the last election).

- Third, in the case of in-person interviews, anticipate and dress for the occasion to make your participant (and yourself) more conformable in the interview setting. If you are interviewing recent high school drop-outs, you may damage your credibility if you show up for the interview in a three-piece suit!

Be alert: Active listening and seeing

Active listening and seeing involves more than sitting quietly and politely; it involves being highly attuned to not only what your interviewee has to say, but also what is communicated through body language.

- First, reflect back your participant's communication style and energy level. So if the participant is laid back and soft-spoken, try to match their interactional style.
- Second, do not interrupt your participant. Your job is to ask your questions, probe when necessary and be highly attuned to what and how the participant responds to questions and their body language.
- Third, allow for silence. Do not attempt to lighten the moment or fill the void with mindless chit-chat. Worse yet, do not respond to the question or try to direct the response. Give your participant the time and space to answer the question, and consider why the silence occurred. Was the participant simply taking a moment to reflect on the question? Is this simply their interactional style? Is the question sensitive or embarrassing? Or has rapport broken down?
- Fourth, consider whether probes are necessary. Has the question been fully answered? Do you fully understand the meaning? Should you ask a follow-up question?
- Fifth, receive rather than offer support or criticism. As a rule, you should keep your opinions to yourself and only use verbal (e.g., 'Oh, I see') or visual cues (e.g., nodding) that encourage the participant to fully flesh out their experiences or understandings.
- Sixth, read participants' non-verbal cues, including their tone, posture, facial expression and gestures. Good interviewers pick up not only what people say but the way in which they say it.
- Seventh: Even if you 'hit it off' with a participant, they are not your friend. You have to find a way to make your interviewee comfortable, while also being professional.

Control your physical and verbal reactions

In theory, good interviewers should make excellent poker players. A good interviewer stays in control and manages their own physical and verbal reactions to the participants' responses.

- First, start off with good body language, including maintaining eye contact, and not doing things such as crossing your arms or slouching in your chair.
- Second, control your physical and verbal reactions. Some interviews involve sensitive or embarrassing topics and behaviours that are not culturally or socially sanctioned. Sometimes your interviewee will tell you something that is far more personal than you were expecting. Looking down or away, flinching, gasping or shifting in your seat may make your participant feel judged or embarrassed and will surely kill any rapport that you have built up.

TRANSCRIPTION DECISIONS

─────────────────────────── Key takeaways ───────────────────────────

- There are two main approaches to transcription: De-naturalist and Naturalist.
- De-naturalist approaches do not record the idiosyncratic elements of the interview or speech, including background noises, stutters, pauses or laughter.
- Naturalist approaches attempt to capture all idiosyncratic elements of speech, including sighs, pauses and stutters.
- Regardless of your approach, make sure you properly label your transcript, including the name or pseudonym of the participant, contact information, location, date of the interview and any other information that may be helpful.

Transcription is rarely discussed other than to comment on the drudgery of the task. Since it serves as the main source of data for interview studies, the practice of transcription is worth reflecting on and will vary depending on the approach and aim of the interview study (see Oliver et al., 2005). Some researchers make detailed notes and only transcribe key quotes from interviews; others subscribe to the belief that the entire interview should be transcribed.

There are two basic approaches to transcription, de-naturalism and naturalism.

De-naturalist transcription

De-naturalist approaches do not record the idiosyncratic elements of the interview or speech, including background noises, stutters, pauses or laughter. This approach is more interested in *what* meaning-making processes are more important than *how* these understandings are articulated.

Naturalist transcription

Naturalist approaches attempt to capture all idiosyncratic elements of speech, including sighs, pauses and stutters. Common in conversational analysis, naturalist transcriptions are appropriate when both the content and the pattern of speech is important. While there is no standard set of transcription symbols, many researchers build on a version of Jeffersonian Transcription Notation. If you create your own symbols, it is a good idea to create a chart or legend to jog your memory.

Table 4.17 gives a few examples of common transcription symbols.

Table 4.17 Common transcription symbols

Symbol	Notation	Example
(.)	Brief pause	I (.) think that it helps patients
(#)	Longer pause timed in seconds	I'm just not sure (5) if the programme really makes a difference
CAPS	Increased volume of speech	I have JUST HAD IT with her
:	Stretched out sound	I am just so gl:ad that it's over
Italics	Emphasized speech	That is *the* worst part of it
(NOISE)	Sound of noise	I know I sound a bit paranoid (LAUGHTER)

MANAGING INTERVIEW DATA

Key takeaways

- There are three basic data managing issues that are easily handled in an Excel file: Recruitment, Participant Information and Labelling.
- Recruitment Data Management is focused on keeping track of who, how and when you contacted potential participants. It also documents potential participants' contact information and the date, time and location of scheduled interviews.
- Participant Information Data Management documents your interviewees, including their name, contact information, demographic information (from a demographic survey, discussed above), any key reflections that you noted in the field, and the status of the transcription.
- Labelling includes properly identifying your materials, including sources, dates, locations and contact information.

Experienced researchers are well aware of the mountains of data that quickly pile up over the course of a research study. Unless you have an encyclopaedic memory, the people, places, strange events, locations and reflections can become unmanageable unless you have a good system in place to store and organize your interview data. Below we present some fairly 'low-tech' and user-friendly, easy to implement options that can be generated in Excel for more novice qualitative researchers who are not yet familiar with various CAQDAS options.[2]

There are three basic data managing issues that are easily handled in an Excel file: Recruitment, Participant Information and Labelling.

---

[2]If you are familiar with CAQDAS options, you are already aware that these programs allow you to store, audio and video recordings, transcripts, photos, journal articles and other information pertaining to your interview study.

Recruitment data management

Once you have identified your sample of participants, you should keep track of a list of potential interviewees and their contact information. You may also need to keep track of when you contacted them, the number of contact attempts, whether they agreed to participate or not, and whether they asked you to phone them back at a more convenient time. If they agreed to participate in an interview, you will want to record the date, time and location of the interview (Table 4.18). You may also want to create a colour-coding or shorthand system so you can quickly identify the status of the potential interviewee.

Maintaining good records has the added benefit of quantifying how successful your recruitment efforts are. If you find that few people have agreed to participate, you should retool your approach, your letter of information or method of recruiting.

Table 4.18   Template: Recruitment data management

Name	Phone number	Address	Date of mailed introduction letter	Phone call attempts	Interview status	Other
J. Peters	888-8765	11 Chestnut Drive	March 1	March 7 March 12	Not interested; do not contact again	
P. Jenkins	888-6543	20 Walnut Street	March 1	March 7	March 15 1 pm Steve's coffee shop	Send reminder email Tuesday
R. Rose	777-6543	15 Lake Drive	March 1	March 7 March 12	Interested, but on vacation for 2 weeks. Call back April 1 to schedule an interview	

Participant information data management

Once you have conducted an interview, you will need to develop some kind of system to keep track of your interviewees, including their name, contact information, demographic information (from a demographic survey, discussed above), any key reflections that you noted in the field, and the status of the transcription. Even if you are at the stage of assigning pseudonyms, it is still a good idea to keep at least one master file of your informants' names and contact information in case you need to reach out to them at another time. This master file should be kept in a secure location that is only accessible to you or other people who have been cleared for access. Most, if not all of this information can be housed in an Excel sheet (Table 4.19).

Table 4.19 Participant information data management

Name	Pseudonym	Phone number	Address	Interview date	Notes/ reflections	Transcript status	Age	Sex	Education	Occupation	Income

Quick tip: The added-value of good record keeping

Using the demographic survey and participant information data management spread-sheet, you will be able to quickly create a variety of summary charts that contain key pieces of information about your participants. These charts provide a snapshot of your participants, and help you and your readers keep track of your interviewees. These charts are routinely included in books, journal articles and theses that draw on qualitative data.

Example: Interviews

Name	Role	Sex	School name	School type	Number of interviewees	Total interviews
Simone	P	F	Verona Street	JK-6	1	3
Richard	T	M	West End Drive	JK-8	1	2
David	CYW	M	Parkville Avenue	JK-8	1	3
Whitney	VP	F	Parkville Avenue	JK-8	1	2
Total					**4**	**10**

Names: Pseudonyms are used.

Roles: P=Principal; VP=Vice-Principal; T=Teacher; CYW=Child and Youth Worker.

CONCLUSION

This chapter outlines concrete strategies for developing an interview study. We review the main types of interviews, including conversational and fixed response and the main methods of interviewing, including face-to-face and internet interviewing. Next, we discuss various kinds of hardware and software options. We then turn to the heart of the chapter – developing an interview schedule. In this section we detail the key steps, considerations and strategies for crafting interview questions and ordering and bundling questions. We also outline specific interview techniques that will improve the quality of your interview. Finally, we address transcription decisions and provide you with important data management tools.

Now that you have the tools you need to conduct an interview study, the next chapter is on the cousin of this approach, focus groups. Focus groups are a useful stand-alone or complementary data collection tool. Focus groups have several advantages, including the ability to interview several people at once. By the end of the next chapter you will have the tools you need to design and execute a focus group.

KEY TERMS

Asynchronous Internet Interview	Internet Interview	Synchronous Internet Interview
Conversational Interview	Interview Schedule	Telephone Interview
Demographic Survey	Naturalist Transcription	Theoretical Bundling of Questions
De-naturalist Transcription	Photo or Video Auto-Driven	Theoretical Questions
Descriptive Questions	Photo or Video Elicitation	Transition Statements
Face-to-Face Interview	Photo or Video Interview	Visual and Verbal Probes
Fixed Response Interview	Semi-Structured Interview	
Guiding Interview	Summative, Theoretical, Methodological and Personal Memos	

5

HOW TO DO FOCUS GROUPS:
MAKING THE MOST
OF GROUP PROCESSES

─────────────────────── **Learning objectives** ───────────────────────

By the end of this chapter you will have the tools to:

- Develop a focus group discussion guide
- Choose a location for your focus group
- Set up and facilitate a focus group discussion
- Moderate a focus group interview
- Understand the advantages and disadvantages of focus group discussions

─────────────────────── **Chapter summary** ───────────────────────

This chapter presents information on focus groups, including key considerations for the focus group com-position, and group dynamics, and the location of the focus group interview. It outlines the steps needed to create an effective interview discussion guide. It also outlines the main roles in the focus group interview, including that of moderator and that of note taker. The chapter then presents information on selecting a location to host the focus group. It also outlines some of the advantages and disadvantages of using a focus group discussion.

INTRODUCTION: WHAT IS A FOCUS GROUP?

Khan and Manderson (1992: 57) define the role of the focus group to be a method for 'describing and understanding of a particular issue from the perspective of the group's participants'. Focus groups are often referred to as 'focus group interviews' or 'focus group discussions'. Each term conveys an important piece of what focus groups are: an opportunity for multiple interviewees to interact with one another and have a conversation in a group setting. Throughout this chapter we will refer to them interchangeably as focus groups, focus group interviews or focus group discussions. The key, however, is to remember that a focus group is truly about a *group process*, and not merely a gathering of individuals to be interviewed.

Focus groups can be used for exploratory research, explanatory research, evaluative research or policy-oriented research (Hennink et al., 2011). They are particularly useful for exploring new topics, as an abundance of data can be gathered at one time. They also allow for the collection of a wide range of viewpoints. One key aspect of focus groups is that they allow for the understanding of group processes, including 'observing how an issue is discussed, how participants influence each other or how a strategy or outcome is decided' (Hennink et al., 2011: 138). Focus groups are also often used as one methodological component of a broader study. They are frequently paired with quantitative data or other qualitative methods, such as survey research or in-depth personal interviews.

Focus groups are not just an easy way to gather information from a lot of people in a short period of time. There are times when personal interviews are better suited for gathering data, and there are times when focus groups will be more effective. Focus groups are also not a good method for gathering in-depth individual-level information as they place the group and their interactions as the main source of the data; this is not merely what individual respondents are saying about a particular topic, but also how their thoughts, feelings and opinions were formulated and shared (Morgan, 2012). It is important to keep your research question in mind when deciding which type of method will be most useful.

THE FOCUS GROUP

-------------------------------- Key takeaways --------------------------------

- Group size should be determined by the subject of the research.
- The number of focus group discussions and length of each is determined by the diversity of the topic and the point at which saturation is reached.

Group size

There is no 'right answer' when it comes to the question: How many people should be in a focus group? The existing research suggests anywhere from as few as four to as many as 12 participants (Warren and Karner, 2010). Morgan (1998) suggests 6–10 members, but he elaborates that the number of participants truly depends on the topic at hand. Smaller groups are better if the topic is of an emotional nature or when you can expect that each individual will have a lot to say on the particular topic. Larger groups are better for more general topics, and when the researcher wants to hear brief thoughts from as many people as possible. Smaller groups are easier for a moderator to manage, but the group is more vulnerable to negative group dynamics (for example, if there are one or two domineering participants, this will be quite noticeable if there are only five participants in total). Larger groups will have a greater number of opinions, experiences and stories to share, but it may take some time to ensure that everyone has an opportunity to share their thoughts and feelings. Table 5.1 outlines when to choose a smaller group or a larger group.

Number of group discussions

No matter what your topic is, one focus group will not be sufficient. Just as one interview does not tell you a lot about what people, in general, think or feel about a subject, having only one focus group may not be representative of other groups. However, you do not want

Table 5.1 Determining Group Size

Small groups	Large groups
Emotionally charged topics	Neutral topics
Each participant has time to discuss	Wider range of responses, ideas, opinions
Easier for moderators to manage heated discussions	Easier for moderators to manage due to lower level of involvement
Limited range of experiences to be shared	Exploratory research
Vulnerable to group dynamics	Not overly vulnerable to group dynamics

to have too many focus groups, either! Morgan (2012), suggests that most projects should consist of four to six focus groups, but notes that the number will vary dependent on both the range of topics and the diversity of participants. Once you are no longer gathering any new information from the focus group discussions, you have reached *saturation*. Saturation also occurs with personal interviews, and is a desirable point to reach as you know that you have completed extensive research and should begin to analyse your findings.

Length of focus group

Typically, focus group discussions range from one to three hours. From 90 minutes to two hours is an ideal length for a focus group discussion; anything less will not provide enough data, and anything longer can become cumbersome to your participants.

GROUP COMPOSITION

Key takeaways

- Groups can be homogeneous or heterogeneous.
- The decision on group type is contingent upon the nature of your research topic and research question(s).

The composition of the group will depend on the goals of your research. In some cases, having a homogeneous group will be most beneficial, but in other cases a heterogeneous group will provide the greatest information. Regardless of the group's make up, the goal is to create a comfortable environment so that productive discussion can occur.

When planning your groups, think about demographic information such as age, race, sex, social class, religion, income, education, etc. It is important to have all relevant groups represented, which means you will need to have a number of focus group discussions to ensure everyone is included and as many different perspectives as possible can be captured.

But, you will need to decide whether your groups should be homogeneous or heterogeneous. For topics like perceptions of school violence, a heterogeneous group would be a great way to gain a number of different views from people of all ages, races, etc. However, for exploring a topic such as intimate partner violence, it would not be a good idea to have men and women in the same group; therefore, a homogeneous group would be the best choice.

Group homogeneity

A homogeneous group is beneficial because the participants are often willing to share their thoughts, feelings and opinions with others who are similar to them and can understand their point of view. If individuals feel that others in the group are more knowledgeable or more powerful than they are, they may be reluctant to share their ideas or opinions. A homogeneous group is desirable when sensitive topics are under investigation, or when the research requires participants to have shared a common experience or have a common background understanding about the research topic. One benefit of homogeneous groups occurs during data analysis, as the researcher is able to determine whether participants vary in how they discuss or respond to an issue (Hennink et al., 2011).

Most commonly, groups are segmented based on a particular characteristic like gender. *Segmentation* occurs when groups consist of particular categories of participants. Using the example of intimate partner violence from above, having homogeneous groups segmented by gender – with groups for male participants and separate groups for female participants – would be one way to ensure that participants felt comfortable sharing their views within the focus group setting, and did not feel re-victimized. For other topics, segmentation based on age, socioeconomic status or life status (especially if authority relationships are involved) may be more appropriate. Groups can also be segmented by multiple categories, for example by age *and* gender. Thus, groups would consist of young men, young women, older men and older women. Some research suggests that men and women interact differently in mixed focus groups, but there is debate within the literature (for examples, see Fern, 2001; Hennink, 2007; Krueger and Casey, 2000 and Morgan, 1997). On the one hand, segmented groups allow comparison between groups: for example, allowing you to see how men and women differ on a particular topic, or how older men's views differ from younger men's views. On the other hand, the use of segmented groups means that the total number of focus groups necessary to achieve saturation may multiply greatly; it is unlikely that only one group per segment will be enough to gather strong data (Knodel, 1993; Morgan, 2012).

Group heterogeneity

A heterogeneous group is beneficial because the participants will likely have different views and opinions. This can open up the dialogue, allowing individuals to explain why they hold a particular viewpoint. It might also create some disagreement among the participants, which will ensure that there are varied opinions presented. The more expla-nation that is given for why individuals hold their views and opinions, the richer the data will be.

Should the participants know one another? This is one aspect of focus groups that is widely debated, and there are pros and cons to each answer. On the one hand, sometimes attempting to recruit individuals who have no connection to one another is challenging. Participants may not want to come and chat about their opinions and feelings without hav-ing a friend, co-worker or family member present. Holbrook and Jackson (1996) reported that they had great difficulty when attempting to find respondents with no personal con-nection, as nobody wanted to participate alone. On the other hand, when 'natural groups' are utilized – those that occur on their own without the influence of the researcher, such as a group of friends, students or co-workers – people may not share as detailed informa-tion about their opinions and experiences, assuming that the other group members already understand where they are coming from. Morgan (1998) suggested that in cases where the details and background are important, then a group of strangers is a better option than a natural group (Bryman et al., 2012). However, in certain contexts (for example, dense neighbourhoods or small organizations), it is next to impossible to draw a sample where the respondents are strangers.

Use of pre-existing groups

Groups that already exist, such as through a particular social group or even a counselling group, can be recruited for focus group discussions. In these situations, recruitment is usu-ally quite easy, and often rapport already exists within the group. However, participants will also have knowledge about one another. This can be a benefit, for example if respondents are able to remind each other of details that they may have forgotten; it can also be a draw-back, as participants may not share as much information, assuming that their peers already know what they were going to say. There is also a concern about confidentiality. Individuals may not share as much personal information because they do not want their group mem-bers to know particular things about them or their family.

GROUP DYNAMICS

———————————————————————— Key takeaways ————————————————————————

- The group dynamics must be managed so all participants can have an equal opportunity to share their thoughts.
- The group interactions are an important part of focus group research and are key components of the data.

Have you ever held back from sharing your opinion with others because of the group that you were in? Maybe you did not want to draw attention to yourself, so you did not share your thoughts or feelings. Or, maybe you spoke up in order to be different from the rest of the group and stand out from the crowd. This happens in focus group research as well. How people work as a group and how they present themselves in a group setting can vary, and is something the researcher must take into consideration.

In a personal interview, respondents will certainly act differently than in a small group. Hollander (2004) found that men and women interacted differently, possibly as a result of the diversity of the small group. In conversations about violence, women shared stories about their concerns whereas men did not. Similarly, Karner (1995) found that men's presentation of self differed greatly between personal interviews and focus groups; during personal interviews the men shared much more emotion but in the focus group setting they attempted to appear tough or strong (Warren and Karner, 2010: 140).

Though each group will be different, there are some personality types that will likely emerge within each focus group interview. Hennink et al. (2011) call these the *quiet participant*, *dominant participant*, *rambling participant* and *self-appointed expert*. Table 5.2 outlines the characteristics of each of these participant personalities, as well as some strategies that the moderator can use to manage them (adapted from Hennink et al., 2011: 160–1).

Table 5.2   Types of Participations and Methods of Management

	Characteristics	Facilitation tips
Dominant participant	Monopolize discussion	Body language: Turn away from participant; look at other participants; avoid eye contact
	First to respond	
	Respond to every question, even if they have nothing productive to contribute	Verbal cues: Thank participant and ask others to contribute to discussion
	Interrupt other participants	
Quiet participant	Only speak when asked directly	Body language: Turn toward participant, smile and nod while they answer
	Remain quiet during discussion	
	Only provide short answers	Verbal cues: Probe for more detail; reinforce that everyone's opinions are valued; ask person directly if they have anything to share
Rambling participant	Monopolizes discussion	Body language: Turn away from participant; look at other participants; avoid eye contact
	Provides very long, elaborate answers	
		Verbal cues: Interrupt participant by thanking them; redirect discussion and invite others to share
Self-appointed expert	May state outright that they are an expert/ have extensive knowledge on the subject	Verbal cues: Moderator should reiterate that everyone's values are encouraged and respected, and that everyone in the group is an expert on the subject
	State their opinions as though they are facts	

Managing the group can be challenging. If certain individuals are either domineering or too quiet, the whole point of a focus group is lost. The facilitator needs to step in to actively encourage the quiet participants to share their thoughts, and to keep the domineering participants at bay. Statements like 'That's an interesting opinion on the topic. Does anyone else have an opinion?' can help keep the conversation flowing.

Encouraging group discussion, and not merely having each respondent answer in turn is crucial to conducting a focus group interview. Though it is considered an interview, a focus group is considered a *non-directive interview*, where the goal is to gather data from the discussion, the disagreement and the interactions among participants (Hennink et al., 2011). Ample discussion and interaction will ensure that respondents are probing each other, asking for clarification or for additional information to back up their point (in other words, doing the job of the moderator!). On the one hand, if the respondents disagree and question one another, the researcher is able to see various viewpoints and understand diverse perspectives on the topic. On the other hand, if the respondents agree with one another, the researcher can feel confident that their data is supported. This is only achieved, though, when there is ample discussion and interaction among the group members.

Group interaction

The interactions within the groups are an important part of the focus group process and the data to be gathered and analysed. In order to fully understand how the focus group participants view the issues under discussion, noting the types of interactions, the agreements and the disagreements is crucial. Hollander (2004) argues that

> the relationships among the participants and between the participants and the facilitator, as well as the larger social structures within which the discussion takes place - affect the data that are generated in ways that have not yet been widely acknowledged by focus group researchers. (603)

Since it is the group environment itself that brings about such a wide range of issues and variety of perspectives, the details from the group interactions are key components of the data.

INCENTIVES

———————————————— Key takeaway ————————————————

- When planning focus group interviews, the researcher should consider offering incentives to their participants, such as money or food.

Many focus groups will pay respondents for their time, or provide them with other incentives such as a gift card to a local establishment (e.g., a coffee shop or book store) or a water bottle or travel mug. This serves to thank the respondent for their time and effort. Any incentives that are being used should be highlighted during recruitment to help entice respondents.

How much should you offer? Think about how long you expect your respondents to be there for, how far they have to travel, whether they will have had to hire a babysitter, etc. Thinking about your respondents and their life situations will help you answer this question. For example, if you are interviewing parents of small children, you know that they will have to arrange for a babysitter and pay them; work this into your compensation. Remember that your respondents are doing you a favour by participating. Any incentives or payment offered should be a reflection of their sacrifice.

Offering snacks or a light meal after the focus group is a nice way to thank your respondents for their participation, and to provide some closure to the group. If food will be offered, this can be mentioned to your respondents during recruitment so that they know whether or not they should pack their own snacks, and also so they can inform you of any serious dietary concerns. Food can be put out before the focus group as a way of encouraging respondents to mingle and meet. It also gives them something to do in the awkward few minutes before the focus group discussion begins. However, food can serve as a distraction if the respondents bring it to the table. Imagine someone taking a large bite of a sandwich and then trying to share their opinion … it is not an ideal situation. Refreshments can cause other challenges, specifically if the focus group respondents include individuals from religious or cultural communities, where a certain preparation might be required or a particular type of food should not be consumed (Barbour, 2007). At the very least, offer your respondents some water so that they do not feel parched while they are talking.

ROLES

Key takeaways

- There are three main roles in a focus group interview: the Moderator, the Second Interviewer and the Note Taker.
- The style and facilitation skills of the moderator are key for an effective focus group discussion and managing the group dynamics.
- The moderator has four main tasks: Introductory tasks, Ethical tasks, Group Cohesion tasks and Facilitating Discussion tasks.

The moderator

The moderator plays a key role in the successful execution of a focus group interview. The moderator serves to guide the questioning of the group, and also plays the role of a facilitator to ensure that discussion occurs, that each participant's voice is shared, and that the conversation stays on topic. The moderator's role is similar to the interviewer's role in an in-depth interview, as they are both tasked with developing rapport, asking questions, responding to the flow of discussion, and probing for detail. The moderator is also tasked with ensuring that a group of respondents are all able to share their views, speak their opinions and not dominate the group, and with managing the group dynamics that will inevitably differ with each group of people. The amount and type of direction that the moderator provides can influence both the quality and the type of data that comes from the group (Stewart et al., 2007).

Hennink et al. (2011) outline four main tasks that moderators perform during a focus group interview: (1) Introductory tasks; (2) Ethical tasks; (3) Group Cohesion tasks; (4) Facilitating Discussion tasks. *Introductory tasks* are those that help to welcome the group and set up what the next hour or two will be about for the participants. The moderator should be sure to introduce themselves, and also the note taker, or any other individuals that are present. They should broadly outline the research and how the information gathered from the focus group will eventually be used. The moderator should outline any guidelines or rules for how the focus group participants should conduct themselves. *Ethical tasks* include ensuring informed consent and dealing with any questions regarding tape recording, confidentiality or data storage. The moderator should make sure that they receive consent from each member of the focus group discussion. *Group Cohesion tasks* are related to creating an encouraging and welcoming environment where all members feel comfortable, and include positive body language and creating a friendly atmosphere. Finally, *Facilitating Discussion tasks* include managing the group dynamics as they arise, probing all group members to ensure thorough responses, ensuring the discussion remains focused on the research topic, and watching the timing of the questions and overall discussion.

The level of structure that the focus group takes will impact the moderator's role and the style of discussion. A focus group with more structure will need a moderator who has a high level of control over the group. The moderator will have to control the questions and the topics, and to focus the group discussion. The moderator can also take control of the group dynamics, facilitating the interactions among participants and ensuring that there is equal participation (Morgan, 2012). Groups with less structure have more flow to the discussion, as the moderator can let the participants steer the conversation without much interference. In this instance, some participants may dominate the conversation while others may barely share anything at all. The biggest difference between the two forms of groups is that 'a less structured discussion means that the group can pursue its own interests, while a more structured approach means that the moderator imposes the researcher's interests' (Morgan, 2012: 277). Finding a balance with the level of structure is often best for both the researcher and the participants.

When should the moderator intervene? This is a tricky question. Minimal intervention is the best situation, as it will allow the conversation to flow as naturally as possible. However, sometimes the discussion can go completely off topic and the moderator needs to bring the group back to task. The moderator should be careful in these instances, as seemingly unrelated conversations can sometimes actually be peripherally related to the topic at hand, and might reveal some significant information. The moderator's main task is to facilitate data collection, and they should be familiar with the research to a point that they can make the best decision whether to intervene or allow the discussion to continue. Hennink et al. (2011: 159) note that 'a focus group discussion is therefore working effectively when the moderator has limited input yet is subtly managing the discussion'.

A word of caution: research has demonstrated that the *deference effect* can be present in focus groups. The deference effect is when respondents share information that they think the moderator wants them to share instead of what they really want to say (Bernard, 1994). The moderator should be careful to remain impartial, and to encourage both positive and negative opinions and viewpoints to avoid the deference effect occurring (Hennink et al., 2011).

Second interviewer/note taker

It is wise to have a *second interviewer* or a *note taker* present in addition to the moderator. While the moderator is the person who will ask all of the questions and keep the discussion flowing, the second interviewer or note taker can take on some of the peripheral tasks to ensure the smooth flow of the focus group discussion. The second interviewer will play a supportive role, for example writing notes on a chalk board, handing out any supplies needed for activities, such as writing utensils, paper, etc. A note taker – which should be used whether a second interviewer is present or not – writes down the key issues that are being discussed, and takes down enough detail of the focus group discussion that it could be recreated should the tape recorder fail or should the group refuse to allow the discussion to be tape recorded (Hennink et al., 2011). The note taker should also record any non-verbal information, such as the respondent's body language.

LOCATION

─────────────────────── **Key takeaway** ───────────────────────

- Choose a location that is easily accessible for participants, is thoughtfully arranged and free from avoidable distractions.

───

When focus groups occur on TV or in movies, they are usually based on market research and not social science research. They often take place in rooms with two-way mirrors, where the subjects are all sitting around a table discussing their views on a particular topic, and there are people behind the two-way mirror interpreting the responses. This is an option for the types of focus group interviews discussed in this chapter, but not many researchers have the facilities or money to conduct their focus groups in this type of location.

Focus groups can be conducted in a variety of locations to suit the needs of the researcher, research topic and participants. You will want to make sure, though, that the location is quiet, private, easy to locate and distraction free. The physical layout of both the group and the room are important aspects of the location to consider. Below are some key considerations when planning out where to hold the focus group discussion.

Proximity

Focus groups that are held in familiar and comfortable locations, such as a shopping mall or recreation centre are easy for participants to access, have ample parking, and are often perceived as more attractive to participants (Stewart et al., 2007). If a group of professionals, such as doctors or nurses, are being asked to participate, try to have the focus group at or near their place of work, such as a private conference room in the building where they work. If you use a location that requires paid parking, arrange to have your participants' parking validated or provide them with pre-paid parking passes to alleviate any financial burden on them. No matter what type of location you select, you should make sure that you visit it beforehand to ensure that it is physically accessible to all of your respondents (Barbour, 2007).

Indoor versus outdoor

There will likely be more distractions to contend with outside (birds, bugs, wind) but depending on the topic you are studying, it may be more conducive to creating a comfortable environment for your participants. Be sure to inform your participants beforehand if you will conduct a focus group outside so they can wear the appropriate clothing, sunscreen, insect repellent, etc. Microphones are sensitive to background noise, and a location that is windy, has traffic or even has a stream nearby, could affect the quality of the tape recording.

Seating arrangement

Stewart et al. (2007) claim that respondents will feel most comfortable when they are seated around a table. A table serves as a barrier between respondents which can give more reserved members of the group a sense of comfort. It also gives each participant their own personal space and a location to put their hands, rest their elbows, and place their food or water. A table also provides cover for legs, and can make individuals feel more comfortable if they are in a group with both men and women. We recommend seating the participants in a circle or oval, so that everyone is a part of the discussion and can have eye contact with all of the other respondents. This will help facilitate a true discussion. We also recommend that the moderator sit as a member at the table, so that they can facilitate the discussion in a smooth manner, and see each of the respondents as well.

Name tags

One way of encouraging conversation and rapport among participants is to offer a name tag. It's best to only put first names on the tag to maintain as much privacy as possible. Having the name tags sit on the table facing the other respondents ensures that they are always visible, and not covered by a scarf or crossed arms, for example, which is one concern with name tags that are worn on the chest. Make sure that the moderator has a list of all participants' names, and where they are seated to ensure that they can address everyone personally.

Distractions

Be sure to eliminate as many physical distractions as possible. Wall decorations should be kept to a minimum, as paintings, artwork or other decorations can serve as a distraction from the group conversation. If props are being used as part of the activities, try to keep them out of view until they are about to be used. If food and refreshments will be provided after the focus group, keep them out of sight or in another room so they do not attract the attention of hungry participants. Similarly, if you are having a catering company set up refreshments, make sure they do not come in to set up while you are in the middle of a focus group interview!

THE DISCUSSION GUIDE

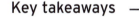
Key takeaways

- The discussion guide has four key parts: Introductory Remarks, Opening Questions, Body Questions and Closing Questions.
- Probing respondents and having activities can help to guide the discussion.

Like the interview schedule, discussed in Chapter 4, the discussion guide includes all of the topics and questions that the researcher or moderator will ask during the focus group discussion. Unlike the interview schedule, the discussion guide should be quite short; remember that you are directing the questions to a group of people and therefore you will ideally receive a wide range of views and opinions for each question, which takes much more time than an individual interview. Focus group discussion guides often include too much information and attempt to ask too many questions. This can turn the focus group interview into a group-survey, as opposed to an interactive group discussion (Stewart et al., 2007). Because of the variety of participants within a focus group, the discussion guide should serve as a checklist to ensure topics are covered, even when they do not play out in the same order during the focus group discussion. Having a moderator who is flexible will allow for a more fluid discussion (Hennink et al., 2011).

A focus group discussion guide follows the structure of a funnel, beginning quite broadly and becoming more focused as the questions and discussion progress. Typically, the discussion guide will begin with *Introductory Remarks*, where administrative details are outlined along with a brief discussion of the research topic. This provides the participants with some idea of what to expect during the rest of their time together. Following the *Introductory Remarks* are some *Opening Questions*. These are usually general or broad questions, designed to develop rapport among the participants and make them feel at ease when sharing their opinions and ideas. These questions often do not add anything to the analysis; in fact, 'information from these questions is rarely analyzed' (Hennink et al., 2011: 144). Moving the group forward, the *Body* questions become more focused and directly related to the central research issues addressed. These questions are the main thrust of the focus group, and from them you will generate the data for your analysis. Placing them toward the middle of the focus group discussion ensures that the participants are more comfortable, relaxed and honest with one another. The final section consists of *Closing Questions* which help to conclude the discussion. In addition to these main sections, the discussion guide often includes transition statements and probes (see Chapter 4 for a more detailed discussion on transition statements). Table 5.3 provides an overview of a general focus group discussion guide.

Table 5.3   Generic focus group discussion guide

	Section One: Introductory Remarks
A1	
	Transition Statement
	Section Two: Opening Questions
B1	Warm-up
B2	Warm-up
	Transition Statement
	Section Three: The Body
C1	Central
C2	Central
C3	Central
	Transition Statement
	Section Three: Closing Questions
D1	

Section one: Introductory remarks (Table 5.4)

This section serves to provide your respondents with information about the research topic. It also is an opportunity to discuss any administrative information, such as the use of a tape recorder. This section should outline how the interview process will occur, including the requirements for an open, honest and polite dialogue, that everyone will be encouraged and invited to participate, that questions can and should be answered by anyone, and that those who have a differing or dissenting opinion from the one presented should share their opinion as well (Berg and Lune, 2012).

Table 5.4   Section one: Introductory remarks

1. Moderator introduces her- or himself, along with any other members of the research team and note taker
2. Thank the participants for their participation
3. Provide a brief description of the research in broad terms
4. Establish the project's purpose
5. Establish how you will use the information
6. Handle administrative details including:

    - How long the focus group will take
    - Review and sign ethics forms

    If applicable ask for permission to record the interview and for how you will use the recording

7. Ask the participants if they have any questions or concerns before the interview begins

Section two: Opening questions (Table 5.5)

The opening questions allow the group to warm up to one another; these questions are designed to 'break the ice'. Typically the questions in this section are generally about a term or a concept related to the research. The moderator will take time to probe the respondents for complete answers and encourage them to answer in a conversational manner. This way, the opening questions also serve to teach the respondents how they should answer the remaining questions.

Example: 'A lot of our discussion today will focus on X. Can you describe your experiences with X? How do people you know/in your family feel about X?' Probe: 'Can you tell me what the term X means to you?'

Table 5.5   Section two: Opening questions

1. Ask participants to introduce themselves
2. Ask general questions related to the main themes or concepts of the study

    - Take time to probe for complete answers, and encourage interaction and dialogue

Section three: The body (Table 5.6)

After a brief transition – either a question or statement – the respondents are directed to the *Body* of the focus group discussion. These are the key questions of the most importance to the research at hand. Typically, there are two or three main topics of discussion with two or three questions related to each topic. They are usually the most challenging questions for the respondents to answer, and can lead to debate, disagreement or very insightful discussion. This is the most important section of the focus group interview as most of the data for analysis will be generated from the responses to the body questions.

Table 5.6   Section three: The body

1. Introduce the first key topic of discussion

    • Ask two or three questions about this topic

2. Introduce the second key topic of discussion

    • Ask two or three questions about this topic

3. If there are any other key questions, ask them now

Section four: Closing questions (Table 5.7)

The questions in the closing section will once again be more general and provide some closure to the focus groups. Often, the moderator will provide a brief overview of what has been discussed, summarizing the key points and insights that have been made, and then turn it back to the group to ensure that their opinions are being accurately reflected.

Example: 'We're now reaching the end of our conversation. Does anyone have anything that they would like to add to the discussion before we conclude? Is there anything you were hoping we would ask about but we didn't? I would like to thank you for your participation in today's discussion. The opinions, views and experiences you have shared are very valuable to the research process.'

Table 5.7   Section four: Closing questions

1. Establish that the focus group interview is coming to an end
2. Summarize the key points and insights that have been made
3. Thank the respondents for their time
4. Remind the respondents of potential follow-up with the researcher or research team
5. If applicable, ask the respondents to fill out a post-discussion questionnaire and offer them some refreshments
6. Thank the respondents again

Probes

The use of probes during a focus group is an important way for the moderator to keep the group focused. The moderator can probe the respondents individually or the group as a whole. Table 5.8, adapted from Hennink et al. (2011) describes eight different types of probes used in focus group discussions.

Table 5.8   Probes

Type of probe	Explanation	Examples
Individual	Prompt one individual to elaborate, clarify, or otherwise extend their statement	Can you elaborate? Can you tell me what you mean by the term 'respect'?
Group	Ask the group as a whole to highlight a concern or perspective that one participant has raised and seek input from everyone	How does everyone else feel about that? Does anyone have an example of that?
Group explanation	Ask the group as a whole to explain/elaborate on an issue when everyone is in agreement	Is this everyone's experience? You all seem to understand. Can you explain it to me?
Ranking	Ask the participants to order a number of items. Follow-up by asking why they placed them in that particular order	Here is a list of 10 types of school safety measures. Rank them in order from what you think will be most effective at preventing school crime and violence, to those that are least effective
Participant gesture	Note a participant's body language or non-verbal cues to draw them into the conversation	You look confused. What don't you understand?
Diversity	Ask the group for different or divergent views	Does anyone have a similar/different perspective?
Silent	Remain silent for seven seconds. People are often uncomfortable with silence and will try to fill it by talking	
Activities	Share an activity with the group	See the section (below) on Activities

Additional information

Often, you will want to collect personal information from the focus group participants. You can collect demographic information either before or after the focus group. One suggestion is to have a brief questionnaire with demographic information ready for respondents to fill out when they arrive, so they have something to do while they are waiting for everyone to congregate. Some information, however, you will want to wait and collect after the focus group discussion has concluded. If you are doing a survey on the research topic, this should be done after the focus group discussion concludes so as to not potentially influence the discussion topics by raising issues before the focus group interview begins. At the close of the focus group discussion, you can direct the participants to fill out the post-discussion questionnaire, and to help themselves to some refreshments (if any will be provided). This provides a nice way to end the focus group, and will make your respondents feel that their time and effort has been appreciated.

Interview schedule versus focus group discussion guide

You will note that there are similarities between an interview schedule and a focus group discussion guide, especially in terms of the organization of the questions. However, focus group questions are designed to be asked of a group and therefore should promote group discussion. This means that there will be fewer questions in a focus group discussion guide than in an interview guide. It also means that direct personal questions should be avoided (those are best for personal interviews). Focus group discussion questions should be open and conversational in nature (Hennink et al., 2011). The questions should be written so that participants can answer in various ways (not just 'yes' or 'no'), and feel as though they are engaging in a conversation with one another. Use of group probing or an activity can help facilitate the discussion and make the participants feel more at ease (see below for more information on use of activities with focus groups).

Taking advantage of what you learn in one focus group and adapting the questions accordingly is referred to as 'emergence' (Morgan, 2012). Morgan (2012: 274) argues that 'standardization is actually a matter of degree', with predetermined and fixed questions on the one end of the spectrum, and emergent questions on the other end. Thus, the focus group discussion guide takes on a life of its own, changing and becoming more relevant with each focus group interview that takes place. Though standardization is advantageous – you can directly compare the results from one focus group to another, if the questions are the same from group to group – there is a severe disadvantage when the questions are determined before entering the field, if they are not necessarily the most relevant for gathering data from the group (Morgan, 2012).

The discussion guide should be well developed, and even pre-tested on a small group (if you can, use your friends, colleagues or classmates to help you pre-test the order and wording of questions). A discussion guide that is well developed will provide the moderator with the necessary information to introduce the research topic, open the discussion, develop rapport within the group and eventually close the discussion. Whenever possible, the moderator should facilitate the pre-test so that they can have practice with the questions and topics. Some questions to consider during the pre-testing of your focus group discussion guide include:

- Did the introductory remarks provide enough of an overview of the research, but not steer the participants toward particular answers?
- Was the wording of the questions clear?
- Was there flow to the discussion?

- Was the order of questions and topics easy to follow?
- Did the answers to the questions aid in answering the overall research questions?
- Is the discussion guide long enough, or too long, for a typical focus group discussion?
- Was the discussion guide clear enough for the moderator to follow?
- Did the moderator facilitate the conversation well?
- Were enough or too many probes used?

Activities

Focus group interviews can include activities that the participants are asked to engage in. These might range from drawing a picture representative of something relevant to the research; writing a list of concerns, issues or important points; word association techniques or sentence completion tasks; watching/hearing a vignette or scenario and discussing responses to it; to ranking or sorting items provided to them. Activities allow participants to focus on the task at hand, thus making it easier for them to talk as the activity can be used to promote discussion. For example, if there is a quiet participant in the group, the moderator could ask them to share what they had written down, or to explain why they drew a picture in a particular way. Additionally, activities produce additional data that researchers can use in their analysis; all of the pictures, lists or ordered material can be gathered and analysed after the focus group discussion has concluded. Group activities will take up some of the discussion time, and thus the number of questions should be reduced if an activity will be used.

RECORDING

——————————————— **Key takeaways** ———————————————

- Video or audio recording of focus group discussions allows for more detailed analyses after the discussion concludes.
- Large numbers of focus group participants can make transcription challenging and recording devices should be used to manage these challenges.

Whenever possible, and with consent of your respondents, you should attempt to record the focus group discussion for later transcription. This will allow the moderator to focus on the discussion at hand, and ensure that you do not miss anything that someone has said. In an interview, you can ask the respondent to repeat what they said or to pause while you jot down some notes. In a focus group setting, however, it is important to maintain the flow of discussion without interruption. There is little research to suggest that a recording device will alter the group discussion; the very nature of the group setting already means that the comments are public (Stewart et al., 2007).

However, there are challenges associated with recordings. You need to decide if you will use an audio recording or a video recording. If using video recording, be sure to not draw much attention to the cameras, or the respondents may focus their attention on the video camera and not toward one another. Video recording is only advised when it is important to see the respondents' body language in addition to their conversation. Remember that the note taker can also record information about people's body language and non-verbal communication (such as if people are uncomfortable, fidgeting, etc.). Any type of recording you choose should be discussed at the outset of the focus group discussion.

If you choose to use an audio recorder, you will need to be careful to think about the placement of the machine. Many audio recorders are quite small and do not provide much distraction to the respondents. We recommend using more than one recording device if the table is large (an oval or rectangle); placing one recorder at each end of the table ensures that the respondents at the end of the table can still be heard, and it also serves as a backup should one recorder malfunction.

Transcribing focus groups can prove to be challenging, especially if there are many people talking all at once or if some respondents have faint voices (or others are quite loud). Transcribing focus groups may take longer than transcribing individual interviews, as there will be more information covered and it could prove difficult if some voices are muted or if individuals talk over one another. One way of making the transcribing process easier is to have the note taker jot down the start time and the name of each person who is speaking. The note taker can even write the first few words of the respondent's statement, which may help the transcriptionist immensely. Similarly, no matter how many cameras or audio recording devices are present, not every facial expression or non-verbal communication will be captured. The use of a note taker is the best way to moderate these disadvantages.

ADVANTAGES AND DISADVANTAGES OF FOCUS GROUPS

Each method has advantages and disadvantages associated with it. It is important to reflect on the advantages and disadvantages when planning your methodology in order to accentuate the strengths and minimize the weaknesses within your project. Additionally, it will allow you to ensure that you are choosing to use focus groups for the right reasons.

Much of the available literature on focus groups outlines the various advantages and disadvantages (Berg and Lune, 2012; Bryman et al., 2012; Hennink, 2007; Hennink et al., 2011; Holloway and Wheeler, 2010; Liamputtong, 2009; McParland and Flowers, 2011; Morgan, 2012; Stewart et al., 2007). A summary of the advantages is as follows:

- Participants are able to question one another's reasoning.
- Results may be more realistic or naturalistic than in an interview because people may challenge opinions and views in real life.
- A wide variety of perspectives on one issue may be generated at one time; insights may be generated about the sources of motivations and behaviours.

- There is opportunity to witness interactions and uncover how meaning is jointly constructed and shared collectively.
- Issues are debated and justified; new issues can be identified.
- Individuals may feel more comfortable sharing perspectives than in face-to-face interviews.
- Participants can ask questions and achieve clarification easily, which reduces the opportunity for misunderstanding.
- Focus groups can be used for a wide variety of topics, research questions and types of groups.

There are also disadvantages outlined by the various literature on focus groups:

- Individuals may modify what they have said after hearing someone else's opinions.
- If certain individuals are either domineering or too quiet, the conversation could turn to an argument; group dynamics could hinder the participation of some members.
- The amount of data that is produced may be so great that it is difficult to manage.
- Researcher control is limited once the group is engaged in the conversation.
- Attitudes and perspectives may become more extreme and polarized after the discussion.
- Participants could potentially conform to the ideas of the other group members, or not share their personal views and opinions in front of others.
- Generalizations to larger populations can be problematic because there are small numbers of individuals participating and because the group members' responses are not independent of one another.
- Bias may occur if the moderator - whether knowingly or unknowingly - shows favour toward certain types of answers over others.
- A limited number of questions can be asked in the allotted time.
- Only group responses, not individual responses, are obtained.

Focus group interviews provide the researcher with less control over the proceedings than is available during a personal interview. Some researchers see this as a disadvantage, though others see the lack of researcher control and the group's influence over the direction as being advantageous (Bryman et al., 2012).

CONCLUSION

This chapter outlines concrete strategies for developing a focus group discussion. First, we outline the key aspects central to any focus group, including group size, the number of interviews and the length of each. We discuss concerns regarding the group composition and group dynamics. We review the key roles associated with facilitating an effective focus group interview; namely, a moderator and a note taker. We also provide an overview of other key concerns, such as location, seating arrangements and recording of the focus group interview. Then we provide a thorough discussion and steps for creating an effective focus group interview discussion guide. Finally, we review the advantages and disadvantages of using focus groups as presented by the literature.

The following chapter will outline the various types of field research that can be conducted by qualitative researchers.

KEY TERMS

Deference Effect	Group Heterogeneity	Note Taker
Dominant Participant	Group Homogeneity	Quiet Participant
Emergence	Introductory Tasks	Rambling Participant
Ethical Tasks	Moderator	Saturation
Facilitating Discussion Tasks	Natural Groups	Second Interviewer
Group Cohesion Tasks	Non-Directive Interview	Segmentation
		Self-Appointed Expert

6

HOW TO CONDUCT FIELD RESEARCH:
GETTING IN AND GETTING OUT WITH HIGH QUALITY DATA

——————————————————— **Learning objectives** ———————————————————

By the end of this chapter you will have the tools to:

- Identify and select a research setting
- Find the theoretical framework that links to your research question
- Conceptualize strategies for entering the field and negotiating roles
- Identify the right time to exit the field
- Make meaningful observations and write field notes

——————————————————— **Chapter summary** ———————————————————

Field research is a form of qualitative data collection based on understanding, observing and interacting with people in their natural settings. Theory and field research are mutually reinforcing: theory focuses research and field research grounds theory in social life. This chapter provides a step-by-step guide on how to conduct field research.

INTRODUCTION

> It seemed as if the academic world had imposed a conspiracy of silence regarding the personal experiences of field workers. In most cases, the authors who had given any attention to their research methods had provided fragmentary information or had written what appeared to be a statement of the methods the field worker would have used if he had known what he was going to come out with when he entered the field. It was impossible to find realistic accounts that revealed the errors and confusions and the personal involvement that a field worker must experience. (Whyte 1993 [1943]: 358)

Observational field research is one of the backbones of qualitative methods. While it may seem quite straightforward – getting into the field and observing people's behaviour – in fact, field research involves some of the most complex planning and negotiation in qualitative methodologies. The above words of William Foot Whyte capture the messiness of field research that often requires substantial revisions of the research design. In contrast to survey research that seeks to uncover the frequency of behaviour, observational methods focus on its meaning. The goal is to shed light on the day-to-day life of individuals. Thus, researchers go to the 'natural' settings where social life occurs to gain insight into the question, 'What is going on here?'.

Observational research requires more researcher involvement than other types of research and is labour intensive. It generally necessitates immersion in a setting for an extended period of time and the ability to build relationships. Although developing a strong research design is a key to success, once in the field, researchers often are able to collect more data on some aspects of social life than others. Thus, observational methods require the ability to remain flexible and re-evaluate one's research design when necessary.

To outline the tools needed to conduct observational research, this chapter presents the following sections:

Field Research Options: Where, When, How? We review the where, when and how of selecting a field.

Developing Data Collection Resources. We give guidelines for developing a theoretical link between your research question and your fieldwork options.

Gaining Access. Once the where and when have been identified, it is time to consider the 'how' of getting in. We provide a discussion of tools for success.

You're in, Now What? Negotiating Roles in the Field. We discuss what the consequences of being an insider and/or outsider to the research setting, including ethical dilemmas.

Time Matters: How Long Is Enough? In this section we examine the difficult question of when and how to leave the field.

Field Notes: Data Recording and Organizational Devices. We outline approaches to observation and writing field notes.

FIELD RESEARCH OPTIONS: WHERE, WHEN, HOW?

──────────────── **Key takeaways** ────────────────

- The 'field' can include physical spaces, people, objects, public places, groups, social milieu ('scenes'), organizations, online chat rooms, blogs, visual representations and artefacts, and other organizational documents and discursive materials.
- Fieldwork helps us uncover mechanisms and processes that can answer 'how' and 'why' questions.

William F. Whyte (1993 [1943]) documents in his appendix, written 12 years after the first edition of *Street Corner Society* was published, the haphazard manner in which he found a suitable community to study and, once he found it, his clumsy attempts to communicate and gain acceptance by the community's members. After graduating from Swarthmore in 1936, he became a junior fellow at Harvard University, which provided support for three years of research. He first engaged the community he named Cornerville as a representative of a private agency concerned with housing matters to do a survey with tenants about living conditions. Of this choice, he states,

> This brought me into contact with Cornerville people, but it would be hard now to devise a more inappropriate way of beginning a study such as I was eventually to make. I felt ill at ease at this intrusion, and I am sure so did the people. (288)

After several more false starts, Whyte was introduced to 'Doc' through a social worker at a settlement house, and Doc became his main informant. He would spend the next four years living in this Italian community, becoming a pioneer of participant observation.

Different approaches to field research

- **Phenomenology**: An approach based on the idea that different people experience the world in different ways.
- **Symbolic interactionism**: A social situation has meaning only in the way people define and interpret happenings and events. People interact on the basis of shared meanings and understandings.
- **Ethnomethodology**: An approach to the study of social life that focuses on the discovery of implicit, usually unspoken assumptions and agreements.
- **Ethnography**: A study of the 'World View' of different groups, offering detailed thick description.
- **Institutional Ethnography**: A research technique in which the personal experiences of individuals are used to reveal power relationships and other characteristics of the institutions within which they operate.
- **Naturalism**: An approach to field research based on the assumption that an objective social reality exists and can be observed and reported accurately.

Whyte was fortunate to find an informant who opened the door for conducting his research. However, his initial awkward attempts to gain access as an outsider may have ended very differently, causing distrust among community members and preventing further attempts to study this population. Whyte's experience demonstrates the importance of carefully choosing a research site, crafting a design grounded in the literature, and reflecting on the potential effects that the research may have on the participants who are being studied. All of these components are central to approaches and decisions one must consider before entering 'the field'. The first consideration is to establish what constitutes the field one will study.

The concept of 'the field' is often left rather vague in ethnographic research. Hammersley and Atkinson (1995: 1) define ethnography as participation 'overtly or covertly, in people's daily lives for an extended period of time, watching what happens, listening to what is said, asking questions – in fact, collecting whatever data are available to throw light on the issues that are the focus of the research'. Ethnography's origins date back to the social anthropology of Malinowski in the 1920s and the 'natural ecology' of the Chicago School from 1917 to 1942 (Deegan, 2001). This legacy treated the field as 'laboratory' or a site of discovery for 'privileged sojourners' (Geertz, 1997: 194). In past decades, social scientists have criticized the idea that there exists a 'natural' environment in which to conduct field research. Contemporary ethnographies tend to take into account important questions about the relationship between the researcher and her or his participants and the types of objects that will be studied in the field.

Traditional dimensions of field research have included physical spaces, people and/or objects. It may include public places, groups, social milieu ('scenes'), organizations, online chat rooms, blogs, etc. If one is studying hospitals, for example, decisions must be made about how many hospitals to include, which wards to study and where the researchers should locate themselves. Strauss et al. (1964) argue that choosing one location can circumscribe the researcher's perspective. To counter this pitfall, a site should be chosen that allows the maximum mobility possible for comparisons between different groups. Another important consideration in deciding the field is time considerations. Are there particular activities that must be observed during particular hours and over a particular length of time? This aspect of fieldwork is discussed in more depth below in the section on Time Matters. Once the 'where' and 'when' questions have been answered, the researcher needs to decide what people (if any) to include. Will the research project involve a certain group of patients, for example, such as those with mental illness? Decisions about sampling are outlined below in the section on Gaining Access.

In recent years, the idea of the field has expanded to encompass visual representations and artefacts – photographs, video, etc. – and other organizational documents and discursive materials. The field may also include cyberspace, studying online communication and interaction, as well as related mediated and interactive spaces, such as virtual universities, communities, care systems, organizations, telemedicine, teleshopping, marketplaces, households, and so forth. Institutional artefacts, archival data and historical documents can also be important elements of data collection.

Quick tip: Are you a suitable candidate?

Here are some questions to ask when considering whether to conduct fieldwork (note: the importance of these questions will depend on the actual site/project):

- Do I feel relatively comfortable in new situations where the rules for behaving are not clear? Can I work for extended periods of time in situations that are ambiguous and unstructured?
- Am I comfortable playing the student role? Or do I prefer to be in the expert role?
- Am I socially awkward in new situations? Or do I find it relatively easy to build new relationships, a rapport, trust? Am I comfortable initiating an interaction?
- Am I able to handle surprising, embarrassing and awkward situations with grace? Or am I easily flustered?
- In new situations, am I overly self-conscious? Am I able to 'go with the flow' and fit in? Am I quick on my feet?
- Am I comfortable asking people I really do not know for something I want (e.g., information, an interview, access, to record what's happening)? Am I good at 'selling' myself, my ideas?
- Do I mind asking questions if I do not understand how things work or what is going on?
- Is there something about my person that will limit my ability to develop a rapport or trust?
- Can I live without many of the comforts and conveniences of home? Will my partner/ spouse understand the time commitment, odd hours, etc.?
- Am I a detail-oriented person? Do I have the discipline to engage in such a labour intensive method of research?

The goal of field research differs from that of quantitative methods, which provide conclusions about characteristics in a population based on a sample of that population. In contrast, there is mounting agreement among social scientists that fieldwork is better equipped to uncover mechanisms and processes that can answer 'how' and 'why' questions (Small, 2009). In deciding the field to study, the researcher needs to identify whether the project will focus on a series of events or an organization, what are the processes involved, and what kinds of interpersonal dynamics are included. These tend to manifest as 'how' questions: Is the researcher trying to understand *how* an event or organization functions, *how* something is accomplished, *how* participants experience or respond to a particular process, or *how* participants interact?

Thus, the first step in developing a field research project is to consider carefully what constitutes the field and how the field relates to one's topic of research and question. In order to accomplish this step, we argue for the importance of theoretically developing the project. Developing theory guides answers to the questions of where, when and how, which are central to field research. We address this important component in the next section.

DEVELOPING DATA COLLECTION RESOURCES

Key takeaway

- Three possible paths to developing theory through ethnographic methods are Theoretical Discovery, Theoretical Extension and Theoretical Refinement.

Overall, the identification of a topic for field research requires theoretical clarification of the object of study. Sociologists sometimes bemoan the lack of theoretical development – 'processes by which theories emerge, change, and grow in scholarly work' – that sometimes occurs within ethnography (Emerson, 1987; Snow et al., 2003: 185). Generally, attention to theory in the beginning stages of fieldwork, as well as later on, guards against a conceptually impoverished study that may be interesting but does little to answer the 'So what?' question (Lofland, 1970). Snow et al. (2003) identify three paths to developing theory through ethnographic methods: Theoretical Discovery, Theoretical Extension and Theoretical Refinement. We discuss and outline an example of each below.

Sociological ethnographic research often seeks 'discovery' as a way to develop theory. For example, Lofland (1970) embraces an inductive approach where the researcher begins with as few preconceptions as possible and allows theory to emerge from the data. This form of discovery seeks to develop taxonomies and mini-concepts through 'detailed coding and emergent constant comparative analysis of observational data' (Snow et al., 2013: 186). It is consistent with the highly influential methodology of Glaser and Strauss in *The Discovery of Grounded Theory* (1967), who stress the importance of comparing cases to maximize differences in the contexts of varying phenomena.

Whyte's *Street Corner Society* (1993 [1943]) offers a classic example of theoretical discovery in its development of concepts to explain the processes of stratification and mobility at the community level. Whyte (1996) described his interest in economics and social reform that led him to seek a poor urban neighbourhood in Boston's North End to conduct his study that focused on gangs of young men who hung around the street corners in a tightly knit Italian-American community. His review of the literature revealed that no real community study had been conducted of such a district. Thus, he set out to discover the patterns and organizational structure of this community. He uncovered the complex relationship between street-corner gangs and the political and economic structures of the community in which they were immersed.

Theoretical discovery in Whyte's research was not based on expanding extant theory. Instead, he developed concepts and theoretical principles that emerged from ethnographic observations. This type of theoretical discovery has produced significant findings used by qualitative and quantitative researchers alike to generate research and hypotheses on various groups, neighbourhoods and communities. In contrast, Snow et al. (2003: 186) warn that the prevalence of this tradition 'has blinded ethnographers to alternative forms of theoretical development'. They argue that most theoretical development in fieldwork comes from the other two paths of extension and refinement.

A second path to developing theory seeks to extend prior theoretical models to other 'groups or aggregations, to other bounded contexts or places, or to other sociocultural domains' (Snow et al., 2003: 187). Sharon Hays (2004), who conducted ethnographic research on the effects of welfare reform in the United States, provides an example of theoretical extension. In her book, *Flat Broke with Children*, she applies the concept developed in previous research on the cultural contradictions of intensive mothering to her fieldwork on welfare reform, thereby extending her analysis of the political processes of cultural contradiction, distortion and exclusion to the case of single mothers. She found that stereotypes deriving from and perpetuating these distortions led to policies that buttress conditions of poverty. Ultimately, similar to her research on intensive mothering, Hays was interested in the ways that ideas about welfare reform reflect national values. She chose to study these issues in two welfare office sites in different states, one in the downtown area of a quaint historic city and the other in the centre of a larger city. While there were different regulations and interactions between caseworkers and clients in the two sites, Hays found important similarities in the cultural contradictions between the market logic and the logic of care and commitment.

A third way to develop theory is through theoretical refinement, or the adaption of an existing theory based on new data. Snow et al. (2003) note that this possibility is consistent with analytic induction because it implies that the theory is modified on the basis of new evidence. In her book, *The Challenger Launch Decision*, Diane Vaughan (1996) offered new perspectives on the series of events that led to the doomed *Challenger* launch decision. Vaughan was interested in studying the NASA case as an example of organizational misconduct. Yet, she found that the data contradicted the starting theory: the explanation of NASA's history of booster decision-making involved conformity rather than misconduct. Thus, she refined theories of disaster to attend to the 'normalization of deviance' through: 1) the 'production of culture' that allowed the erosion of the O-ring to become normalized; 2) the 'culture of production' that permitted managers and engineers to see cost/schedule/safety compromises as normal and non-deviant; and 3) the structural secrecy that existed in the organization where patterns of information obscured the seriousness of the problem. Vaughan's method was historical ethnography, which sought to elicit structure and culture from documents created prior to an event in order to understand how people in another time and place made sense of things.

These examples demonstrate the importance of identifying upfront the specific ways that your project will build theory. The role of guiding research questions is particularly important in pinpointing theoretical development and determining where, when and how the research will be conducted. Whyte's (1993 [1943]) theoretical approach of discovery was based on an open and general question: How is the social structure of a 'slum' organized? To answer this question, he identified a community of first- and second-generation Italian immigrants who lived in an urban area, and conducted fieldwork for a number of years to *discover* how the relationships of group members related to the political structure of the community. For Hays (2004: 10), the important question to ask was: How does the 'cultural logic' of the 1996 welfare reform law, including cultural norms, beliefs and values, organize and regulate the lives of poor single-mother families living in poverty? She chose to study the cultural impact of welfare reform in two different welfare offices in two different states, logging 600 hours in the field. This design made it possible to *extend* the theory of cultural contradiction to the case of welfare mothers. Vaughan (2004: 323) asked a cultural question that led to meticulous analysis of documents and allowed her to *refine* existing theories of risk and disaster: 'Was NASA's a risk-taking culture, where production pressures pushed schedule ahead of safety, as the Report implied'?.

Thus, planning for field research – whether the research question demands a more inductive or deductive approach – requires theoretical conceptualization (Table 6.1). The theoretical approach may change as the researcher delves into fieldwork and analysis, but this first important step will provide necessary direction and depth to the project. The next important step, and for some lines of inquiry perhaps the most difficult, is establishing a plan to gain entry in the field.

Table 6.1   Linking research question to method to theory

Research question	Data collection	Theoretical strategy
How is the social structure of a 'slum' organized?	William Foote Whyte (1993 [1943]) spent over three years conducting participant observation in a community study of Italian-Americans. Whyte collected in-depth ethnographic data to examine the interactions among group members, including patterns of reciprocity and exchange	Whyte's theoretical strategy was one of discovery. He sought to understand the political and economic structures of street-corner gangs and their relationships with the rest of the community. Rather than simply detailing disorganization or pathology – the dominant way at the time to describe these communities – he found a complex organization of relationships that participated in a highly developed social structure
How does the 'cultural logic' of the 1996 welfare reform law, including cultural norms, beliefs and values, organize and regulate the lives of poor single-mother families living in poverty?	Sharon Hays (2004) spent over three years observing welfare offices in two cities and conducted over 90 in-depth interviews with welfare caseworkers and female welfare recipients. Her fieldwork provides a window into the impact of the welfare reform law on the wellbeing of recipients	Hays' theoretical strategy can be characterized as theoretical extension In her first book (Hays, 1996), she introduced the concept of the 'cultural contradictions of motherhood' to theorize the contradictory nature of 'intensive mothering' among women trying to simultaneously raise their children and pursue a career. Her 2004 book considers the contradictory values of the welfare reform law between work and family. The law requires participation in the work force and paradoxically promotes marriage as a way out of poverty
Was NASA's a risk-taking culture, where production pressures pushed schedule ahead of safety, as the Report implied?	Diane Vaughan (1996) employs an historical ethnography, spending the better part of a decade studying archival records – an astounding 122,000 pages of documents, including 9,000 pages of the 160 post-accident interviews – to reconstruct a thick description of the events as seen by those in NASA culture	Vaughan's theoretical strategy exemplifies refinement. She began with the dominant theory that the events at NASA represented organizational misconduct, but found that she must apply a different theoretical framework to capture the 'normalization of deviance' in the organizational and environmental context in which the decision was made

GAINING ACCESS

---------------------------------- Key takeaways ----------------------------------

- One of the greatest hurdles to field research can be gaining access. Efforts to get into the field should be recorded as data.
- You must decide early on whether to enter the field overtly or covertly. This decision will influence all subsequent experiences in the field.
- Gatekeepers who guard the boundaries of public and private field research sites can present problems for access, especially when you are studying elite organizations or institutions.

Establishing contacts and gaining access into the field are often time-consuming and stressful aspects of doing ethnographic research. There are no simple formulas or set rules for how to access the field, and strategies will largely depend on the project itself. In fact, negotiating access is a task that is never readily accomplished in fieldwork, and it must be managed cooperatively and negotiated with intended participants. Managing the necessary steps to gain access is not only methodologically important but can also generate important insight into structure of the field. It can help identify what defines the field and who are the key players. Thus, the ordeals, detours and false starts that researchers often experience in gaining access to the field not only present problems to be solved but also opportunities for discovering significant aspects concerning the structures and the boundaries of the field. At times, however, trials and tribulations can discourage the research process. The worst-case scenario means changing the focus of the study due to barriers and gatekeepers who may block access.

Research snapshot: Gaining access to difficult to reach populations

Jessica Braimoh (2015) conducted a case study of a *single* youth organization that works across rural and urban settings to understand how geography shapes organizational supports for marginalized youth. She did not anticipate some of the challenges that she would face entering the field.

To gain entry into the field, Jessica began hanging out at the sites of the organization during regular hours of service. Although she began to connect with youth across both sites, she was only successful at gaining interviews with youth in the rural setting. The challenge was how to get urban youth to agree to an interview.

After a couple of months in the field, Jessica learned from staff that other researchers had conducted interviews in the past with youth in the urban location but *not* the rural community, and these researchers remunerated urban youth for their time. Jessica revised her research protocol and advertised that all youth research participants (both rural and urban) would receive a $20 gift card to either McDonald's or Tim Horton's for their participation in the study.

Jessica's *original plans* to gain access to young people included the following:

- Speaking with staff about herself and what the research was about.
- 'Hanging out' during regular hours both inside and outside of the organization to connect with youth.
- A local cell phone number that would be free for youth to call to learn more about the project and to schedule an interview time.
- Advertisements that were posted in all common spaces of the organization and in 'hang-out spots'.
- Conducting interviews in spaces where youth felt safe.

After receiving the approval on the amendment to her ethics protocol, Jessica's *revised approach* added the following:

- Changing advertisements to reflect remuneration.
- Locating the youth who had already completed an interview and providing them with a gift card.
- Buying gift cards ahead of time.

Lincoln and Guba (1985) stress the importance of preparation before entering the research setting. Knowledge about the individuals, communities and 'objects' of study, and familiarity with their norms and routines, is essential to the ongoing negotiation of access. Thus, an important step is immersion in the literature. This knowledge can help you to identify key informants and gatekeepers who may be willing to share their insights and contacts.

There is general agreement that researchers need to address existing networks to seek a 'known sponsor' or 'orienting figure' able to offer referrals or facilitate access into the field (Monahan and Fisher, 2014: 3; Patton, 2002; Weiss, 1994). Doc is a recognized example who provided William F. Whyte with contacts and acted as a guide. Whyte also rented a room from a local family as a strategy to gain understanding and acceptance in the community. Ashley Mears (2013) tells the story of being approached during her first year of graduate school by a model scout in a coffee shop, who praised her 'look' and promised that she could 'make it big' in the fashion industry. Mears jumped at the opportunity for accessing the industry but found dependence on her agents and bookers to be a challenging aspect of fieldwork.

An important decision to make is whether to enter the field overtly or covertly; one that can critically influence the data you are able to collect. Covert research might include observation of public behaviour involving anonymous participants or joining an organization in some integrated role to conduct research clandestinely. Arguments have been made for the benefits of conducting covert research to observe interactions or organizational processes that might not be possible otherwise. A prominent example is the research on casual homosexual encounters conducted by Humphreys (1970), a study that required concealing his identity as a researcher. Playing the role of 'watch queen' at a public bathroom where men met for brief homosexual encounters, Humphreys discovered that many had wives and families. His research pointed to the fact that homosexuality was not a disease, as was the common understanding at that time. Covert research, however, is often fraught with controversy. Such cases require careful consideration of the actual social or scientific benefit to ensure not to abuse the rights and privacy of the research subjects, which could cause harm. For example, research in public institutions where the accountability of officials is at stake could require conducting research without voluntary participation of participants for the study to be meaningful (Rainwater and Pittman, 1967). However, the idea that a researcher can imperceptibly slip into the field to conduct observations unnoticed is highly implausible even as an ideal. Thus, most researchers conduct fieldwork overtly (see Chapter 7 for more discussion of covert methods).

Another important element of gaining access involves the identification and management of 'gatekeepers' who guard the boundaries of public and private field research sites. Morrill et al. (1999) point to several important aspects in managing access to organizations with formal gatekeeping mechanisms: whether gatekeeping involves individual or collective actors, whether it operates from the top down or on multiple levels of an organization, and how external factors affect those in different managerial roles in ways that might impact the research. They also point out that gatekeeping negotiations can lead to useful data, including information about how an organization operates and its managerial structure.

Gatekeepers can be especially difficult to manage when one studies more powerful groups, such as 'elite' informants who are able to control access to their domains. Monahan and Fisher (2014) offer the following strategies for accessing elite organizations with strong formal gatekeeping, many of which we find illuminating as tactics for gaining access in general. 1) Attend industry or government conferences, which may allow contact with informants of an organization and/or may provide the opportunity to treat presentations as sources of data. Heath (2012) used this strategy to gain access to study a statewide marriage-promotion initiative by meeting with representatives of the organization at a national marriage conference. 2) Determine the names of key informants and make cold calls. 3) Communicate succinctly your institutional legitimacy and the importance of your research. Organizations or individuals may have had negative past experiences with journalists (or other researchers) that make them wary of participation. Clear communication strategies, such as explaining the difference between journalism and research, are important to establishing legitimacy. 4) Understand the complex ways in which potential informants might view researchers as potential threats to their organization, and be ready to take steps to diminish this perception. 5) Make unexpected or barely announced visits. Although not an ideal strategy, this may work if you are traveling from a distance or there is an inconvenience to your schedule that puts the onus on the organization to give you access. 6) Immersing yourself in the community that surrounds a research site might be a way to gain data about the organization. Finally, we want to stress again the importance of recording these efforts as part of your data (see our discussion below of strategies for taking inclusive field notes).

YOU'RE IN, NOW WHAT? NEGOTIATING ROLES IN THE FIELD

———————————————— Key takeaways ————————————————

- In negotiating your role in the field, it is important to consider how your social location, and your insider/outsider status, might limit what or where you can study.
- Building rapport and sustaining trust with participants is key to successful managing of roles in the field.

Often it is hard to determine exactly the moment you have made it 'in' to the field, and a constant negotiation of roles takes place as you interact with new and established participants. As field relations vary over time, from person to person, and situation to situation, the ability to spontaneously respond and alter your role in the field is key to successfully navigating it.

Successfully negotiating roles in the field requires awareness of one's ascribed characteristics – age, gender, social class, social status, and race and ethnicity, as well as one's social identity. These characteristics can influence access and the ways that interactions take place. Mazzei and O'Brien (2009) point out that gaining access and establishing rapport with participants often means acknowledging and strategically acting within the socially constructed meanings assigned to our ascribed attributes that take on more or less relevance depending on the field setting. They note:

> The field setting determines which of a researcher's 'key attributes' are most important and that socially constructed meanings, 'scripts,' are attached to these and other attributes, ... [which] contain messages about what individuals in particular groups - female, Latina, white, black-female, American, male, gay white male, etcetera - are 'typically like,' and therefore what is expected of them. (360)

A central consideration in managing your role as a researcher depends on identifying these established scripts in the process of building rapport.

One's status in the field also depends on whether one is viewed as an 'insider' or 'outsider' to the group or organization being studied. Conducting field research often requires toggling the dual role of recognition as a group member and as a researcher separate from the group. Seeking to 'fit-in' has inevitable trade-offs. Ashley Mears (2013), who conducted long-term participant observation as a fashion model, detailed the perils of negotiating her insider role within a stratified field. As a model, she was situated at the bottom of a social hierarchy that subjected her to continual and public judgment on her appearance, her weight and her personality. Like others, she found herself struggling to slim down and being constantly subject to criticism that she endured without remark for risk of being expelled from the field. Furthermore, her role as participant observer circumscribed her ability to ask pressing questions to the bookers and clients she worked for about meanings attached to ideals of beauty. Negotiating her insider/outsider role, she waited until the end of her participant observation to step into the role of formal 'researcher' and interview important players. Still, her insider role as a model and as a young graduate student placed her in a hierarchical relation that made it difficult to ask certain questions concerning gender. In the end, this insider/outsider stance shaped the data Mears gathered and allowed her to uncover the stratification system that makes modelling a form of precarious labour.

A key aspect of managing your role in the field is building rapport and sustaining trust with participants. This is a particularly challenging aspect of fieldwork, and unexpected events and/or opportunities in the field can lead to fresh data but can also jeopardize established relationships. Peter Magolda (2000) explains that during his fieldwork involving a residential college community he gained knowledge that put him at the centre of a contentious relationship between two groups: an invisible and marginalized clique of students who held illegal parties that included the use of marijuana, and the resident assistants (RAs) who sought to prevent drug abuse. He could not engage in open conversations with the RAs about the illegal activities of the students and protect the latters' confidentiality, nor could he openly discuss the RAs' strategies to deter illegal activities while maintaining the confidentiality of RAs. He explains, 'Establishing rapport with groups whose agendas are competing complicates the conventional wisdom that advocates self-disclosure and candidness. Trust and confidentiality usually go hand-in-hand, but not always' (143).

Establishing trust is generally more circuitous than the linear process that is often assumed to take place in field research, from a wary regard from participants to eventual acceptance and full disclosure. You should expect setbacks or times when trust is called into question. Successfully managing your role in the field requires keeping detailed field notes to document how unexpected events might affect rapport.

TIME MATTERS: HOW LONG IS ENOUGH?

 Key takeaways

- Methodologically, you must determine when your data collection has reached saturation.
- In some instances, you may not have a choice about when to leave the field.

While gaining access to the field requires an ongoing process of negotiating roles, personal relationships and social interactions, these concerns remain important considerations in completing fieldwork and deciding when to leave the field. How long is enough, and how do you handle the relationships that you built while in the field? The answers to these questions will depend on both theoretical and methodological factors that are specific to your project. Below we outline some important considerations in deciding when and how to leave the field.

First, methodologically, it is important to determine when your data collection has reached saturation. Also known as informational redundancy, saturation occurs at the point when you find no new or pertinent information emerging. In other words, the themes you identify have become anticipated and/or redundant. Ask yourself: How robust is the theory I've developed? Are there any gaps? These questions can be difficult to answer, since it is possible that unforeseen insights can be gained by continuing your time in the field. Frequently it is necessary to make a decision based on an assessment of diminishing returns. Will collecting more data cease to contribute important insights to theoretical development? Saturation is not generally determined by time in the field or sample size but by assessing variations in your collected data and their importance to emerging theory.

Quick tip: Strategies for reaching saturation

Here are some strategies to help you reach saturation quickly and efficiently without sacrificing depth (see Chapter 3 for more details on designing your project):

- The sample should be cohesive. Too much variability among demographic groups will make saturation challenging. Remember that the goal is not generalizability.
- While cohesiveness is important, ensure that your sampling frame is not so narrow that you will reach saturation prematurely. Make sure that you are not just skimming the surface of the phenomena you are studying.
- Purposive sampling can help to balance the need for cohesiveness and breadth. Select your participants based on the need to build and validate emerging theory.
- Make sure you will have enough time in the field. Sustained fieldwork can uncover the intricacies of the research setting and help you identify redundancy.
- Search for negative cases to identify possible gaps in your theoretical development.

There are times when the researcher has little choice about when to leave the field. The group or institution being studied may determine the period of time in the field or you may run out of funding. If you must travel to conduct field research, it is often necessary to decide in advance a window of time in which to complete the research. If you find that saturation has not been reached during that window, it will be important to plan a second stint of fieldwork to ensure there are no gaps in your theoretical framework.

Issues of conflict and/or safety can also precipitate when to leave the field. Ruth Horowitz (1986) described the process of negotiating multiple identities in her research on Chicano gang members and the girls who hung around with them in the park. Early on, the male members identified her as a 'lady reporter', an identity that resolved the tensions that arose by the nature of her involvement as a woman who spent substantial time in this largely masculine world. She cultivated this identity as a way to stave off perceptions of her as sexually available, in contrast to other girls who hung out with gang members who were either girlfriends or potential objects of desire. Over time, some of the young men began to redefine her identity as potential girlfriend, making her sexual identity salient. After 18 months studying gang members, she found it necessary to shift her fieldwork to focus on studying the young women at the park: 'I was unable to negotiate a gender identity that would allow me to continue as a researcher' among the male youth (1986: 423).

Horowitz's experience also speaks to the emotional aspects of leaving the field. Exiting can bring strong emotions both for the researcher and the researched. The more time spent in a research setting, the more difficult it can be to complete fieldwork in an ethical manner. It is important to avoid distressing a research community. For example, Shaffir et al. (1980: 259) state:

> Personal commitments to those we study often accompany our research activity. Subjects often expect us to continue to live up to such commitments permanently. On completing the research, however, our commitment subsides and is often quickly overshadowed by other considerations shaping our day-to-day lives. When our subjects become aware of our diminished interest in their lives and situations, they may come to feel cheated – manipulated and duped.

Every field situation is unique, and you must consider the specific relationships you have cultivated when considering the best way to leave. In most circumstances, you must prepare the community members for your exit. At the same time, you must also prepare yourself. Relationships are two-way streets, and personal emotional commitments built during fieldwork can have an impact both for you and for those you study.

Carolyn Ellis (1995) offers a germane example of the emotional and ethical 'quagmires' of leaving and returning to the field based on her research experiences studying two isolated fishing communities in which she did fieldwork from 1972 to 1984. Over time, rather than a researcher and outsider, she became 'just Carolyn coming to visit' (1995: 71). After she completed her fieldwork, she did not discuss during her subsequent visits the book that she published in 1986 about their community. Because most in the community were illiterate, she assumed they would never read her book. She was wrong. In 1989, another researcher from a nearby college read parts of Ellis' book to the community, particularly 'the "sinful" things I had written about sexual practices' (1995: 73). This damaged her relationships with many and caused much emotional pain, both for those who felt that the stories they had shared with her had been exposed and for Ellis herself who recognized the impact of the pain she had caused. Ellis did not leave the field suddenly without returning, and she cared about the people with whom she had built relationships. Still, she recounts the mistakes she made in not discussing her publishing plans and in not confirming parts of the book with community members before it was published.

Accordingly, some cases require a quick exit, or a shift away from a potentially dangerous situation, as was the case for Horowitz. In other fieldwork situations, a more gradual exit may be best (Glaser and Strauss, 1967). As Ellis' account exemplifies, however, these decisions are fraught with possible ethical challenges that can be very difficult to manage. One tool to help manage these choices is the act of recording and taking notes on the process of leaving. While Ellis would never have anticipated that another researcher would read portions of her book to community members, outlining the pros and cons of giving the community more information about her plan to write a book might have ended in a different decision. Next, we turn to considerations in taking good field notes as a key source of data collection in field research.

FIELD NOTES: DATA RECORDING AND ORGANIZATIONAL DEVICES

Taking precise field notes is the backbone of conducting a successful field research project. Feld notes allow you to record in a systematic way the behaviours, activities, events and other aspects of the setting being observed. There are multiple strategies for taking comprehensive field notes. In this section, we outline important steps to consider in deciding your approach.

Quick tip: The what, when and where of field notes

- Draw on your research question and study design for theoretical guidance in deciding the what, when and where of taking field notes.
- Establish your relationship to the field and to the members of the setting, and decide the best mechanism(s) for remembering the behaviours, activities and events you observe. Jotting down your thoughts periodically is an important memory tool.
- Set a regular time and place to write field notes, generally directly following observations, or as soon after as possible.
- Include the date, time, location and all details of the main informants at the top of the page of each field observation.
- Every hour in the field will require about an hour to write up.
- Distinguish between descriptive, methodological and analytic field notes.
- Keep a separate record of your personal reactions and reflections.
- Organize your field notes in a manner that allows for easy manipulation, especially if you are using a qualitative data analysis program.

The first important decision to make about taking field notes is how to remember what you observe. In some research settings, it is possible to use your computer, notebook or iPad to take field notes directly onsite. Heath (2012), for example, conducted participant-observation of marriage-promotion classes where it was possible to bring her computer and take field notes during the sessions. Her note taking was not conspicuous, since other participants also took notes during the class. In many research settings, however, taking field notes while observing can be disruptive both to your ability to perceive details and to the flow of events, conversations, etc. Note taking may also make participants uncomfortable.

There are many challenges to keeping an accurate record of your observations while in the field when you are unable to take simultaneous field notes. If the duration of fieldwork is relatively short, you will likely be able to take more complete field notes right after exiting while events are still fresh in your mind. Fieldwork that lasts for a longer duration, more than two hours, presents many difficulties. First, you may become fatigued and your ability to observe may be diminished. Other concerns include how accurate your memory will be after a long stint in the field, or whether you will be able to recall conversations concerning who said what. Finally, your memory may favour the extraordinary or last event, rather than the ordinary or earlier events. Planning ahead, you will want to limit the time you remain in the setting to ensure you are able to write up high quality field notes.

During observation, find a creative way to take notes. In the past, field researchers often jotted notes on small notebooks that they kept in their pockets, or to be less conspicuous on a napkin or even their hands. Today, smartphones make it easier to 'jot' notes in the field since it is not out of the ordinary for a person to text or surf the web. Most smartphones have an application for note taking, and the app in iPhones syncs with other devices. If possible, build in breaks that allow you to jot down key phrases and cues. If you are able to find a quiet spot, the use of a recording device may be more efficient. You should also record the sequence of events, indicating what occurred before each action and following the noted event. Outlining the sequence of events will enable you to recall more details later when you do the write-up. You may also want to create a personal style of shorthand for jotting observations to allow you to take notes more quickly. Finally, it is key to balance the need to record events and conversations with the possibility that you will miss important nuances in your observations if you spend too much time writing. This balancing act is also important when more complete field notes are taken onsite.

Another tool that can aid in documenting events in the field, and can be a source of data as well, is taking photographs or use of video recording. If you are able to gain permission from participants, video recordings or photos are extremely helpful devices for remembering sequences of events.

Once you leave the field, it is important to write up your field notes as soon as possible. We recommend doing so directly after exiting. You should allow about one hour of write-up for every hour of observation (for beginners, three to four hours!). There are many extenuating circumstances that can make writing up soon after leaving the field difficult or impossible. If you are too fatigued, this can affect the quality of your field notes. Or, you may have an opportunity to conduct an interview or another set of observations right away. In these cases, you need to do your best to record the bare bones of what you can remember to better jog your memory when you can sit down to write with more detail. In other words, you would expand your jottings before writing the more complete notes. It is important, however, to be wary of putting off writing up field notes to a later time. Annette Lareau (1996) describes the serious mistake she made in falling behind on writing her field notes. She states: 'Missing sessions of writing field notes can, like skipping piano practice, get quickly out of hand ... exponentially, in fact' (218). She developed what she called the 'Lareau Iron Rule of Scheduling': she would never go into the field unless she had the time in the next 24 hours to write up her notes. This seems to us very good advice.

When writing up notes upon returning from the field, you need to 'fill in the blanks'. Admittedly, this can be a painful process. Again to quote Lareau (1996: 217–18): 'painful, because it forces you to confront unpleasant things, including lack of acceptance, foolish mistakes in the field, ambiguity about the intellectual question, missed opportunities in the field, and gaping holes in the data'. While it is important to record your frustrations and personal reflections, these should be kept separate from field notes. Below we outline some options to record your personal experiences, but first we discuss what good field notes look like.

You should decide on a system of standardization for typing up your field notes (see the Example below). This will aid with data retrieval later on and help ensure that you include comprehensive details. Every entry should contain the time you entered and exited the field, the date of the field experience, and a title that captures the essence of the field session. Make sure to include page numbers. We recommend saving separate documents for every field observation rather than a long running document. This will help you better organize the data, especially if you will be using a qualitative data analysis program to analyse your data.

Example: Field notes, marriage promotion classes, Heath (2012)

February 3, 2004, Christian PREP, JC Baptist Church

Time In: 10:30 am

Time Out: 12:30 pm

10:30 am   JC Baptist Church is located about 20 minutes outside Oklahoma City. I was a few minutes late for the Christian PREP class, because I had trouble getting into the church. When I arrived, the parking lot seemed empty and the door was locked. I called the church's number, but no one answered. Five minutes later a tall white man in his fifties wearing work clothes opened the door, and I was able to enter. [*I was feeling very nervous because I did not know what to expect from the class or who would be present. My anxiety heightened my frustration when I found the door locked.*]

The church stood on a smallish lot not surrounded by other buildings. It was an ordinary stucco white church, built as a rectangle, small, and no frills. Upon entering, the man who had opened the door was nowhere to be seen. I wandered through the hall past the sanctuary and towards some small classrooms. The hallway was bright with several pictures on the walls representing the teachings of Jesus. Finally, I heard voices and found the PREP class in a small room painted white that appeared to be used mainly for small group meetings, such as Sunday school.

The instructor was a white woman and appeared to be in her early fifties. Her short blond hair was styled in a bouffant, and she wore a skirt and flats. She introduced herself and I told her my name. There were two couples present, each sitting at a different table. All were white. One couple was older than the other, and the latter had just been married for a year. The instructor brought me a Christian PREP workbook, and said, 'We provide one of these per couple. Do you have another person joining you?' This seemed a polite way of asking if I were taking the class alone. I told her, 'No.' And, she said, 'That's fine.' She returned to her table to prepare, and I thought this would be a good time to ask permission to attend the class. I approached her and gave a brief introduction to my project, specifying that one of the PREP employees had said it was fine to attend the class if it was okay with her. She responded, 'Oh, you are a trained observer.' [*I immediately sensed her discomfort.*] I shook my head in affirmation. [*Also feeling discomfort.*] She gave permission but seemed annoyed, saying something about forgetting a portion of her workbook and feeling unprepared.

You will want to create a system to distinguish the different types of notes you record. There are three potential kinds of field notes: descriptive, methodological and analytic (see Table 6.2). Most of your notes will be descriptive based on what you see and hear in the field, providing a straightforward and detailed account of what exactly took place. The emphasis is on describing what you observed rather than summarizing or making generalizations. In other words, provide vivid details about observations such as body language and behaviour (e.g., 'Laura slouched down on her desk, head in hands', instead of 'Laura appeared upset'). Make sure to elucidate the setting and the participants, including when they come and go and the spatial configurations of how people are placed. Your notes should detail the actions and interactions that occur, such as what is said, how it is said, and the types of conversations that people have. Are you involved in these conversations? Are you listening in? Describe any physical responses that you notice. How do the participants themselves describe the meaning of the events and/or interactions?

Aspects of descriptive field notes may become redundant when you are documenting the same descriptions of individuals, locations and settings. You may find it better to decide on a referencing system to refer back to the detailed accounts of particular settings, items, events or people that reoccur frequently in your notes. Or this might be a place to summarize when you have recorded more detail in previous entries.

You may want to create a section to record methodological considerations. Do you find yourself speaking mostly to one group over another? What strategies might you use to gain access to another group? Horowitz (1986), for example, suggests that she took methodological notes on the change in her status during her interactions with gang members from 'lady reporter' to 'object of desire'. She describes seeking to stave off the undesirable transition, the challenges she faced, and finally the point where she was no longer able to focus her research on these members. Eventually, she published a methodological paper on the challenges inherent to negotiating multiple identities in a research setting. Methodological field notes can thus allow you to grapple with the particular obstacles that you face in a fieldwork setting and can be generative to finding solutions and perhaps to publishing based on your methodological experiences.

You will probably write fewer analytic notes than any other type of field note, but this aspect of your research is very important. This is the place where you begin to theorize the concepts that emerge out of your observations and link them back to your research question. What themes can you begin to identify? What questions will help focus your observation on subsequent visits? Can you begin to draw preliminary connections or potential conclusions based on what you observed? These notes are important for the process of coding, as you will begin to identify themes and concepts that you will want to code more systematically.

Finally, you will want to record the impressions and feelings that you experienced while in the field. This will include your interpretations of what happened and your reactions in contrast to those of the participants. For example, did others share the righteous indignation that you felt at an injustice that became apparent in your fieldwork? It is also important to record your place in the setting and your relationship with participants. Is there evidence that you have established trust? Are there aspects of your fieldwork that make you an insider? How do you negotiate your outsider status?

As noted above, you will want to mark your personal experiences separately from other field notes. This can be done in many different ways, and it will be up to you to decide what works best for your organizational process. The strategy that Heath (2012) used was a system of brackets and italics interspersed in the descriptions and methodological writings (see the Example above). You might use the 'Comments' function in a word processing program or a system of columns. You might also want to keep your personal writings in a separate log or diary. These personal reflections are extremely important for revealing things like personal biases. They may also become aids in analysing your data. Sometimes they are just a way to let off steam or celebrate particular experiences.

Table 6.2   Field notes options

Type	Example
Jottings: Brief words or phrases written quickly while in the field or after to help jog your memory for writing more complete field notes. Try to record direct quotes as much as possible	Lesson on 'oneness' Example of name change Quote: 'Ladies, we change our names. This is an outward manifestation that we have become one with our partner. Men have to do this internally. We give our name away'
Descriptive: The meat and potatoes of fieldwork. Descriptive field notes record what you have observed and heard in the field as carefully and in the most detail possible. They will constitute the majority of your field notes. Descriptive field notes should describe *not* summarize	The instructor delved into the lesson about how two people are made into 'one' in marriage. She stated, 'Ladies, we change our names. This is an outward manifestation that we have become one with our partner. Men have to do this internally. We give our name away'. The two couples listen attentively. She gives an example of the compromises necessary to make a relationship work. She tells us that her husband loves golf. When they got together, she thought she would learn, but it turns out she has very little interest. She says, 'I will never catch up'. Though not stated directly, her example suggests that the compromise for her was to try golf and for him to let her give up
Methodological: Concerns the technique of collecting data. These can be helpful to separate as a way to reflect on the methodological challenges while in the field. These reflections will be important in writing up your methods section in a thesis, dissertation, article or book, and as a possible journal article on methodology	The undertone of discomfort that the instructor sought to hide when I asked permission to attend the class has occurred in other instances. Gaining permission is problematic when I am not able to get approval beforehand (and this has been in most cases so far). Some instructors seem happy to let me attend, but others seem a bit put off. Comments have pointed towards a fear that I will be evaluating them. I have learned to emphasize in my introduction that I am not conducting evaluative research, but that I am simply observing to learn what takes place in the classroom

(Continued)

Table 6.2   (Continued)

Type	Example
Analytic: Articulate your ideas about how the culture/organization/activity is organized. Start to identify dominant themes and connect these back to theoretical frameworks. Questions to ask yourself: What themes can I begin to identify? What questions will help focus my observations on subsequent visits? Are there preliminary connections or potential conclusions based on what I have observed?	The discussion of 'oneness' teaches about the need to accept the patriarchal model where the wife submits to the husband's leadership. This is emphasized over and over in the examples offered, such as the fact that the wife demonstrates that she becomes one with her husband by taking his name. It is not 'oneness' of each giving an equal share but oneness where the wife becomes part of the husband. This fits with the biblical story where God uses Adam's rib to create Eve
Personal: Record your experiences, impressions and feelings separately from other field notes. Think about your reactions in comparison to those of the participants' reactions (are others similarly angered, pleased, etc.?)	While making comments on 'oneness', the instructor talked about how amazed she was that homosexuals were getting married in San Francisco. I had a hard time hiding my emotions as she made fun of the idea that same-sex couples could marry

Ruth Behar (2003: 16) offers a poignant summary of the important contribution fieldwork can make to understandings of the social and cultural context in which human behaviour occurs: 'The beauty and mystery of the ethnographer's quest is to find the unexpected stories, the stories that challenge our theories'. In this chapter, we have not engaged debates over the role of sociological theory, or the lack thereof, in various traditions of field research, such as grounded theory. (For an interesting perspective on these debates, see Waquant, 2002.) Instead, we draw on the typology offered by Snow et al. (2003) as a useful device for generating theoretical development. They emphasize the need for a systematic approach to conducting fieldwork and analysing data that 'promotes the linkage of field data to relevant theoretical traditions' (194). We believe that it is important to familiarize yourself with numerous theoretical perspectives as an aid to conducting rich ethnographic field research.

Deciding to conduct fieldwork is a quest that requires self-knowledge. You must be able to recognize both the strengths and the limits of your data, and to identify how your presence in the field impacts those you are studying. To conclude, we quote the words of Gary Alan Fine (1993: 290) who discusses the compromises we must make when conducting fieldwork:

> We contextualize events in a social system, within a web of meaning, and provide a nameable causation. We transform them into meaningful patterns, and in so doing, we exclude other patterns, meanings, or causes ... We ethnographers cannot help but lie, but in lying, we reveal truths that escape those who are not so bold.

Our final words for this chapter: Be bold, and be careful!

KEY TERMS

Ethnography	Homogenous Sample	Rapport
Ethnomethodology	Insider	Saturation
Field	Institutional Ethnography	Symbolic Interactionism
Field Notes	Naturalism	Theoretical Discovery
Gaining Access	Outsider	Theoretical Extension
Gatekeeper	Phenomenology	Theoretical Refinement

7

HOW TO USE
UNOBTRUSIVE METHODS:
THE BEAUTY OF SOCIAL, PHYSICAL AND VISUAL ARTEFACTS

─────────────────────── **Learning objectives** ───────────────────────

By the end of this chapter you will have the tools to:

*   Access the types of unobtrusive data
*   Develop the tools needed to design a study using unobtrusive methods

─────────────────────── **Chapter summary** ───────────────────────

Data collection that does not directly engage participants often falls under the umbrella of 'unobtrusive' research methods. Data includes everything from gathering social artefacts that people leave behind (e.g., garbage), create (e.g., graffiti, blog posts), and use (e.g., wear patterns). In some cases, data involves how people use a space or respond to a particular condition that you created or manipulated. In this chapter we discuss some sources of unobtrusive methods and provide you with the tools you need to collect this kind of data.

INTRODUCTION

Unobtrusive methods refer to data collection that does not directly engage participants. The type of data collected includes observing people and gathering 'social artefacts' (e.g., digital media, newspapers, periodicals, and legal documents and film). Researchers use unobtrusive methods to capture the human experience, provide insight into the people, groups or institutions of interest, and access difficult to reach segments of the population (e.g., young children). The nature of unobtrusive methods may seem a bit odd given that so much of qualitative research demands frequent and intense interaction with the subjects under study. Yet, there are three very good reasons for using unobtrusive methods as standalone or complementary sources of qualitative data.

First, many types of unobtrusive data collection methods avoid the problem of 'reactivity', the process by which participants react to being researched. Other forms of qualitative methods such as interview studies and participant observation introduce, in Webb's term, a 'foreign element'. In such studies, you not only generate the data collection materials – interview schedules, questionnaires or other instruments – but you often participate in the very creation of data.

Second, the reliance on volunteer participants introduces another source of bias. Many types of qualitative research methods rely on the willingness of people to agree to participate. Bias is introduced if there is a tendency for certain kinds of people to participate in certain kinds of projects, or if there are barriers that prevent some groups from participating. Summarizing the first and second potential challenges, Webb and his colleagues note (1966: 1):

> Interviews and questionnaires intrude as a foreign element into the social setting they would describe, they create as well as measure attitudes, they elicit atypical role and response, they are limited to those who are accessible and who will cooperate, and the responses obtained are produced in part by dimensions of individual differences irrelevant to the topic at hand.

Third, unobtrusive methods may inspire you to see the social world in a new and interesting way. We are surrounded by visual, physical and audio traces of human behaviour, culture and consumption. Historical documents, graffiti, music and images produced by Google Street View are just a few viable sources of unobtrusive data (for an example see Odgers et al., 2012). Unobtrusive methods may allow you to explore not just what people say, but also how they actually behave and the products of that behaviour.

As in other chapters, we emphasize that any benefit or challenge associated with this research method is highly contingent. Factors such as the skill of the researcher, the characteristics of the researcher and the people being observed and nature of the research influence the quality of the study.

This chapter starts off at the point at which you have decided to use unobtrusive methods as a main or complementary source of data and have decided on a sampling strategy. These decisions are discussed in great detail in Chapter 3. To outline the tools needed to collect unobtrusive data, this chapter is divided into two parts:

Types of Unobtrusive Data: We will review social behaviour and physical trace sources of unobtrusive data.

Collecting Unobtrusive Data: Key Considerations and Tools: This section will outline practical tools needed to collect various kinds of unobtrusive data, including Contrived and Systematic Social Observation studies.

TYPES OF UNOBTRUSIVE DATA

──────────────────── **Key takeaway** ────────────────────

- The craft of unobtrusive observation involves the rigorous examination and recording of social behaviour and physical traces.

Perhaps the most obvious choice of unobtrusive research is observing what people do, how they behave and how they interact in various social settings. Another separate or complementary option is to examine physical traces, or remnants of human behaviour, including documents, archival materials and even garbage (Table 7.1).

Table 7.1 Examples of unobtrusive research

Type	Description	Examples/approaches
Social behaviour	How and what people do, how they interact	Natural and contrived observations
		Covert and non-covert
		Systematic and non-systematic social observations
Physical traces	*Remnants of human behaviour* produced by erosion or accretion	Documents, pictures, historical/archival materials
	Erosion, or wear and tear, of a physical space. Erosion indicates frequency of use	The condition of tiles or carpeting
		Litter, graffiti, blog postings, Twitter
	Accretion is additions or changes to physical space and what people leave behind	

Social behaviour

> While nearly everyone who goes to a zoo sees the animals there, and many even watch some of those animals, very few can be said to observe their behavior. (McCall, 1984: 264)

Non-participant observation is the main method for examining social behaviour in an unobtrusive manner. Non-participant observation is 'focused on situations in which the observer has no control over the behaviour or sign in question, and plays an unobserved, passive and nonintrusive role in the research situation' (Webb et al., 1966: 112). However, just like the quote above implies, observation in the context of research involves much more than passively seeing and watching social behaviour; instead it involves the rigorous examination of what people do, how they do it, and how they interact with people and objects.

Webb and his co-authors (1966) discuss four types of data gathered when examining social behaviour:

- **Exterior physical signs**: Personal appearance and affects such as hair, tattoos, dress and shoes. These symbols may indicate personal and group identity, consumer culture, religion and even social hierarchy or organization.
- **Expressive movement**: Expressive movement includes non-verbal cues such as eye movement, touching and body language.
- **Physical location**: Physical location includes how people use and maintain space in social interaction. It also includes culturally sanctioned rules about physical location and personal space. Researchers can also examine how a setting is spatially organized (Hall, 1966).
- **Conversations**: Researchers also may record conversations in public spaces, either in person or online.

Physical traces

Physical traces include a wide range of social artefacts, or remnants, of human behaviour, attitudes, culture, likes and dislikes and social interaction. You can tell a lot about a person, group or neighbourhood just by how people wear down parts of their environment and all the 'stuff' people create.

There are endless amounts of data that could be collected for physical traces – wear and tear of floor tiles, the music people have on their iPods, the types of books taken out at a library, the kinds of items that are stolen at a convenience store, and the contents of our garbage. These few examples are types of evidence about a social group's attitudes, preferences, behaviours, social values and cultural norms.

There are two main types of physical trace data:

- **Erosion**: Erosion measures are evidence of what people use, how they use it and how they utilize a physical space. These measures include:

  o   Wear and tear of the floor or furniture.
  o   The depletion or theft of items.
  o   Researchers have also collected information on the size, shape and movement of material objects and people (e.g., streetcar transfers as an indicator of physical mobility, see Lee, 2000: 19-20).

- **Accretion**: Accretion measures are additions or changes to physical space and what people leave behind. Accretion is the build-up or layering of social activity, including:

  o   Visuals may be from government and non-government sources and may be current or historical. Visuals include photographs, art, advertisements, film and television (Banks, 2001; Pink, 2001).
  o   Documents may be from government and non-government sources. The documents may be current or historical. You can gather records that can be observed over a long period of time such as marriages, births and deaths, and job advertisements; and researchers can gather personal documents, photos and diaries or newspapers and official reports.
  o   Netography includes data generated from sources such as blogs, records of email exchanges, wikis and message boards. Unlike synchronous and asynchronous internet interviews, you do not solicit information and instead gather what is already on the internet.
  o   Beyond physical objects, researchers have also examined how people leave a space or an object. Webb et al. (1966: 39) for example describe a car dealer who had his mechanics record the radio stations his customers were tuned into when they brought their cars in for repair. The car dealer then placed advertisements at the radio stations that were popular with his customers.

Example: A natural netography

Beside social research, netography has also been used for product development research. A sporting goods company conducted a netography of five online basketball communities. The members of these communities were 15-25 years old, in school, and interested in basketball and related products. Members frequently shared their opinions of products, discussed specific product features and made suggestions for improvement. Over six months more than 240,000 posts in more than 18,000 discussions were screened and analysed using NVivo. The sporting goods company found that the netography generated a tremendous amount of good feedback, both positive and negative, and members of these communities posted a lot of innovative ideas for improving basketball products (Jawecki and Fuller, 2008).

COLLECTING UNOBTRUSIVE DATA: KEY CONSIDERATIONS AND TOOLS

--- **Key takeaways** ---

- You will need to consider whether you plan to conduct a natural or contrived, covert or non-covert, systematic or non-systematic, or manifest or latent research project.
- These approaches are not mutually exclusive. So you may design a project that is natural, non-covert and systematic, for example.

You will need to take four things into consideration before embarking on a project that includes unobtrusive data.

- Natural Observation and Contrived Observation.
- Covert and Non-Covert research.
- Systematic and Non-Systematic Social Observations: People.
- Manifest and Latent Approaches: Things.

These considerations include deciding whether to observe the social setting in its natural state, or whether you will vary it in some way. You also need to decide whether you will examine people or settings covertly, or whether your participants will know that they are being observed. If you are observing people, you will need to decide whether you will pre-specify and systematize what you plan to observe, or whether you will approach your project more inductively. And finally, if you are observing things (e.g., documents) you will have to decide between manifest, latent or a combination of both approaches.

For clarity, we have separated these considerations; however, they are not mutually exclusive. So you may design a project that is natural, non-covert and systematic, for example.

Natural and contrived observations

Natural observations do not manipulate or alter the research setting. Researchers who use this approach are not interested in how people respond to a particular stimulus or change, but rather how they behave and interact in a particular context. Projects that are 'natural' include everything from observing people at a park or viewing what people post on an online message board.

Contrived observations are when the social setting has been altered or varied in some way by the researcher. Researchers typically add or remove material in an environment to see how participants add, erode or respond to them.

There are many ways a contrived observation can be designed. Below we provide one example.

In the boxed Example, the researchers were interested in observing whether a change in condition or setting affects how people respond to the same stimulus. In Condition 1, the parking zone was clean. In Condition 2, the parking zone was covered in graffiti. The researchers asked: Are people more likely to litter when the environment is disorderly (graffiti) or orderly (clean) (Table 7.2)?

Table 7.2 Example of contrived observation

	Time 1	Time 2	
Condition 1: Clean parking lot	Alter setting (e.g., place flyer on a windshield)	Observe erosion or accretion and social behaviour in condition 1	
Condition 2: Littered parking lot	Alter setting (e.g., place flyer on a windshield)	Observe erosion or accretion and social behaviour in condition 2	Compare and contrast conditions 1 and 2

Example: Testing broken windows theory

Keizer et al. (2008) were interested in testing 'Broken Windows Theory' (BWT). BWT suggests that the presence of one kind of disorder (e.g., broken windows, litter) triggers others kinds of disorder (e.g., theft). To test BWT, the research team created six field experiments. One of the experiments examined how the presence or absence of graffiti in a bicycle parking zone influenced whether people littered a flyer the researcher team attached to the handlebar of each bike.

In condition 1, the parking zone was clean and there was no graffiti. In condition 2, the parking zone wall was covered with graffiti (Figure 7.1). In both conditions there was no trash can nearby, so the only option for participants was to take the flyer with them or to litter. Observing from the sidelines, the team found that in condition 1, 33% of bike owners littered. The team found that in condition 2, almost 70% of people littered. They repeated this field experiment in other settings and found similar results. The results of their experiments lend support to BWT.

Figure 7.1   Testing broken windows theory

SOURCE: Keizer, Kees, Siegwart Lindenberg and Linda Steg. 2008. 'The spreading of disorder.' *Science* 322: 1681-5.

Covert and non-covert research

If the project involves people, you will also have to decide on your role in the field. Should you be known or not known to the people you are observing? You and your ethics research board will need to work out a variety of issues, including: What are the potential ethical issues, and how are they influenced by whether the research is conducted in a covert or non-covert manner?

Covert research

Covert research reduces reactivity even further, since not only are you not participating, but participants will not be aware that they are being observed in the first place. In the case of contrived research, covert research may generate more authentic reactions if the participants are not actively looking for alterations or variations in the social setting.

Covert research, however, may give rise to a variety of ethical issues. First, participants will not have the opportunity to make an informed decision about whether they would like to participate in a research project or not. Importantly too, you may violate your participants' right to privacy, particularly if they have a reasonable expectation that their presence, statements or actions will remain private. In some cases, these potential ethical dilemmas are contingent on the nature of research (e.g., covert research at an AA meeting is a different animal than observing people in a shopping mall food court).

Second, you will be limited in your ability to record information in real time unless there is some logical and natural reason for jotting down notes, audio recording, or taking pictures or videos. Writing down notes at a mommy-and-me play group will seem rather strange (especially if you do not have a child with you!), while furiously typing on a laptop during a university lecture will appear perfectly natural and appropriate. Finally, as a covert researcher you may risk violating the very tenets of unobtrusive research if members of the group under study ask you to participate or join the group in some way.

Non-covert research

Non-covert research may introduce observer effects, even in the context of unobtrusive methods. Just because you are not participating or interacting with the participants does not mean that your presence will not affect how they behave or interact. And in fact your lack of participation – and your presence on the sidelines 'watching' – may intensify reactivity. Contrived observation may be compromised in non-covert research if the participants anticipate or look for alterations or variations in the social setting.

Non-covert research also has many potential benefits. First, it allows for informed consent. You will have the opportunity to inform participants about your research project and ask for their cooperation and participation. Second, since the participants know that they are being observed, you are less restricted in your ability to record in the field. Third, participants who understand the unobtrusive nature of the research will be less tempted to ask you to participate in group activities.

Systematic and non-systematic observations: People

If you are planning on observing people and their environment, you will also need to decide on the degree to which the recording of behaviours, social interactions, physical artefacts and events are pre-specified and standardized. To simplify our discussion, we will differentiate two approaches that are situated at opposite ends of a long continuum of observational methods: Systematic Social Observation (SSO) and Non-Systematic Social Observation (NSSO) approaches.

Systematic social observation

Systematic social observation approaches specify from the outset what and how observations will be recorded. SSO studies allow for replication since rules are decided on in advance (see Reiss, 1971). The observations, recording and even some analysis occur simultaneously. SSO projects are used to revise or evaluate theories, test hypotheses and examine patterns. SSO projects are also highly amenable to quantitative analyses, and have been used in a variety of mixed-method studies. Standardization allows for comparability across individuals and settings and the approach is suitable for multi-site and multi-researcher projects since it specifies what and how data will be collected in advance (see Maxwell, 2013: 87–8).

The main data collection tools for SSO projects include using a sign-code system. For qualitative researchers, a sign-code system may be complemented with other methods of data collection, including interviews, pictures or other artefacts and non-systematic social observations.

Sign-code system

The sign-code system of observation specifies a list of physical artefacts, social interactions or events that have been determined in advance to be methodologically and/or theoretically important. You can record in real time using a checklist or retrospectively by recording the people and the environment of interest with video recording equipment and coding the physical and social environment afterwards with the pre-scripted checklist.

Robert Sampson and Stephen Raudenbush have written extensively on social and physical disorder using systematic social observation. One of their most well-known projects was conducted by observers trained at the National Opinion Research Center (see http://www.norc.org/Pages/default.aspx). In total 23,816 Face Blocks, the block segment on one side of a street, in 196 Chicago census tracts were recorded. A stratified probability sample was used to sample census tracts. Face Blocks were observed by four observers in an SUV: a driver, a videographer and two observers who were taking notes.

> As the SUV was driven down the street, a pair of video recorders, one located on each side of the SUV, captured social activities and physical features of both face blocks simultaneously. At the same time, two trained observers, one on each side of the SUV, recorded their observations onto an observer log for each block face. The observers added commentary when relevant (e.g., about unusual events such as an accident or drug bust) by speaking into the videotape audio.. (Sampson and Raudenbush, 1999: 616)

Although Sampson and Raudenbush quantify their results (not to mention that their project was fairly elaborate and costly by most standards of research), their work is an exemplary example of SSO. Adopting a similar approach, you could easily use the principles of SSO to craft a qualitative or mixed-method project by using additional research tools (see Example: Researcher profile below). A mini-SSO is also a perfectly reasonable assignment in a course, and is a great way for students to 'get their feet wet'.

Given the standardization and ease of the checklist, researchers can include a fairly long list of descriptive categories to capture the physical space (e.g., presence of garbage, signs) and social activities (e.g., loitering) or behaviours (e.g., fighting). In the example in Table 7.3, you will notice that this checklist includes social behaviour (e.g., loitering), erosion (e.g., sign of disrepair) and accretion (e.g., litter). Before you begin, you should specify or operationalize your measures to ensure that your observations are consistent. 'Disrepair', for example, can mean a lot of different things, and one person's idea of loitering may be quite different from another person's. Operationalizing each measure in advance will improve the reliability of the study (see also Odgers et al., 2012).

Table 7.3 Example of a sign-code system checklist

Project: Examining Neighbourhood Disorder
Date: Time:
Location: Block (circle): North   South   East   West

Physical disorder			**Extra notes**
1 Is the lawn maintained?	Yes	No	
2 Are there signs of disrepair on the building?	Yes	No	
3 Is there graffiti on the building?	Yes	No	
4 Is there litter on the ground?	Yes	No	

Social disorder			
1 Is there loitering?	Yes	No	
2 Are adults fighting or arguing?	Yes	No	
3 Are there adults drinking alcohol?	Yes	No	
4 Are there prostitutes on the street?	Yes	No	

Quick tip: Event-sampling and time-sampling

Researchers can also build in Event-Sampling (recording every time a particular event takes place) and Time-Sampling (repeatedly recording observations at fixed regular intervals) elements into their sign-code checklist.

Event-sampling is when the researcher records a behaviour or event every time it happens. Recording every time a child interrupts his parent is an example of event-sampling.

Time-sampling, on the other hand, is the designation of time periods in which observations will take place. Researchers can designate the days, time of day and the interval of observations (e.g., 10 minute intervals). Below is an example of a simple time-sampling sheet.

Category: Girls Talking to Peers

Description: Girls talking when teacher is delivering a lesson or providing instruction to the class

X = Occurrence: O = Non-Occurrence

DATE					Total
	9:00	**9:10**	**9:20**	**9:30**	
May 1	X	O	O	X	2
May 7	X	X	X	O	3
May 14	X	X	O	X	3
May 21	X	X	X	X	4
May 28	X	O	X	O	2

Example: Researcher profile

Darren Cyr (2014) was interested in examining neighbourhood disorder and its impact on student behaviour and achievement. Lacking Sampson's monster budget (see Sampson and Raudenbush, 1999), Darren conducted a W-SSO, or Walking-Systematic Social Observation, of neighbourhoods surrounding 168 schools in Hamilton, Ontario to examine neighbourhood disorder around schools and its effect on educational outcomes. The term 'walking' means just that – Darren spent a summer walking along a set number of blocks surrounding each school and recorded signs of physical and social disorder on his sign-code checklist.

Darren then placed a small sample of four schools into high, medium and low disorder categories based on the results of the W-SSO. At these four schools and the surrounding communities, he conducted interviews with teachers, students, business owners, police officers, news reporters and real estate agents to examine their perceptions of physical and social disorder and its relationship to student behaviour and achievement. Darren also visited these four schools at 3 pm for three weeks to examine patterns of disorder (e.g., whether litter found one day was cleaned up the next day).

Darren found that low disorder schools always appeared 'orderly', whereas the downtown schools always showed signs of disrepair and strewn garbage. However, based on his interviews, the presence of disorder did not appear to trigger student deviance or poor achievement. Instead, other factors such as lack of parent and student engagement were more likely to be associated with poor student behaviour.

Non-systematic social observation

Non-Systematic Social Observation (NSSO) projects are usually designed more inductively, and do not specify or systematize the parameters of observation. Descriptive and theoretical categories are developed (or 'emerge') after at least some data collection has been completed, rather than specified at the beginning of the project (see Chapter 3).

If your data collection involves observing social behaviour, you will typically write field notes either during or after the observation. You are encouraged to use 'thick description' when describing the people, the settings, the interactions and the events.

Denzin (1989) and others (Ponterotto, 2006) have noted that thick description has the following characteristics:

- **Biographic Information**: The researcher includes detailed information about the people and their circumstances.
- **Historical Information**: The researcher places people and events into the context based on their histories, and the historical development or circumstances of the people, events or institutions of interest.
- **Situational**: The researcher paints a vivid picture of what happened and how it happened.
- **Interactional**: The researcher embeds the people, issues and events into the fabric of social relationships.

If the data collection involves physical traces, much of the same kind of data is collected, including erosion and accretion and observations of human interaction in person and online (see the list of categories discussed by Webb et al., 1966); however, it is less structured and systematic. The Example of a study about student cheating is a good illustration. Rather than trying to observe (or catch) students cheating, the researchers decided to collect cheat sheets, an accretion measure of student cheating.

Example: Student cheating

As any educator will tell you, cheating is a problem. Researchers know a lot about the characteristics and antecedents of cheating, but little about the technique of cheating. Pullen et al. (2000) came up with an innovative unobtrusive method for examining one way students cheat: cheat sheets that were discarded at their university.

They coded the cheat sheets for a variety of characteristics, including discipline, size, content and timing in the semester. The average cheat sheet was rectangular and the size of a match book, to fit comfortably in a person's hand. They found that most of the cheat sheets were from business, a discipline emphasizing more factual information. Cheat sheets from disciplines that required applied proficiency (e.g., maths) were rare. Most cheat sheets were found near the end of the term, and none were found early in the term. Their findings suggest that while students may not start off a term intending to cheat, they may do so near the end of the term to improve their grade or pass the course.

The researchers acknowledge the study's weakness, namely it only captures students who not only cheat but also who discard the cheat sheet on the university grounds; however, in essence the cheat sheet is a record of academic misconduct that exposes how some students accomplish cheating using a cheat sheet.

Manifest and latent approaches: Things

If you are planning on analysing things, you will also need to decide on the degree to which the recording of artefacts is more systematic and pre-specified or whether your project demands a more inductive and subjective approach to data collection. By 'things' we mean any erosion or accretion measures such as diaries, government documents, pictures or Twitter feeds.

To simplify our discussion, we will differentiate two approaches: Manifest and Latent. Manifest approaches are amenable to quantitative data analysis, while latent approaches focus on subjective meanings. Each approach may be used separately, or together. So a researcher may record the frequency of words, themes and items in a document (manifest) and then re-analyse the entire document for the implicit meanings embedded in the text (latent).

Manifest approaches

Similar to social observations of people, systematic approaches to things usually specify in advance easily identifiable and countable elements like a particular word, shape or item. A systematic document analysis, for example, may include counting the number of times a particular word appears, the number of pictures or the number of pages. Just like the sign-code system of systematic social observations, there are an infinite number of items that you could record; and the categories will depend on the nature of the study (Table 7.4). A project examining photographs will generate different categories than a project examining job advertisements, for example.

Given the standardization and ease of manifest approaches, you can include a fairly long list of categories that have been determined to have methodological and theoretical significance.

Table 7.4 Example of manifest coding categories

Content	Examples
Words	The frequency or placement of a particular word
People	Who is included and their characteristics (e.g., men, women, old, young) The frequency or placement of a particular person May also include the groupings of people (e.g., mom is always with baby)
Size and composition	Shape, size and colour of content Amount of space occupied (e.g., size of advertisement)
Things	The frequency or placement of things Groupings of things (e.g., pictures of mom with a vacuum cleaner, pictures of dad with sporting equipment)
Action	What people, animals or things (e.g., car racing down a track) are doing
Visual content	The content of the images presented in mediums such as art, film and online
Physical layout	How people, animals or items are positioned in the text or visual representation The social distance between people, animals or things The physical layout of the space
Themes	The frequency of themes (e.g., mom frustrated that dad does not help with housework)

Latent approaches

Latent, or 'hidden', approaches look for underlying meaning. Rather than search for specific words, themes or other characteristics (e.g., colour, shape), latent approaches rely on a set of interpretative guidelines that are no less rigorous than manifest approaches. You should review the content more holistically, looking more broadly for the meaning or essence of the object (e.g., diary) under study. Latent approaches usually demand that you have a substantial stock of knowledge about the context, people or events surrounding the materials so you are able to interpret them in historically, culturally and institutionally sensitive ways.

Example: What insurance claims tell us about the value of children

Viviana Zelizer used a latent approach to examine the economic and social value of children. Combing through hundreds of historical documents, including insurance claims and newspaper articles, Dr Zelizer illustrated how our economic system tells us a lot about our cultural values. One of her most famous books is *Pricing the Priceless Child* (1994). In the past, children were valued for their ability to contribute to the family's economic wellbeing. Insurance claims in wrongful death cases, for example, were a rather straightforward calculation of the lost revenue that would have been generated by the child. However, early in the 20th century, children were no longer valued for their economic utility, but instead seen as economically useless and emotionally priceless. Strangely, economically useless children became more valuable, evidenced by skyrocketing wrongful death settlements and the introduction of tough child labour laws.

CONCLUSION

This chapter outlines concrete tools for using unobtrusive methods. To review, we first discussed types of unobtrusive methods, including examining social behaviour and physical traces. Next, we outlined key considerations and techniques, including natural and contrived observations and systematic and non-systematic approaches. As we detail in this chapter, unobtrusive methods provide almost a limitless range of data and may be perfectly suitable as stand-alone or complementary sources of data.

KEY TERMS

Accretion Measures	Natural Observations	Social Behaviour
Contrived Observations	Non-Covert Observations	Systematic Social Observations
Covert Observations	Non-Systematic Social Observations	
Erosion Measures	Physical Traces	

PART III

ANALYSING AND WRITING UP YOUR RESEARCH

8

HOW TO DO DATA ANALYSIS:
THE BEGINNER'S
GUIDE TO CODING

———————————————— **Learning objectives** ————————————————

By the end of this chapter you will have the tools to:

- Prepare your data for coding, including proper labelling, preparing your documents and pre-coding your data
- Develop a codebook
- Make an informed decision about manual, Word or Excel, or CAQDAS data analysis tools
- Understand the basic structure of coding, including Codes, Categories, and Themes
- Conduct pre-coding, First Cycle and Second Cycle coding

———————————————— **Chapter summary** ————————————————

As researchers, we always start a project seeking that perfect 'ah-ha' moment. Yet as Richards notes below, the 'grand moment of discovery' does not arrive out of thin air. Instead, most discoveries are the product of good research design and ongoing analysis. In this chapter we present one of the main ways qualitative researchers bring order to qualitative data: coding. We take you from the early stages of preparing your data all the way to First and Second Cycle coding.

INTRODUCTION

> The majority of projects arrive at a good conclusion through analysis processes rather than a grand moment of discovery. Arrival will be confirmed by growing confidence that you really know what is going on. It happens, in other words, over time, through thinking and working with the data. (Richards, 2009: 143)

We have written this chapter for qualitative researchers who are relatively new to the process of data analysis. Qualitative data analysis can be quite daunting and confusing, so we have avoided the 'everything and the kitchen sink' approach adopted by some qualitative methods books. These books usually give students little bits and pieces of information that typically amount to a shopping list of definitions. In our experience students gain a surface understanding of what is available, but still have no clue as to how to actually execute any one of the data analysis strategies discussed.

Our goal is to offer concrete strategies for bringing order to qualitative data by 'coding'. We recognize that there are other ways to analyse qualitative data, and coding is simply inappropriate for some projects and approaches to qualitative methods (Saldana, 2013: 2). Our discussion is also largely focused on analysis of texts such as transcripts, field notes, documents and online materials.

We felt it was important to give more novice qualitative researchers a focused set of instructions that will suit most qualitative projects. Once qualitative researchers have a good understanding of at least one of the main methods for analysing qualitative data, they can easily expand their methodological toolkit.

For a more detailed discussion of qualitative data analysis, we recommend two books. Each book provides an excellent in-depth examination of qualitative data analysis and coding. We refer to these books many times throughout the chapter. These books are suitable for novice and experienced qualitative researchers and are part of our library of 'must have' books.

- Miles, Matthew B., A. Michael Huberman and Johnny Saldana. 2014. *Qualitative Data Analysis: A Methods Sourcebook*, 3rd Edition. Thousand Oaks, CA: Sage Publications, Inc.
- Saldana, Johnny. 2013. *The Coding Manual for Qualitative Researchers*, 2nd Edition. Thousand Oaks, CA: Sage Publications, Inc.

The chart below details the generic timeline of qualitative data analysis discussed in this chapter. Some of these steps, such as developing a codebook, start early and continue throughout the data collection and analysis phases of the project. Others, such as deciding on the tool you will use to analyse your data, occur only once. We have positioned these types of tasks in the middle stages of data analysis; however, more experienced researchers will likely come into a project knowing that they intend to use a particular CAQDAS program for example.

Generic stages of data analysis

Labelling

    Developing a Codebook

        Pre-Coding

           Making Decisions about What to Code*

              Decide on Data Analysis Tool*

              Formatting

              To Hard Copy or Not*

                  First Cycle Coding (Codes)

                      First Cycle and Second Cycle

                    Coding (Codes and Categories)

                          Mainly Second Cycle

                      Coding (Categories and Themes)

Early Stages-------------------------------Half-way through Data Collection----------------------Later Stages

Italicized = Ongoing throughout data collection and analysis

* = One time decision

To outline the tools needed to analyse qualitative data, this chapter is divided into two parts:

Getting Prepared: We will outline how you should prepare your data, including developing a code-book and selecting the tool you will use to analyse your data.

Pre-Coding, First Cycle and Second Cycle Coding: We will explain how you should approach data collection, including pre-coding your data *while* you are collecting it and are still in the early phases of data analysis. Next, we will show you how to conduct First Cycle and Second Cycle coding.

GETTING PREPARED

In this section we discuss preparing your data, creating a codebook, writing memos and selecting the tools you will use to code. We want to stress that these tasks should *not* be left until the completion of data collection. Tasks such as labelling your materials, pre-coding and developing a codebook should not be viewed as chores that 'have' to be completed once you have conducted your last interview or written your last field note; instead, they should be seen as part of the data analysis process itself. Treating your data analysis as an ongoing process will allow you to gain a deeper and holistic familiarity with your materials and will likely generate more meaningful and analytical memos that you will be able to harvest during later stages of coding.

Preparing your data: Early considerations and tasks

As you collect your data, it is important that you prepare your data for analysis.

- *Labelling*: Make sure transcripts, field notes, pictures or any other qualitative materials are organized and properly labelled. A label should include all the information you need to readily retrieve and identify the data such as the name, location, contact information and date of data collection.
- *Making Decisions about What to Code*: In all likelihood you will not be able to code all the data you have collected. In the process of selecting a community group, for example, you may have collected quite a bit of information about many others. Depending on your research question, these data may no longer be useful and be relegated to a paragraph in your methods section about how you ended up selecting group 'A' over groups 'B', 'C' and so forth. It is also not uncommon for researchers to make decisions about whether they want, at least initially, to code the entire transcript or sections of the transcript. Your interview schedule, for example, may have been divided into several sections to capture a reasonably wide range of topics, with only one or two being truly germane to the research question at hand. In the case of collaborative projects, decisions may have been made early about which part of the interview each person 'owns'.
- *Preparing Documents*: If you have transcripts or field notes, Saldana (2013) recommends double spacing text or creating 'stanzas' (Gee et al., 1992). Stanza is a term used to describe grouping text that represents a particular topic or line of discussion. Line spaces are used to separate

stanzas to represent a new topic or direction. In the example below, we have divided up the text into three separate stanzas to differentiate the discussion about parent engagement, worries about friends, and friends as bad influences.

QUESTION: What does the term parent engagement mean to you?

PARTICIPANT: Well it's like being there, you know. Being supportive.

QUESTION: Can you elaborate on what you mean by 'being there' and 'supportive'?

PARTICIPANT: Being engaged means that I take responsibility for raising my kid, not the school or anyone else. I make it a point to know what is happening at school, you know in terms of the curriculum, deadlines, homework, what teachers expect, what Sara should be working on to succeed. We work with Sara every night on her homework. We check it. But beyond school stuff, being engaged also means knowing your kid's friends, and what your child is doing. I guess for me it's hard to articulate because it's so pervasive. There's no one thing, it's really everything. School, after-school, what they're watching on TV, who they're texting, what's on their phone ... monitoring their friends. Wow that's a big one.

QUESTION: How so?

PARTICIPANT: Oh man, the friend thing is so huge now. All this texting and hanging out. Kids coming over to the house. As a parent you're always wondering, who is this kid, do I want them hanging around my house? Who are their parents? What are they up to? You wouldn't believe the stuff that I've heard.

QUESTION: Like what?

PARTICIPANT: Well there are so many kids that are just bad influences. One kid, I thought I knew her, seemed so sweet. Well she was selling drugs, out of her mom's car no less. And I heard about another one, I can't recall his name. But anyway, another bad egg. He stole a case of wine from his job, he was bussing tables. Of course he got caught. These kids, they think they're so clever sometimes. But anyway, you just have to be so careful. Here's this kid, who looks sweet, has good grades and is all 'yes sir, please and thank you', when they come to your house, and next thing you know they're busted for selling drugs. Really scary stuff.

- *Formatting*: If you are importing your data into CAQDAS, make sure materials are formatted to the software program specifications. Some programs handle documents saved in rich text, others can import materials in a variety of formats, including .doc and .docx files. The variation of the programs and ongoing program upgrades makes it impractical to list all of the formats here. Consult the specifications of the software program.

- *To Hard Copy or Not*: Even if you plan on importing materials into CAQDAS, some researchers find it helpful to have a hard copy handy. As you code you can use the hard copy as a reference guide, and refer to your pre-coding notes. If you have accretion measures (e.g., photos) you can lay out your materials on the floor or use a corkboard to display them. While some may scowl at the idea of printing out documents, pictures or other materials, others simply find it helpful to physically see, touch and arrange their materials before and during data analysis.

The codebook

You should also start your codebook, a 'bible' of sorts that specifies how you have operationalized each Code. A codebook 'is a set of Codes, definitions, and examples used as a guide to help analyze data' (DeCuir-Gunby et al., 2011: 138). Starting a codebook should be part of the planning process, but it is an ongoing task that gets added to and modified along the way as you reflect on and refine your analysis. The point of the codebook is to formally operationalize your Codes, and maintain consistency across coding and in some cases coders. A very elaborate and multi-person project may require a lot more detail, while a researcher working alone may require short and simple descriptions to stay on track.

You can specify each Code, define what each Code means, and the limits or exclusions of each Code. You should also include a representative quote to remind you of the essence of a particular Code. Modifying MacQueen et al. (1998) and others (Saldana, 2013), a codebook usually includes the following information:

- Code Name: The label that you have assigned to the Code
- Code Definition: A short description of the Code
- Inclusion and Exclusion Criteria: The criteria or central characteristic that justifies the material's inclusion or exclusion from a particular Code
- Examples: One or two examples (e.g., interview quote) that best represent the Code

There are other Categories that you may include in your codebook. Saldana (2013) suggests including a 'close, but no' Category to specify material that could be mistaken for a particular Code (in other words, the 'close but no cigar' example). MacQueen et al. (1998) list six components for each Code, including a brief description *and* a full description. Some researchers also suggest separating the 'inclusion' and 'exclusion' criteria into separate Categories. If a particular Code is related closely to one of your interview questions, you may also want to include an 'Interview Question' column.

While it sounds very technical, a codebook can be developed using a simple Word document or Excel file. Rather than be too prescriptive about the format of the codebook, we have provided you with a simple template that could be easily modified to suit a range of topics and organizational preferences (Table 8.1). Some researchers may want to organize Codes alphabetically, others may prefer to organize their codebook by topic, concept or theory.

Table 8.1 Codebook template

Code	Description	Inclusion/exclusion	Example

Data analysis tools: From manual to CAQDAS options

Finally, you will need to decide on the tools you will use for data analysis. There are three basic data analysis options: a) Manual; b) Word or Excel; and c) CAQDAS.

Manual options (Table 8.2)

Table 8.2 Coding manually

	Possible tools
Researchers use a colour-coding system to differentiate codes, patterns or themes	Printed transcripts, memos or unobtrusive data
Researchers often write in the margins	Pens, highlighters, recipe cards, Post-it notes, scissors
Some researchers write chunks of text on recipe cards or cut transcripts up by text passages. Each card or strip of paper serves as one code, and researchers organize the cards or strips into broader categories and themes	

Obviously the most low-tech option is to code manually. There are two basic strategies for manual coding. The first strategy is to simply use a hard copy of the data – transcript, field notes and so forth. Some researchers like to colour-code text with a highlighter or marker, using different colours to signify a particular Code or Category (e.g., green for 'hate school' and yellow for 'love school'). Post-it notes can be used to add notes or memos on the side.

Other researchers prefer to write the main text on recipe cards, with each recipe card containing one passage of text. Similarly, some researchers prefer to cut text directly out of the transcript, with each strip of paper containing one passage of text. Researchers arrange and re-arrange the cards or strips of paper into different piles that each correspond to a particular Code or Category (e.g., pile 1 = hate school; pile 2 = love school). Regardless of the method, researchers eventually arrange Codes and Categories into larger Themes.

Manual coding is not without its drawbacks. Most obviously, manual coding can be extremely labour intensive and can easily become unmanageable if the project involves a lot of qualitative data or multiple researchers. However, for pilot projects and small class projects, manual coding is a perfectly reasonable option. For newer and less experienced researchers, manual coding may help them feel closer to the data and gain a deeper understanding of the process of coding. And some researchers just prefer to code manually for personal or methodological reasons.

Word or Excel (Table 8.3)

Table 8.3   Coding using Word or Excel

	Possible tools
In a Word document, researchers can do one or more of the following: • Highlight text and use a colour-coding system to differentiate Codes, Categories or Themes • Cut and paste sections of text, grouping text by Codes, Categories or Themes • In the 'Review' toolbar, use the 'New Comment' function to add memos or comments on the side • In the 'Insert' toolbar, use the 'Text Box' function to add memos or comments within the body of the document	Word: • Highlighting • Cut and paste function • New Comment function
In an Excel document, researchers can: • Create columns relating to Codes, Categories or Themes Create rows that relate to each individual piece of data or person	Excel: • Cut and paste function

The middle-ground option is to code data using a Word or Excel file. This option is suitable for interview and focus group transcripts and field notes. In a Word document, you can colour-code text, cut and paste sections of text into different Codes, Categories or Themes, or do both. Similar to manual coding, each section of text or colour represents a different Code, Category or Theme. You can also use tools such as Textboxes to make notes on the side, or Comments to act like Post-it notes along the side of the document.

In Excel, you can organize columns and rows in a variety of ways to separate your data into different Codes, Categories or Themes. The most straightforward option is to place each interviewee or set of field notes into a separate row, and then create columns that correspond to a particular Code, Category or Theme.

CAQDAS options (Table 8.4)

CAQDAS programs are wonderful organizational tools for storing, organizing and coding qualitative data. Qualitative research projects tend to generate mountains of data that can become quite unmanageable, even for the most experienced researcher. It is not surprising that many share Saldana's sentiment about CAQDAS programs: when one considers the ability to quickly move back and forth between analytical tasks and 'recode, code, uncode, rename, delete, move, merge, group, and assign different codes to shorter and longer passages of text with a few mouse clicks and keystrokes … the advantages of CAQDAS over paper and pencil soon become apparent' (Saldana, 2013: 33–4).

Table 8.4   Coding using CAQDAS

	Possible tools
Once the materials are imported into the selected program (see software specifications for formatting), most CAQDAS software allows researchers to:	ATLAS.ti MAXQDA NVivo Weft QDA

- Organize and store a large amount of data. Researchers can import a variety of data including documents, jpegs, videos, mp3 files and pdfs
- Assign data to Codes and develop broader umbrella Categories and Themes
- Organize Codes separately or into a family-tree-like structure to signify a pattern, relationship or hierarchy
- Assign a passage of text, picture or other to more than one Code
- Create, add, delete, merge or modify Codes and their content as the project develops
- Review materials line by line, picture by picture and so forth
- Search for key words or phrases
- Link one piece of data with another
- Write memos
- Conduct a content analysis
- Create various kinds of displays (e.g., matrix) or data maps

Programs will vary, but many of the most popular brands allow researchers to import a variety of data, including documents, jpegs, videos, mp3 or other audio files and pdfs. Once the data are imported, CAQDAS programs will allow you to create Codes. The coding structure may vary a bit, but most will allow you to create stand-alone Codes (e.g., NVivo refers to these as Free Nodes) or Codes that are structured like a family tree (e.g., NVivo refers to these as Tree Nodes).

Family-tree-like Codes are usually organized hierarchically, with the master or parent Code first, followed by 'child' Codes and even 'grandchild' and 'great-grandchild' Codes following it. NVivo, for example, offers researchers a lot of flexibility. Stand-alone Free Nodes can be left as is, or developed into more elaborate Tree Nodes as the project develops; or conversely a Tree Node may be broken apart into many different Free Nodes. And you may decide that a 'child' node should become a 'parent' node at some point. The options are really endless, but you can think about this process as the software version of manual coding, allowing you to move around, arrange and re-arrange your coding (just like you could move around recipe cards) as your understanding of the data matures as you move from First Cycle to Second Cycle coding.

Figure 8.1 is an example of Janice Aurini's project on parent engagement using NVivo. Similar to manual coding, you will be able to then assign data to the Codes. You can assign data to more than one Code at a time, and make changes to the Codes, assignments or the data itself at any point. You can also assign the same passage, quote and so forth to several Codes. The beauty of these programs is that while only segments of data are typically assigned to a Code (e.g., a passage of text), you will be able to readily see where any one piece of data came from. So if you are working with transcripts, each small coded passage of text will include the label you have assigned to it (e.g., Mary Smith, Parent, East End School, July 1, 2014). You will also be able to readily access the entire transcript with a click of a button if you want to re-read the entire transcript again or simply the text just before or after the passage.

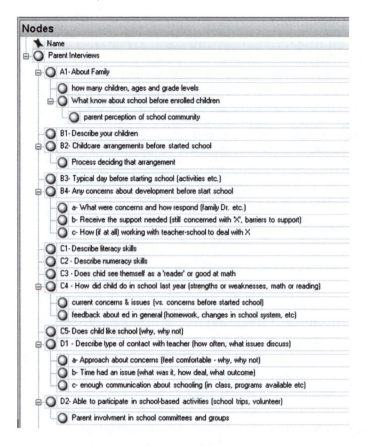

Figure 8.1   Coding example using NVivo (NVivo 10-2012)

Figure 8.2 is another example of Janice's project. By clicking the title, 2012\\Ava_North End School_Parent_Aug 3, 2012, she can return to the original transcript within seconds.

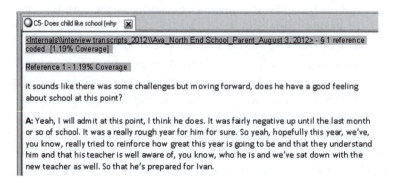

Figure 8.2   Access to interview transcripts using NVivo (NVivo 10-2012)

One of the biggest questions qualitative researchers have about CAQDAS is 'What is the "best" qualitative software'? It is not practical for us, in the capacity of writing a textbook, to make such a recommendation. There are many very good programs that will get the job done.

For a good review of different software packages we recommend:

- The CAQDAS project at the University of Surrey (http://www.surrey.ac.uk/sociology/research/researchcentres/caqdas/support/choosing/index.htm). The website provides up-to-date and unbiased information about the CAQDAS programs on the market.
- Silver, C. and A. Lewins. 2014. *Using Software in Qualitative Research: A Step-by-Step Guide*, 2nd Edition. Thousand Oaks CA: Sage Publications, Inc.
- Lewins, A. and C. Silver. 2009. 'Choosing a CAQDAS Package.' http://eprints.ncrm.ac.uk/791/1/2009ChoosingaCAQDASPackage.pdf.
- If you are new to qualitative data analysis, it is also a good idea to speak to colleagues who have some familiarity with CAQDAS since it will be difficult for you to anticipate the features that you will need at this point.

It is also not practical to provide you with specific instructions for using CAQDAS software. Once you have selected your software, most brands provide detailed and easy to follow instructions (e.g., how to import documents, how to create Codes). QSR International, the makers of NVivo, offer online tutorials and sell very good training guides for novice *and* more experienced NVivo users. NVivo trainers also offer in-class workshops, some may even be sponsored by your postsecondary institution. Other software options offer similar levels of training and support. There are also very detailed books available on specific CAQDAS programs (for an example see Bazeley, 2007).

There is a lingering misconception that CAQDAS programs code for you. This misconception used to generate a lot of fear-mongering about the dangers of CAQDAS. The field has matured and most qualitative researchers appreciate that while many programs allow you to search for words (e.g., auto code), it is ultimately your responsibility to verify the accuracy and authenticity of the Code by manually going through each coded passage to ensure that it belongs. In short, coding that is sloppy, selective, distanced from the data, or directed by a zealous allegiance to a particular theoretical stance can occur whether one uses manual or CAQDAS data analysis tools. *Responsible and ethical coding that captures the essence of your data is the result of careful and thoughtful data analysis, not the specific tool or program you use to code.*

PRE-CODING, FIRST CYCLE AND SECOND CYCLE CODING

The terms 'pre-coding', 'First Cycle' and 'Second Cycle' coding generate an image of a neat and orderly process that occurs in distinct and compartmentalized stages. More experienced researchers know that coding is an iterative process that evolves as the data collection and analysis progresses. Importantly as we and others (e.g., Miles et al., 2014; Saldana, 2013) recommend, data analysis and coding should occur throughout the data collection phase.

In this section we outline a condensed version of what Saldana (2013: 64) refers to as 'generic coding'. This approach spans a number of qualitative methods and is quite amenable to grounded theory, one of the most widely used methods of analysing qualitative data. As Miles et al. (2014: 10) observe, most approaches to qualitative coding (e.g., grounded theory, ethnography) share the same basic steps. Below we present a condensed and slightly modified version of their list that we will expand on in the remainder of the chapter.

- Pre-Coding: Assign preliminary Codes to collected text (e.g., transcripts, field notes, websites) as you collect your data. You can do this manually, in a Word document, or start a project in your selected CAQDAS program.
- First Cycle Coding: Review pre-coding and make changes as needed. Continue to assign Codes to collected text (e.g., transcripts, field notes, websites). First Cycle coding tends to be more descriptive and captures the central characteristics embedded in the data. You should start to develop tentative propositions about what you think is going on, patterns and even some possible Categories and Themes.
- Second Cycle Coding:
  - Early Stages: Review First Cycle Codes and start to reorganize and subsume, where appropriate, First Cycle Codes into broader Categories. You should start to isolate these patterns. If required, you can use these insights to inform the next wave of data collection.
  - Later Stages: Again review Categories and revise or add Categories as needed. Compare and contrast emerging propositions with established concepts, theories and findings. Start to develop two to five master Themes that capture the overarching essence of the data. Themes each subsume, where appropriate, several Categories which are comprised of a collection of Codes.

Throughout pre-coding, First Cycle and Second Cycle coding, document reflections in the field and while reviewing collected data (e.g., memos). Even at the early stages of Second Cycle coding, start to develop a set of propositions about what you think is going on. Your propositions will later inform the Themes that develop at later stages of data analysis.

Getting started: Pre-coding

─────────────────────────── Key takeaways ───────────────────────────

- Assign preliminary Codes to collected text, including transcripts, field notes, and websites throughout data collection.
- Pre-coding can be done manually, in Word or in your selected CAQDAS program.

Saldana (2013) and others (e.g., Layder, 1998) recommend 'pre-coding' your data. As you collect your data, review your materials, make notes, highlight key passages and start to craft preliminary Codes and memos.

Preliminary Codes that can be created in advance, even during the early stages of your data collection and analysis, include (see also Miles et al., 2014: 81):

- Description or Attribute Codes: Attribute Codes capture the basic characteristics of the people, places or things in your study and their characteristics.
- Deductive Codes: Deductive Codes are generated from your research questions, key concepts and theories that you have drawn on to design your study, your research questions and your literature review.
- Interview Schedule: You can also use the questions posed in your interview schedule to create an initial list of Codes.
- 'Potpourri': Given the infancy of data collection and analysis, you should feel free to follow your gut instinct. These Codes may or may not fit with some larger scheme, but strike you as important for their potential empirical or theoretical utility.

You should also begin to write 'memos' – your thoughts, hunches, theoretical musing, questions about the data, problems with the analysis, relationship with the participant, your own emotions, questions about your coding decisions – throughout the pre-coding and coding process.

In Chapter 4, we discussed four types of memos:

- Summative memos are a basic description of the participants and a general overview of what happened during data collection.
- Theoretical memos are conceptual ideas that emerged during data collection, in the field or while reviewing your data.
- Methodological memos relate to any methodological or data collection issues that emerged during data collection.
- Personal memos are all of your reflections about the interview and other issues that may have affected the quality of the data collection.

Memos can be simply written in the margins or created in a separate document. Most CAQDAS programs have some function that allows you to add memos either separately, or connected to a piece of data. Saldana (2013: 42), on the other hand, dislikes using the 'memo' function in CAQDAS programs, and instead prefers to write analytical memos freely first, before determining how to label them or situating them within the larger project. Only you can decide what works for you – a simple pad of paper, notes in the margins of your documents, a Word document that you add to, or CAQDAS memo functions.

Memos are an important part of data analysis and should be written throughout the data collection process. You should not rely on your ability to remember all of your reflections.

Quick tip: How to start coding

As we have repeated throughout the chapter, you should code throughout the data collection phase.

- If you are using CAQDAS, refer to your codebook and create your initial Codes in the program.
- Start slowly and with one transcript, one day's worth of field notes, one internet post and so forth.
- First, read over the data in its entirety. Review any memos that you have written related to that data during the pre-coding phase.
- Start at the beginning of the document, and code small sections of text at a time, while keeping in mind the text in its entirety.

    o   When appropriate, assign pre-existing Codes to sections of text.
    o   Develop new Codes as they emerge or make changes and update the codebook.

While you should be thoughtful, do not get too bogged down with creating the 'perfect' Code. Throughout the process of coding you will have ample opportunity to modify or discard Codes.

Developing Codes: First Cycle Codes

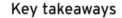 **Key takeaways**

- Segment your data into descriptive Codes that capture the central characteristics embedded in the data. You can start to develop tentative propositions about what you think is going on, patterns and even some possible Categories and Themes.
- First Cycle Codes are developed at the early to mid stages of data analysis.
- The average project will develop 100–200 Codes.

First Cycle coding is when Codes are 'initially assigned to data chunks' (Miles et al., 2014: 73). In the literature this stage is referred to as 'initial coding' (Charmaz, 2006), 'First Cycle' coding (Saldana, 2013) or 'open coding' (Corbin and Strauss, 2008). A '*Code*' is the term used to describe the word or short phrase that captures the main essence of one small dimension of your data. As Charmaz (1983: 186) describes it 'Codes … serve as shorthand devices to *label, separate, compile,* and *organize* data'. It is not uncommon for parts of an interview, pictures, videos and so forth to be assigned to more than one Code, something that is particularly easy to do with CAQDAS.

Table 8.5 is an example of a parent describing her contact with her daughter's school and how she organizes her daughter's after-school time. The first quote was assigned to four different Codes, while the second quote was assigned to three different Codes. As the coding progresses, we could further refine the analysis to differentiate 'Poor' and 'Good' Communication and 'Yes' and 'No' Intervention, for example. For now we will keep our example simple.

Table 8.5 Coding example

Data	Codes
'As a parent it's my job to figure out what is going on with my kid. I'm in constant contact with the school, you know, "How's everything going, how was her day at school, what should I be working on at home, you know in terms of homework". We expect Sara to do well at school, and our job is to make sure she does well. And if I see a problem, it's my job to intervene, find out what is going on and to be part of the solution.'	Code 1: Communication Code 2: Intervention Code 3: Parent expectations Code 6: Home-work
'We do a lot of things after school. I think you can get from our discussion that I'm one of "those" kinds of parents! Sara certainly has free time, but we make it a point to enrol her in a lot of after-school activities like soccer and music classes. Home-work seems to eat up a lot of time nowadays, now that Sara is in Grade 6.'	Code 4: Sports Code 5: Music Code 6: Home-work

Since a Code represents an individual segment of data, an average project will develop 100–200 Codes; however, there are no hard and fast rules about how many Codes you should have. The number of Codes really depends on the size of the project and your approach to coding. Bernard (2011) differentiates between a 'splitter' and 'lumper' approach to Codes. Splitters break down text into very small segments to differentiate each idea expressed in the text, while lumpers create more summative Codes that capture the essence of a segment of text. Splitters will end up with many more descriptive Codes, while lumpers will end up with fewer Codes that are broader and contain more contextual information. As Saldana (2013) observes, there are pluses and minuses with each approach. Splitting may produce more fragmentation and superficial Codes, while lumping may gloss over important nuances in the data. Early in the data analysis, you may want to try both approaches to see which one helps *you* understand your data.

While you are creating these Codes, do not get too bogged down about whether they are 'right' or not. You want your Codes to be thoughtful and true to your data, but remember that most Codes will be revised as your data analysis progresses.

Our list is not as exhaustive as Saldana's (2013), but it will give you a good overview of what and how you may code your data (Table 8.6).

Table 8.6 First Cycle coding options

Type of Codes	Description	Sample quotes	Sample Codes
Descriptive: Nouns	Captures who, what and where	'Our customers are really interested in clean eating. We have locations all over the country, but you tend to find us in more affluent neighbourhoods. We sell a lot of organic products, vitamins … stuff like that'	Code 1: Customers Code 2: Products for Sale Code 3: Affluent Neighbourhoods
Descriptive: Action	Captures actions, interactions and processes as they are described by participants or observed by the researcher	'I have a pretty good relationship with most of the customers. I really enjoy helping customers, you know selecting products. People who are just getting into clean eating often have a lot of questions'	Code 4: Helping Customers Code 5: Answering Questions
In Vivo	In Vivo coding creates Codes from participants' own words or phrases	'The Market pays really **fair wages** too, especially compared to the last place I worked. As an employee, I **feel valued** …'	Code 6: Fair Wages Code 7: Feel Valued
Interpretations	Captures how participants interpret situations or events	'it was really wrong what happened to Steve. He shouldn't have been fired. It wasn't his fault'	Code 8: Wrongful Dismissal
Feelings	Captures participants' feelings and emotions	'I was really angry that Steve got fired. I was so confused. It was so unlike the management …'	Code 9: Angry Code 10: Confused
Belief systems	Questions that examine participants' values, morals or standards	'I just really question the fairness of it all. I just think it's wrong to fire someone without a full investigation'	Code 11: Fairness
Assessment	Captures participants' assessments, estimations or valuations	'I think the impact was huge. I mean the firing just send a chill through The Market'	Code 12: Impact
Frequency	Captures participants' understandings about duration, regularity, or commonality	'It was so unlike the management … it was really unusual. It just doesn't happen here'	Code 13: Unusual Firing
Local causation	Captures how participants understand why something occurred	'I think the firing was really personal. Fred, the head guy, just never liked Steve. There was a lot of personal stuff. I bet he was just looking for any excuse to fire him'	Code 14: Personal Reasons

The emergence of Categories: Early and later stages of Second Cycle coding

Second Cycle coding 'generally work[s] with the resulting First Cycle Codes themselves' by condensing, integrating and laying the Codes into broader and more coherent Categories and

Themes (Miles et al., 2014: 73). Miles et al. (2014: 86–7) refer to the early Second Cycle coding process developing Categories which 'pull together a lot of material into a more meaningful and parsimonious unit of analysis. They are a sort of meta-code' (Miles and Huberman, 1994: 69).

While First Cycle coding is more literal and codes the data at face value, early and later stages of Second Cycle coding interpret and make sense of the data by identifying patterns, relationships and explanations. Part of this process may include re-arranging and structuring the Codes hierarchically to identify Categories. In grounded theory, Second Cycle coding may also suggest that additional data collection is needed in order to further develop a theory that has started to emerge (referred to as 'theoretical sampling'). It is important to remember that during Second Cycle coding, your original Codes may be relabelled, subsumed by other Codes, re-arranged or eliminated.

Developing Categories usually occurs after you have developed a number of Codes and is part of what some researchers refer to as 'pattern coding' (Saldana, 2013), 'focused coding' (Charmaz, 2006) and axial coding (Corbin and Strauss, 2008) (more on this later).

Categorization

Categorization is the process of grouping Codes under larger unifying classifications. As you start to develop Codes, you will find yourself arranging and re-arranging your data into broader classifications or typologies based on the patterns that begin to emerge or for some analytic, practical, methodological or theoretical reason. The same Codes may be used in more than one Category. Since a Category is a grouping of Codes, the average project can include anywhere from 15 to 25 Categories; but again there is no magic number of Categories a project 'should' include or number of Codes each Category 'should' contain.

In Table 8.7, two Categories were created: Parent Engagement and After-School. Category 1 captures four Codes that relate to several dimensions of Parent Engagement. Category 2 captures the three Codes that relate to how parents construct their children's After-School time. Note that both Categories include the Code 'Home-work' since it is related to Parent Engagement *and* After-School activities.

Table 8.7 Categorization example

Representative quote	Categories
'As a parent it's my job to figure out what is going on with my kid. I'm in constant contact with the school, you know, "How's everything going, how was her day at school, what should I be working on at home, you know in terms of homework". We expect Sara to do well at school, and our job is to make sure she does well. And if I see a problem, it's my job to intervene, find out what is going on and to be part of the solution'	Category 1: Parent Engagement Code 1: Communication Code 2: Intervention Code 3: Parent Expectations Code 6: Home-work
'We do a lot of things after school. I think you can get from our discussion that I'm one of "those" kinds of parents! Sara certainly has free time, but we make it a point to enrol her in a lot of after-school activities like soccer and music classes. Home-work seems to eat up a lot of time nowadays, now that Sara is in Grade 6'	Category 2: After-School Code 4: Sports Code 5: Music Code 6: Home-work

Themes

As Saldana (2013: 14) observes, a Theme is an '*outcome* of coding, categorization and analytic reflection, not something that is, in itself, coded'. Specific definitions will vary, but for our purposes think of a Theme as the roughly two to five 'big' ideas that emerge from your data.

Whereas Codes and even Categories tend be more descriptive in nature, Themes tend to be the outcome of interpretive processes (Rossman and Rallis, 2003); they may also relate to an established concept or theory. In short, Themes emerge *after* some pretty significant analysis and reflection, and certainly after the pre-coding and First Cycle coding stages.

In Table 8.8 we have expanded our example to three major Themes: 'Cultural Capital', 'Social Capital' and 'Economic Capital'.

Table 8.8   Putting together Codes, Categories and Themes

Sample Codes	Sample Categories	Sample Themes
100-200 Codes	**15-25 Categories**	**2-5 Themes**
Code 1: Communication Code 2: Intervention Code 3: Parent Expectations Code 6: Home-work	PARENT ENGAGEMENT	*CULTURAL CAPITAL*
Code 4: Sports Code 5: Music Code 6: Home-work	AFTER-SCHOOL	
Code 1: Communication Code 7: Good Relationship with Teacher Code 8: Access to Resources	INFORMATION NETWORK	*SOCIAL CAPITAL*
Code 1: Communication Code 3: Parent Expectations Code 7: Good Relationship with Teacher Code 9: Attend School Events	CONNECTION TO SCHOOL	
Code 10: Private Preschool Code 11: Saving for University Code 12: Tutoring	RESOURCES	*ECONOMIC CAPITAL*
First Stage Coding-----------------------Early Second Stage Coding---------------------Second Stage Coding		

Moving from Codes, to Categories to Themes

You can think of the process of coding like a puzzle. First you start with the individual pieces (Codes); next you put together groupings of pieces that constitute smaller segments of the puzzle (Categories); and after a lot of arranging and re-arranging, you put large sections of the puzzle together (Themes). The completed 'puzzle' is really the story you are eventually able to tell people about your study.

But how do you get there? In our discussion below, we present four coding strategies for advancing your analysis from the more descriptive First Cycle to more explanatory Second Cycle coding by developing the following: a) Patterns; b) Focused Coding; c) Frequencies; and d) Comparisons.

Pattern coding

As your analysis develops, you may start to see reoccurring patterns in your data. Patterns emerge when you find that formally separate Codes are connected, reoccur or develop in similar ways. Such patterns may represent organizational, social–psychological or underlying processes about what is happening, how it is happening, and the assumptions that participants hold to be true about the nature of reality (Charmaz, 1983: 112).

Through this process you may also identify central processes and even an explanation about why or how something has occurred. Miles et al. (2014) also observe that pattern coding can be very useful when there are a very large number of cases or data. Once identified, a pattern Code can serve as a major Category or even a Theme that subsumes several other Codes and even other Categories.

Focused coding

There are a variety of terms that describe the process by which researchers start to 'clump' together 'clusters' of data. As Miles et al. (2014: 279) explain:

> it might be called 'distilling, 'synthesizing', 'abstracting', 'transforming' and even the abhorrent 'reducing' the data. Even though these are different works and processes, they *kind* of mean the same thing ... In all instances, we're trying to understand a phenomenon better by *grouping* and then *conceptualizing* objects that have similar patterns and characteristics.

Unlike the initial stages of coding, focused coding is more selective and develops larger Categories. Focused coding requires the researcher to select the most salient or telling Codes that best represent the data. While initial coding broadly asks 'What do the data suggest?' (Charmaz, 2006: 47), focused Codes are more iterative and represent more theoretically rich Categories.

When conducting focused coding, the researcher takes a limited set of Codes that were crafted during the First Cycle coding phase. The goal is to develop more abstract and inclusive Categories that capture a large amount of data.

Figure 8.3 is an example taken from Janice's former PhD student Emily Milne. After carefully creating dozens of Codes, Emily developed three broad Categories, 'Dynamics of Policy Implementation', 'Schooling Organization' and 'Educators' that were eventually reorganized under the broader Theme 'Dynamics of Policy Implementation'.

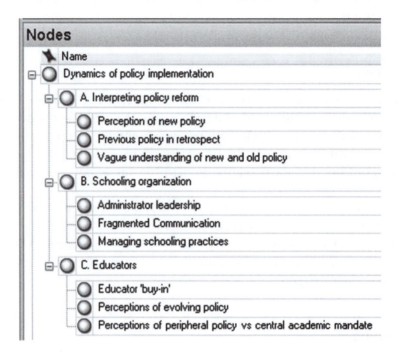

Figure 8.3   Focused coding example (NVivo 10-2012)

Frequency coding

Qualitative researchers tend not to think of themselves as counters. After all, our interest is primarily in the quality not the quantity of whatever dimension of social life we are interested in. However, as Miles et al. (2014: 282) rightly point out 'when we identify a Theme or a pattern, we are isolating something that (a) happens a number of times and (b) consistently happens in a specific way'. You can count a variety of things, including words, phrases and events. Counting can help you identify a Category and even a Theme and it can verify your initial propositions about what is going on in your data. Counting can also keep you 'analytically honest' (ibid.) by forcing you to verify your hunches about what is happening 'a lot' or how your participants understand the social phenomenon under study.

Depending on the search, CAQDAS programs make counting particularly easy. Most programs allow researchers to perform simple word searches, for example, that can be displayed by raw number of counts (Figure 8.4) or more artistically such as the Word Cloud (Figure 8.5) and Word Tree (Figure 8.6).

Word Frequency Query Result ☒			
Word	Length	Count	Weighted Percentage (%)▽
school	6	11870	1.72
think	5	8674	1.26
going	5	6630	0.96
parents	7	6117	0.89
really	6	5943	0.86
things	6	4819	0.70
right	5	4439	0.64
program	7	4313	0.63
teacher	7	3969	0.58
something	9	3745	0.54
teachers	8	3235	0.47
parent	6	3216	0.47
maybe	5	2909	0.42
different	9	2866	0.42
thing	5	2826	0.41
little	6	2801	0.41
people	6	2733	0.40
stuff	5	2558	0.37
child	5	2537	0.37
children	8	2199	0.32

Figure 8.4   Word frequency result (NVivo 10-2012)

Figure 8.5   Word cloud

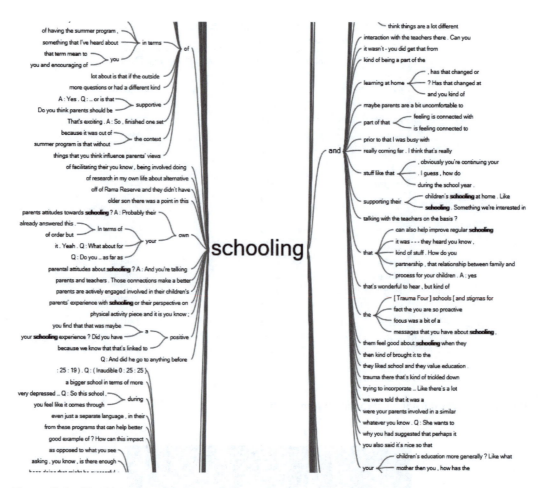

Figure 8.6   Word tree

Comparison coding

Comparisons are a common analytical strategy employed by qualitative researchers. Comparisons can often be anticipated well in advance, either because it makes practical sense or based on prior knowledge generated by other researchers. As you are creating initial Codes, you may have also divided up the data into logical comparison groups (e.g., boys and girls) which allow you to compare and contrast the frequencies in which a particular group responded. These analyses may also shed light into new ways to compare or understand the data.

As we discussed in Chapter 2, you can also look for internally driven comparisons. Internally driven comparisons occur when two or more units of interest (e.g., communities, organizations) are similar or different on the *key attribute of interest*. Method of agreement and method of difference approaches are similar to internally driven comparisons, but examine several cases that had a particular outcome (similar or different) and work backwards.

CONCLUSION

This chapter outlines concrete strategies for analysing qualitative data by coding. We first described preparing your data for analysis and starting a codebook. We also discussed three main data analysis tools: manual, Word or Excel, and CAQDAS options. The main part of the chapter details specific steps to move from stand-alone Codes all the way through to the development of broader Categories and Themes.

The next chapter completes our journey by outlining how to write up qualitative data. While qualitative research is now a widespread and accepted approach, researchers still struggle to publish qualitative data in high quality peer-reviewed journals, books and policy venues. Some granting agencies are also less receptive to qualitative data. Learning how to effectively communicate qualitative research is critical for overcoming these hurdles and effectively disseminating your research.

KEY TERMS

CAQDAS	Comparison Coding	Pre-Coding
Categories or Categorization	First Cycle Coding	Second Cycle Coding
Codebook	Focused Coding	Summative, Theoretical, Methodological, Personal Memos
Codes	Frequency Coding	Themes
Coding	Patterned Coding	

9

HOW TO WRITE UP
QUALITATIVE RESEARCH:
MAKING YOUR
WORDS COUNT

—————————————————— **Learning objectives** ——————————————————

By the end of this chapter you will have the tools to:

- Present qualitative data for various audiences
- Organize a manuscript for a peer reviewed journal article, book or policy document
- Develop a thorough methods section in your manuscript
- Effectively integrate quotations, excerpts and tables
- Make changes to your manuscript based on reviewer feedback
- Articulate changes to reviewers

—————————————————— **Chapter summary** ——————————————————

This chapter is divided into five main sections. Each section outlines specific strategies for writing qualitative data for dissemination. First, we outline how to target writing for a particular audience, such as a book, a peer reviewed journal article or a policy document. Then we discuss tips for integrating data into your work, through the use of charts, tables and quotations or excerpts. We also focus on effective writing skills. Finally, we discuss approaching and responding to reviewer comments.

INTRODUCTION

There is little point in conducting research if you do not write it up. Writing is one way to disseminate the findings from our research in order for others to understand them and use them, whether as the basis for future projects, to advance policy, or to improve current practices in health, education or welfare (Tarling, 2006; Denzin and Giardina, 2010; Liamputtong, 2013). Although many of us would prefer to conduct research and have somebody else write it up for us, the two tasks go hand-in-hand.

As you read qualitative work – or any academic work, for that matter – you will become more familiar with the structure of qualitative pieces of writing. Pay attention to how the structure is created, how the methods are presented, how the findings are written about and how qualitative data, like quotes, are integrated. You will recognize that some pieces of work are more successful than others in these endeavours, and you can begin to learn the techniques of the ones that are most successful.

PRESENTING QUALITATIVE DATA

———————————————————— Key takeaways ————————————————————

- Writing style and organization differs depending on the type of writing you are engaged in, such as books, journal articles or policy papers.
- Most pieces of qualitative writing have a standard organizational style that can be followed.

Understanding your audience

Your audience may change over the course of a single project. For example, you may be writing your dissertation, but either consecutively or concurrently you may also write a grant application, an academic article, a policy report and an op-ed for a newspaper. Each document requires a different focus, different language use, and has different objectives. Thus, knowing your audience and remembering who you are writing for is a priority.

The first step to writing anything is to think about who you are writing for. Are you writing for an academic audience? Are you writing for a policy or governmental group? Are you writing for the public? Are you writing for fellow researchers? Are you writing for healthcare professionals? Are you writing for a funding agency? Who your audience is will determine how you write the paper – it will dictate the language of the paper, the length of the paper and the type of recommendations you suggest. These are very important considerations when approaching a piece of writing, as each group has different needs and expectations (Wolcott, 2009; Hennink et al., 2011; Neuman, 2011; Silverman, 2011; Bessant and Farthing, 2012; Rubin and Rubin, 2012; Yin, 2008; Liamputtong, 2013). With qualitative writing, Fetterman (2010) demonstrates that there are particular considerations depending on the audience, including the format, the style of language and use of specialized terms and jargon, and the levels of abstraction. Liamputtong (2013: 287–8) elaborates that

> research funding agencies, for example, usually want to see the results of the research as well as to assess whether the project attains its objectives. Policy makers will want to know how the findings and recommendations of the research can be implemented and applied. Health professionals may wish to use research findings to improve their health services or the health status of people they care for. Professional social scientists, however, will want to look at the research process, its scientific soundness, and interpretation processes.

Below we will discuss some more common types of writing up qualitative research: books, peer reviewed journal articles and policy documents.

It is common to be completely overwhelmed by the sheer amount and richness of the data. You might be thinking, 'Where do I start?' No matter what type of document you are writing, the answer is: 'Start wherever you want to'. As Richards (2005: 188–9) says, writing is a way of finding out what you know and seeing things that were unclear. To do this does not require that you write a coherent, orderly account of the data. And to sit down to that task is more than most researchers can easily do.

So, start where you feel the most comfortable, the most confident or the most excited. This will help you maintain your stamina and enjoy the writing process. This section will outline the major differences between disseminating qualitative research in a book or manuscript, a peer reviewed journal article and a policy report.

Books

Books are able to publish entire studies, whereas journal articles are only able to focus on one aspect of a much larger piece of research. Books usually do not have a limit on length (within reason, of course!) so the author can take more time to elaborate on each aspect of the research. This is a great option for qualitative research, as the people who are being studied and the methods being used to study them can be described in much more detail than in a peer reviewed article (Liamputtong, 2013).

There is some debate regarding which takes longer to write: a book or a journal article. On the one hand, some argue that it can take much longer to write a book than to write a journal article, partly because books are much longer than articles, and partly because of the effort required to organize and coherently present such a large amount of data (Fetterman, 2010). On the other hand, others argue that publishing qualitative research as a book is much faster because of the high rejection rate of journal article submissions. Similarly, for those manuscripts that are accepted, the wait times at journals can be quite lengthy (McKercher et al., 2007). Depending on the process, the time to acquire reviewers and receive their reviews, the number of 'revise-and-resubmit' opportunities provided, etc., can make the article publishing processes very time consuming (Persell, 1985). When deciding between a book and a journal article, our advice is to think about whether your data would be better presented as a whole (as an ethnography often is, for example), in which case you should choose a book, or if your data would be better presented in a few shorter articles, each highlighting a different aspect of your research.

Peer reviewed journals

Most journals have length requirements (limited page numbers or word counts)[1] that constrain how much we are able to write, and how much detail we are able to provide.

---

[1]In addition to page length or word count, most journals have specific requirements for the type of headings, the citation styles, etc. It is important to know the requirements of the journal you are planning on submitting to prior to formatting the document.

Thus, your research likely will not be able to be presented in its entirety in only one article; it may require multiple articles on multiple topics in order to disseminate all of your research findings. Similarly, each section within the article may need to be condensed to adhere to the journal's length requirements, but enough detail should still be provided to allow readers to understand the complete process and most significant findings and implications. This can be especially difficult when writing up qualitative work, as we must be careful not to sacrifice the depth, richness and thick description that is key to good qualitative research (Morse, 2000; Liamputtong, 2013). To achieve this, Wolcott (2009: 95) argues that we should thus 'do less more thoroughly' and present only one aspect of the findings in each paper, but do so comprehensively; he suggests that 'a strategy for accomplishing this is to look for parts or instances or cases that can stand for the whole... Reporting "part" is all you can possibly do in a journal article...' (103).

Most journal articles have the following components, often in this order:

1. Abstract
2. Introduction
3. Literature Review
4. Theory
5. Methods/Research Design
6. Findings/Results
7. Conclusion/Discussion
8. Bibliography

These headings can vary. For example, instead of 'Findings', many qualitative papers will use the heading 'Themes'. As you read qualitative work, you will begin to see the types of headings commonly used. Being familiar with the conventions of the journal will also help. It is important to check the formatting guidelines with the journal you are planning on submitting to; they may have a particular order or particular length of paper that they require.

Some journals will require a specific order to your paper, and some authors will have personal preferences for the length of each section. For example, some authors write very short introductions and move immediately into the body of the paper, and others will spend more time setting up the paper and outlining the research questions and hypotheses. As you read other qualitative papers you will begin to determine which style you like best and what will work best for you. Pratt (2009) reminds us that while authors have their own voice, so do journals; as such, we need to be familiar with the 'voice' (or style) of the journal we are writing for.

The following descriptions are general guidelines for what should be included in each section of the article.

Abstract

The abstract is a very short synopsis of the paper, typically about 150–200 words in length. (Be sure to check the guidelines of the journal you're submitting to for the required length.) It should be clear and focused. The abstract should outline your entire paper in only a few sentences, focusing on the purpose, the methodology, the findings and the implications of those findings. Remember to keep the writing concise – the details can all be found in the paper. Berg and Lune (2012: 396) outline four key facts that should be included in any abstract: (1) identification of the focus of the study or the key issue under investigation; (2) the type and scope of data that were gathered and analysed; (3) the most important outcomes, findings or results; (4) key implications that have resulted. Almost every abstract will contain these four elements. If you are not able to write an abstract using these guidelines, there is potentially an issue with the clarity and focus of your paper. We suggest writing the abstract after the paper has been completed, to ensure that it is accurate.

Introduction

The first section sets out to introduce the paper. It serves as a guide to the reader for what will come and provides an overview of the main research question and findings. The information in the introduction should be presented in the order that the paper will be written (you want to think of it as a map to the rest of the paper), so you should mention your theory, methods and key findings. It is also the place where you explain the purpose of your paper – Why is your research important? Why should we care? And, most importantly, why should we keep reading the rest of the paper? Many writers will begin their paper by presenting a synopsis or case study of an event that their reader can relate to. Usually this is something that is current and high profile, allowing the reader to relate to the paper (and piquing their interest). A general rule of thumb is that the introduction is about 10% of the overall paper.

Literature review

The literature review presents information on what academic material exists on your topic. What other research has been done in the area? What were the findings? It is important to focus on both depth and breadth. Your literature search should be fairly extensive. Although it is impossible to read or cite every paper ever written on your topic, do not just look at the last few years of research. The current literature should serve as the building blocks for your work, and you should demonstrate the gap in the literature that your work will fill. The literature review sets the context for your own research, critically examines the claims made by previous researchers, and creates the foundation which your own work will rest upon (Rocco et al., 2011; Merriam, 1998). This section should integrate the existing literature; instead of summarizing and presenting each piece of literature you have read in a chronological order or list-like manner, you should be integrating the literature according to themes. Thus, if the themes present in the existing literature are race, class and gender, then those should be three main themes under which you could synthesize the material. If you discuss each study one by one, 'without pointing out how it relates to other studies and to your own findings, [it] will bore you as you write it and bore your readers as they read it' (van den Hoonaard, 2012: 141). Organizing the literature by theme allows you to draw the connections between the various pieces of existing research, and to integrate and interpret the literature.

Theory

This section should provide the reader with the theory (or theories) that you will be discussing to outline your findings. It is important to provide all of the key concepts and terms in this section, and to explain them clearly. The theory section of a paper does not present your research. It is solely about the theory. When you present your findings later in the paper, you will be able to refer to the theory section to demonstrate how the theory guides your findings. This section needs to be robust enough to explain the theory completely, but not too large to overtake the most important part of the paper: your findings.

Methods/research design

The methods or research design section of the paper is where you explain to your readers exactly how you accessed, gathered and analysed the data. Bryman et al. (2012: 311) report that 'quantitative researchers often g[i]ve more detailed accounts of their research design and methods than qualitative researchers'. However, qualitative methods should be spelled out as clearly for the reader as quantitative methods often are. Each step in the project should be outlined, including recruitment strategies, the sampling that was utilized and why, the type of data collection (ethnography, focus groups, interviews, etc.), and the way the data were analysed. This section of the paper should also include a discussion on your 'unit of analysis' and why you chose the particular location, context and unit of analysis. It's important to identify whether your focus is a typical situation/environment/ group, or an outlier – an extreme case that differs from the situation others may expect. A description of the sampling of events, cases or people should be provided. Pratt (2009: 858) demonstrates the importance of outlining the process of arriving at findings from data, and says that 'in explaining how you arrived at what informants thought or believed, be sure to explain what data you drew upon (e.g., observations, documents, interviews, etc.)'.

It is also important to be upfront with your readers about the position you took in the field: What was your relationship with the subjects before the study? If you were employed by or had volunteered for the organization, if you knew some of the respondents, or if you had any other 'connections' – which is sometimes how we are able to get past gatekeepers and into the field – this should be clearly outlined in the methods section. A methodological fit must also be demonstrated; in other words, why did you choose these particular methods for this project? Why were the methods that were used the best choice? According to Richards (2005: 193), 'such a fit is never perfect, so don't try to present it as such. It is important to assess honestly the adequacy of your design and the sufficiency of the data you worked with'. You should mention in the methods section whether you used traditional techniques or modified them, and how they were modified. You should also report if you used any software, such as NVivo, and how it was used during your analysis. Rocco, Hatcher and Creswell (2011: 167) suggest that the methods section can be organized in six parts: '(1) conceptual framework, (2) sample, (3) data collection, (4) data analysis, (5) integrity measure, and (6) data management'. The particular order is not nearly as important as ensuring that there is 'systematic description of the procedures, techniques and tools used' (Rocco, Hatcher and Creswell, 2011: 168).

Information to include in the methods section

- How was the instrument distributed to respondents?
- What did the instrument include? (How many questions? What were the topics?)
- How were respondents located and selected?
- How were respondents given informed consent?
- Why was a particular location selected for a case study or ethnography?
- How were the data collected?
- Was audio or video recording used?
- Where did the interviews take place?
- How long were the interviews? (Report shortest, longest and average of all interview lengths.)
- Were interviews transcribed?
- Were transcriptions verbatim, or were only certain sections transcribed?
- How were other forms of data treated?
- What was your position in the field?
- Why were these particular methods chosen?
- What is the unit of analysis (individual respondent, focus group, case, etc.)?
- How was sampling conducted?
- What type of data were collected?

Findings/results

The findings or results section should be the longest part of your paper. This is where you identify the key themes that you have found throughout the course of your data analysis. The research findings should be presented in a way that is clearly linked to the research questions and their hypotheses. They should also be linked to the theory wherever possible. You will want to use quotations, examples and excerpts from your data to demonstrate the strength of your themes. See the section below called 'Presenting Your Data' for ways of integrating quotations, excerpts and tables effectively.

Conclusion/discussion

Within the concluding section of the paper, return to the research questions and hypotheses that were presented in the introduction and carefully spell out the implications for each: 'linking the findings of the study to the hypotheses and theories introduced earlier allows the authors to discuss whether the hypotheses or theories are supported, and what the implications are for further research' (Bryman et al., 2012: 314). The conclusion, like the introduction, should be a recap of the paper. The discussion section is an opportunity to reflect on the research, the implications and the policy outcomes. In some qualitative pieces, the discussion section becomes merged with the findings – often, the nature of qualitative research requires some interpretation in order to ensure that the findings are clear and meaningful. It is important to be clear in the organization and pay close attention to the structure that best suits the journal's style and your material.

No new information should be introduced in the conclusion. This is your chance to reiterate the importance of your findings. You have presented all of the work you have done, all of the key themes you have found, and now you need to explain why it all matters. Typically, the limitations of the study are also discussed within this section. Not all research is perfect; often, there are aspects that are beyond the scope of our work or were not included in a particular article due to length restrictions. According to Ellinger and Yang (2011),

> limitations are often associated with the sampling approaches used, the data collection and analysis methods, and the concepts of generalizability, among others. It is important to acknowledge elements that have limited the scope, design, or in terms of generalizability so that other authors can carefully interpret the meaningfulness and usefulness of the findings given the limitations. (122)

Good research addresses any limitations and suggests additional areas of research that could fill any gaps within your own work.

Bibliography

The bibliography must include every article that was referenced within your entire article. This can be tiresome and tedious. There are resources that you can use to make it easier for you (for example, Zotero is a free citation software that will 'help you collect, organize, cite and share your research sources' (www.zotero.org, accessed May 26 2015). Microsoft Word also has 'reference tools' that can help you create a bibliography and manage your references. Whether you use a citation manager or write out your own bibliography, it's important to make sure that you keep a complete and detailed record of every source you have used. Keep track of the: names of authors (full first and last names, and middle initials if given); the complete title of the work; the publication year; for journal articles, the name of the journal, the volume and issue number of the journal; for books, the publication location and publisher of the book; for websites, the URL and the date it was last consulted – this information is important for subsequent researchers who are attempting to find the website, especially if it has been changed, updated or moved. Every journal has different requirements for their bibliographic formatting, so you must make sure that you format your bibliography accordingly. Having a complete record of all of the literature you have used will help you make the formatting changes that are required.

Policy reports

Policy reports tend to be shorter than books, but longer than peer reviewed journal articles. The focus is on policy issues; often, these are issues that directly impact the group who are under study. The language tends to be quite different in a policy report than in an academic journal article or a book.

Most policy reports have the following components, often in this order:

1. Title
2. Table of Contents
3. Executive Summary
4. Introduction
5. Theoretical Framework
6. Study Location/Population and Sample Characteristics
7. Research Design/Methods
8. Findings
9. Discussion/Conclusion

The executive summary is unique to policy reports, and serves as an extended abstract. Whereas an abstract is usually 150 words, an executive summary is often two to three pages. Depending on the length of the report, the executive summary may be much longer. The purpose of the executive summary is to allow readers to quickly identify the key points of the report. Like the abstract of a peer reviewed article, it should include the purpose, the methodology, the findings and the implications of those findings. In addition, it should include some of the key policy recommendations and interventions. The discussion/conclusion section of a policy report will include detailed recommendations for policy implementation, suggested interventions and suggestions for future research (Liamputtong, 2013). Typically the details of the other sections are similar to those of a peer reviewed article.

PRESENTING YOUR DATA

—————————————————— Key takeaway ——————————————————

- Qualitative data can be presented through tables, quotations and excerpts which help clarify and elucidate the information.

Tables

Tables are a beneficial way to clearly and succinctly present information. In qualitative writing, tables are often used to convey descriptive information and characteristics of the subjects, such as information about the locations or demographic characteristics of participants. Tables should be supplementary to the discussion, and used as a way to quickly review the information that is presented in the other sections. Do not forget to integrate the tables into the body of the paper; it is important not to just create the table and then forget to mention it.

Quotations and excerpts

Richards (2005: 194) suggests that 'describing a situation vividly and referencing what was said may be more powerful than simply quoting'. By using your research participants' own words, you are able to impart emotion and depth into your writing, while giving a voice to your study population. Be wary of the length of the quotations you choose. Long quotations can often detract from the overall flow of the paper; similarly, Richardson (1990: 41) argues that 'readers are more likely to read short, eye catching quotations than long ones'. However, there are no specific rules for how many quotations are too many, or how detailed they should be. It is often hard to know how much of a quotation to include in order to ensure that it is representative and conveys enough information to the reader. To address this conundrum, Wolcott (2009) suggests that earlier drafts should include 'an excess of illustrative material' that can be shortened and tightened with each draft as you edit. It is always easier to shorten, remove or synthesize information than it is to have to go back through your data to find a particular example or a quotation to illustrate your point.

Something else to consider is that 'the best examples will typically be those that not only show the point you are making but also do so in some utterly human and interesting manner' (Thorne, 2008: 185). When using quotations or anecdotes in your drafts, marking the original location will help you should you need to add more context as you write drafts. For example, if you mark the quote with 'Field Notes Jan. 12, 2015' or with the respondent's pseudonym, you will be able to quickly access the original source should you need to (Wolcott, 2009).

Using pseudonyms

When choosing pseudonyms for your participants, they should be different enough from the respondent's own name to ensure confidentiality but similar enough to be representative of the individual. For example, if your respondent's name is Steph Howells, you would not want to use 'Sarah Howser' as your pseudonym as it is obviously quite similar. But, as van den Hoonaard (2012: 138) points out, you also should not 'use the name "Tiffany" for an older widow or "Christine" for an Iranian Bahai refugee'. Similarly, location names should be representative of the location without giving away confidential information. If you are finding this hard, popular culture is a great reference point: for example, in Howells' (2012) research, she used high school names from television shows and movies as pseudonyms for the actual school locations (you may recognize 'Bel-Air Academy' from *The Fresh Prince of Bel-Air*, 'Degrassi High School' from the popular Canadian show *Degrassi*, and 'West Beverly High School' from *90210*). Similarly, Clarke (2010) used names from the show *Coronation Street* to represent the research participants.

Often, the same people who conduct the research are the ones who write it up; this makes the selection of quotes difficult because you are likely attached to, excited about or moved by a lot of the information. It is important to provide analysis, not merely description. A report that strings together long quotations 'offers bad description and no analysis. You are gaining little ground from the quoted material and going nowhere from the data … But data don't speak for themselves' (Richards, 2005: 196). To overcome this, Richards (2005) suggests that data (in the form of vignettes, anecdotes and quotations) be integrated into the writing as part of the overall argument; she suggests that as editing occurs, the quotations should be pruned and that the author should 'remove all words that don't make the point' (196). The use of ellipses (…) and square brackets ([ ]) are devices that can help you shorten quotations or make the excerpt more direct while maintaining its meaning.

The distinction between observed behaviour and inferred behaviour is one that must be made clear in your writing. It needs to be completely clear to the reader whether the information you are presenting is something you witnessed first-hand (observed behaviour), something that a respondent told you directly (observed behaviour) or something you have interpreted by being immersed in the research (inferred behaviour) (Table 9.1). We can very easily slip up by reporting inferred behaviour as though it was observed, 'with action and intent coloured by the eye of the beholder' (Wolcott, 2009: 28). If we talk about how someone 'felt' we have to be very clear whether they reported a particular feeling to us (observed) or whether we are interpreting their feelings, emotions or meanings (inferred). Whenever possible, reporting what we have actually seen and heard – using verbatim quotes where possible – is the most appropriate. If we must report on inferred behaviour, it should be qualified so the reader understands that the meaning has been created by the author, not the respondents.

Table 9.1 Observed versus Inferred behaviour

Observed behaviour	Inferred behaviour
'Frank stated that he was very angry: "I was so angry with her."'	'His tone of voice sounded **to me** as though he was angry.'
'I saw her stand up and shake his hand.'	'**I thought** it looked as though she wanted to greet him.'

Pratt (2008; 2009) suggests that data should be presented as 'power quotes' and 'proof quotes'. The most important and most common quotes are 'power quotes', which are the quotations that serve to illustrate the key points you are making and appear in the body of your paper as part of your argument. 'Proof quotes' are those that Pratt (2009) suggests you put in tables as supplementary data to bolster your argument and serve as proof of the claims you are making. The tables of 'proof quotes' should be exhaustive, including as many quotes as possible to back up your arguments. Pratt (2009) reminds readers that the tables should be supplementary to the arguments made in the body of the paper, and that 'readers should be able to understand your main arguments without referring to the tables' (Pratt, 2009: 860).

Quotations should always be introduced. Merely plopping in a quotation makes the writing disjointed, and requires your reader to do the work of interpreting the meaning and the context of the quote. Instead, a clear introduction – one that orients the reader to the quotation, tells the reader information about the speaker, and demonstrates the importance of that particular statement – will increase the effectiveness of the example you have chosen. The following excerpt from Steph Howells' (2012) PhD dissertation is indicative of the many tools discussed in this section. It introduces the quotations and sets up their meaning and importance. One quote uses an ellipsis to indicate that it has been shortened. Each quote is referenced with the pseudonym of the respondent and the school. Multiple quotes are used in a single paragraph to demonstrate their similarities. This short paragraph demonstrates the most effective tools that you can use to present clear and effective quotes to your audience:

> Many respondents were hesitant when asked if they felt safe at school, but stated that their hesitancy was only because they had not thought about their own safety at school before. As one respondent, Lilly (a teacher at Sweet Valley High School) noted, 'I've never thought about it before, that's all. The hesitation is because I've never really thought about it'. In fact, as the interview respondents were asked to think about their safety at school and specify what made them feel safe or unsafe, many respondents began statements with phrases like 'Now that I'm thinking about it …'. Thus, until they were forced to think concretely about their personal safety, or the personal safety of their children, school crime and violence had not been a concern for most of these individuals. Furthermore, some parents said that they had not discussed the issue of school crime or violence with their children, as neither parent nor child had any concern with the topic. For example, Edward, the parent of two students (a grade 11 student at Agrestic High School and a grade 12 student at West Beverly High), said, 'in general, it's not a huge topic of conversation in this house, because I think they feel safe'. Again, these are indicators of a relatively low-level of fear, and demonstrate a general lack of concern from parents, teachers, and students about school crime or violence.

Table 9.2 can be used to think about how you are integrating quotations into your own work. Ask yourself the questions at each stage of review to ensure that your answers are consistent and that editing the paper hasn't changed the purpose, clarity, or attribution of the quotation. This table is adapted from Hennink et al. (2011: 281).

Table 9.2   Integrating quotations

Introduction	Is the quotation clearly introduced?
	Is the meaning and importance of the quotation explained?
	Is the reader told whether the excerpt is about inferred behaviour or observed behaviour?
Purpose	Why is each particular quotation selected?
	Does the quotation serve as a typical example or as a unique case?
	Is the purpose made clear in the introduction to the quotation?
Clarity	Is the quotation clear in its meaning?
	Do any words need to be removed (use ...) or added (use [ ]) to improve clarity?
	Is the quotation long enough to impart meaning but short enough to retain reader interest?
Balance	Is there a balance between the number of quotations and your own words?
	Is there a balance between the length of quotations, with some short and some long?
	If you removed all quotations, is there still enough information to understand the issue?
Attribution	Is the proper pseudonym used?
	Has all potentially identifying information been removed?
	Is anonymized information about the speaker provided?

TIPS FOR GOOD WRITING

─────────────────────── **Key takeaways** ───────────────────────

- Proper spelling, grammar, word choice and effective writing style is key to writing a strong piece of qualitative research.
- Editing and having peers review your work are key to presenting polished written research.

A student once asked why we attribute so many marks to the writing, grammar and style of their paper. She asked, 'but doesn't the argument matter more? Aren't the ideas more important than the grammar?'. To some extent, we agree with her: the analysis and synthesis of ideas are the foundations of any solid piece of written work. But in order to fully understand and appreciate the ideas, concepts and sociological contribution, the piece must be well written; if it's not, these key features are lost.

Edit, edit, edit. You have put a lot of time into your paper, and probably read it a hundred times, but you need to make sure that you read it a few times specifically for spelling, grammar and writing style. Since you have put in so much time and effort, your brain knows what the paper *should* say, but you need to see what the paper *actually* says. You can do this in a few different ways. First, try editing on paper instead of on the computer screen. Print it off (double spaced works well), and go somewhere different than your usual workspace. This will get you out of writing mode and into editing mode. Using a pen, go through the paper word-by-word, and sentence-by-sentence. Second, read your paper out-loud (you might want to go somewhere private for this). This will slow down your brain and allow you to really hear each word and each sentence. You will likely notice a few misplaced commas and if you have used the wrong word (e.g., 'world' instead of 'word', or 'form' instead of 'from'). Third, read your paper backwards. This, like reading the paper aloud, allows you to focus on each word or each sentence, and not the writing as a whole. Fourth, when you think that your paper is perfect, ask a friend or colleague to read through it. It's helpful to have someone else read through it for content and for writing; as Morse (1994: 71) says, 'a smart researcher never sends an article to a publisher without both a peer review (for content) and an editor's check (for style and format)'.

Things to consider in your writing

- **Flow**. Do the sentences flow nicely from one to the next? Do the paragraphs flow nicely from one to the next? Are there choppy sentences or sections that jump from one thought to something completely un-related? Each section of the paper should build on the previous one, and the paper should proceed in a clear and ordered manner. Make sure that each paragraph and each section aligns with the theme of the paper and the main research question.
- **Word Choice**. Avoid unnecessary jargon. Sometimes the best word is *not* the biggest word. Try to use accessible language wherever possible – write so that people can learn from your work, not so that they need a dictionary to get through it.
- **Ease**. Well written papers ensure that the reader is not required to make assumptions or re-read sections to understand the information presented, and that there are no leaps of logic or interpretation required on the part of the reader.
- **Presentation**. Make sure that spelling is correct, that grammar is correct, that there are no typos, awkward sentences or run on sentences. A polished presentation allows the readers to focus on the details of the paper, and demonstrates that time and consideration have been put into the piece. A sloppy paper with typos, improper words or spelling errors will distract readers and reviewers from the important qualities of the paper.
- **First Person**. In a paper that you are writing about research that you are conducting, you should write in the first person. Your role as a researcher is integral to the final outcome: 'recognizing the critical nature of the observer role and the influence of his or her subjective assessments in qualitative work makes it all the more important to have readers remain aware of that role, that presence. Writing in the first person helps authors achieve those purposes' (Wolcott, 2009: 17).
- **Active versus Passive Voice**. Writing in the active voice moves readers along (e.g., it helps with the flow) and keeps them interested.

There are numerous articles and books that present guidelines for writing about and writing up various types of qualitative research:

Fox, M.F. (Ed.). 1985. *Scholarly Writing and Publishing: Issues, Problems and Solutions*. Boulder, CO: Westview.

Rocco, T.S., T.G. Hatcher and J.W. Creswell. 2011. *Handbook of Scholarly Writing and Publishing*. Hoboken, NJ: Jossey-Bass.

van Til, W. 1987. *Writing for Professional Publication*. Newton, MA: Allyn and Bacon.

van Maanen, M. 1988. *Tales of the Field: On Writing Ethnography*. Chicago: University of Chicago Press.

Wolcott, H.F. 2009. *Writing up Qualitative Research*, 3rd Edition. Thousand Oaks, CA: Sage Publications, Inc.

Ely, M., R. Vinz, M. Downing and M. Anzul. 1997. *On Writing Qualitative Research: Living by Words*. London: Falmer Press.

Alvermann, Donna E., David G. O'Brien and Deborah, R. Dillon. 1996. 'On writing qualitative research.' *Reading Research Quarterly* 31(1): 114-20.

EFFECTIVELY RESPONDING TO REVIEWER COMMENTS

────────────────────────── Key takeaways ──────────────────────────

- Receiving reviewer comments can be hard to swallow, but ultimately the constructive criticism will make for much stronger written work.
- Responding to reviewer comments should be complete, polite and supported with evidence.

Throughout our lives, most of what we do comes under review, whether it be from our teachers, professors, supervisors; the admissions committee at our graduate school; a selection/hiring committee, etc. Similarly, any time we publish a book or a manuscript it is going to come under review. The difference with an editorial review is that you have an opportunity to address the reviewers' comments and make changes – a second chance that many of us would have loved to have in some of the other situations listed above! Often, the comments we receive from reviewers are difficult to read. We have been slaving for months or years over the piece of writing we submitted, and anything that is not a glowing review can be difficult to take. The reality is, it is rare that we will get the glowing review that we desire. It is important to take the criticism we do receive, consider the comments carefully and objectively, and then respond to the comments in a positive and constructive way. We recommend that you read the reviewers' comments through thoroughly, and then step away from them for 24 hours. This will allow time for your emotions to run their course and for you to come back and re-read them with a clear head. This section provides general guidelines on how to respond to reviewer comments.

When you resubmit your manuscript with the suggested changes, you need to include a letter outlining the changes that you have made. Writing a strong letter takes time and effort, but it will command attention from the reviewers (Samet, 1999). You should begin the letter by thanking the reviewers and the editor for their time and their comments. You can use terms like 'thoughtful' or 'useful' comments. The remainder of the letter should be a very clear overview of each reviewer's comments and how you have made the suggested revisions. Williams (2004) provides three 'golden rules' for responding to reviewer comments: first, ensure that responses are *complete*; second, ensure that responses are *polite*; third, ensure that responses are supplemented *with evidence*.

Complete responses

Authors must ensure that all of the reviewers' comments are addressed. One way to do this is to create a worksheet – like a database – with all of the reviewers' comments. You can label each reviewer (Reviewer 1, Reviewer 2, etc.) and then number each of their comments (Comment 1, Comment 2). This will serve as your to-do list for you as you address the comments in your work, and will ensure you do not miss anything when crafting your response to the editor. It also will ensure that you understand each of the comments, and that you can take the time to think about what the reviewer is actually saying. It is important that you address the comments in the order that they were provided to you, so make sure that your labels reflect the order of each reviewer's comments. Sometimes the comments you receive will be compliments, but these should also be addressed in your letter to the editor. The more complete your responses are, the easier you have made the editor's job. Annesley (2011) suggests that you state both the page and line number of any changes you make (revisions, corrections, adding or deleting of text) and that you make sure to remove the original text completely from the revised source, and not use track changes or strikethrough on your re-submission.

Polite responses

Every comment that you receive should be addressed politely and respectfully. Remember that reviewers put in a lot of time to read your work, and you owe them for that. Sometimes we receive comments that we disagree with. No matter how off-base we think the reviewers' comments are, we need to address them and we need to address them politely. There are many ways to disagree that do not hurt or offend reviewers, such as 'We respectfully disagree with Reviewer 2's assessment …' or 'although Reviewer 1 was right to point out the challenges, we believe that …'. If you do feel that you have been wronged, then it is your responsibility to speak up – politely. Unfortunately, not all reviewer comments will be politely worded; this is your opportunity to be the bigger person and write a polite response. Annesley (2011: 554) notes that 'perhaps most important of all, expressing more humility and gratitude is wiser than that you might really want to say'.

Evidenced responses

Using evidence to back up your claims is pertinent if you disagree with a reviewer's comment. If you do disagree, do not just say 'I disagree with you'; you need to ensure that you (politely) explain *why* you disagree. Using evidence from published work, or clarifying your position will help you to respond completely and politely. For example, if the reviewer requests that you change/add/remove something but you feel that it would detract from your paper if you do so, you should clearly explain why that would be the case. Remember, there needs to be a strong case!

Occasionally reviewers may give you conflicting advice. Although this might seem frustrating, it can actually work in your favour since you are able to choose which set of comments fit best with the aims of your paper. You can address this within the letter by (politely) outlining the fact that the comments seemed to conflict and which direction you chose to go with and why you made that decision. You can also contact the editor for advice and clarification.

Reviewers might also miss something in the text and ask about it in the comments. Remember that reviewers are human; we all make mistakes. Politely point out this oversight and indicate where the answer can be found in your work.

If you are asked to shorten your work, you may have to make some difficult decisions about areas to cut. Occasionally the discussion section is a good place to cut. It is also a good idea to have an outsider (a friend, colleague or someone un-related to your paper) read it and see if there are sentences, paragraphs or entire sections that do not directly answer your research question (and can therefore be removed).

CONCLUSION

This chapter outlines the key considerations for disseminating qualitative data clearly, thoroughly and effectively. We introduced the need for understanding your audience before you begin. Next, we discussed the key considerations for presenting qualitative data in books, peer reviewed journal articles and policy documents. We focused on the methods section, indicating how to discuss your methodology clearly and concretely. Then we focused on the task of writing, providing tips for demonstrating the data effectively through the use of quotations and tables, and general guidelines for strong writing. Finally, we outlined strategies for effectively responding to comments from reviewers.

KEY TERMS

Active Voice	Observed Behaviour	Power Quotes
Inferred Behaviour	Passive Voice	Proof Quotes

REFERENCES

Abbott, Andrew. 2004. *Methods of Discovery: Heuristics for the Social Sciences*. New York: Norton.

Anderson, Elijah. 1999. *Code of the Street*. New York: Norton.

Anderson, Gary L. and Janelle Scott. 2012. 'Toward an intersectional understanding of process causality and social context.' *Qualitative Inquiry* 18(8): 674–85.

Annesley, Thomas M. 2011. 'Top 10 tips for responding to reviewer and editor comments.' *Clinical Chemistry* 57(4): 551–4.

Bagnall, Anne-Marie, Jane South, Mark J. Forshaw, Christopher Spoor, Paul Marchant, Karl Witty and Alan K. White. 2013. 'Self-care in primary care: Findings from a longitudinal comparison study.' *Primary Health Care Research and Development* 14: 29–39.

Baker, Lynda M. 2008. 'Unobtrusive research.' pp. 904–5 in *The SAGE Encyclopedia of Qualitative Research Methods*, edited by Lisa M. Given. Thousand Oaks, CA: Sage Publications, Inc.

Banks, M. 2001. *Visual Methods in Social Research*. Thousand Oaks, CA: Sage Publications, Inc.

Barbour, Rosaline. 2007. *Doing Focus Groups*. London: Sage Publications, Ltd.

Barnett, George A. 2011. *Encyclopedia of Social Networks*. Thousand Oaks, CA: Sage Publications, Inc.

Bauer, M. 1996. *The Narrative Interview: Comments on a Technique for Qualitative Data Collection*. London: Methodology Institute.

Bazeley, Pat. 2007. *Qualitative Data Analysis with NVivo*. Thousand Oaks, CA: Sage Publications, Inc.

Becker, Howard S. 1953. 'Becoming a marihuana user.' *The American Journal of Sociology* 59(3): 235–42.

Becker, Howard S. 1970. *Sociological Work: Method and Substance*. Chicago: Aldine.

Becker, Howard S. 1986. *Writing for the Social Sciences: How to Start and Finish your Thesis, Book or Article*. Chicago: University of Chicago Press.

Behar, Ruth. 2003. 'Ethnography and the book that was lost.' *Ethnography* 4(1): 15–39.

Bennett, Andrew and Colin Elman. 2006. 'Qualitative research: Recent developments in case study methods.' *Annual Review of Political Science* 9: 455–76.

Berg, Bruce L. and Howard Lune. 2012. *Qualitative Research Methods for the Social Sciences*, 8th Edition. Harlow: Pearson.

Bernard, H. Russell. 1994. *Research Methods in Anthropology: Qualitative and Quantitative Approaches*, 2nd Edition. Beverly Hills, CA: Sage Publications, Inc.

Bernard, H. Russell. 2011. *Research Methods in Anthropology: Qualitative and Quantitative Approaches*. Lanham, MD: Rowman Altamira.

Bessant, J. and R. Farthing. 2012. 'Presenting research to different audiences.' In *Research and Research Methods for Youth Practitioners*, edited by S. Bradford and F. Cullen. London: Routledge.

Biernacki, Patrick and Dan Waldorf. 1981. 'Snowball sampling: Problems and techniques of chain referral sampling.' *Sociological Methods & Research* 10(2):141–63.

Booth, Wayne C., Gregory G. Colom and Joseph M. Williams. 2008. *The Craft of Research*, 3rd Edition. Chicago: University of Chicago Press.

Braimoh, Jessica. 2015. 'Unequally placed: A study of the organization of social services for rural and urban youth.' Doctoral dissertation, McMaster University, Hamilton, Ontario.

Bryman, A., E. Bell and James J. Teevan. 2012. *Social Research Methods*, 3rd Canadian Edition. Don Mills Ontario: Oxford University Press.

Buzan, T. and B. Buzan. 2000. *The Mind Map Book*. London: BBC Books.

Carswell, Andrew T. 2012. *The Encyclopedia of Housing*, 2nd Edition. Thousand Oaks, CA: Sage Publications, Inc.

Charmaz, Kathy. 1983. 'The grounded theory method: An explication and interpretation', pp. 109–26 in *Contemporary Field Research: A Collection of Readings*, edited by R.M. Emerson. Boston: Little Brown.

Charmaz, Kathy. 2006. *Constructing Grounded Theory: A Practical Guide through Qualitative Analysis (Introducing Qualitative Methods Series)*. Thousand Oaks, CA: Sage Publications, Inc.

Cheek, Julianne. 2008. 'Research design.' pp. 761–3 in *The SAGE Encyclopedia of Qualitative Research Methods*, edited by Lisa M. Given. Thousand Oaks, CA: Sage Publications, Inc.

Clarke, D. 2010. *A Sociological Study of Scholarly Writing and Publishing: How Academics Produce and Share Their Research*. Lewiston, NY: Edwin Mellen Press.

Collier, John Jr. 1957. 'Photography in anthropology: A report on two experiments.' *American Anthropologist* 59: 843–59.

Colquitt, Jason A. and Cindy P. Zapata-Phelan. 2007. 'Trends in theory building and theory testing: A five-decade study of the *Academy of Management Journal*.' *The Academy of Management Journal* 5(6): 1281–303.

Corbin, Juliet and Anselm Strauss. 2008. *Basics of Qualitative Research: Techniques and Procedures for Developing Grounded Theory*, 3rd Edition. Thousand Oaks, CA: Sage Publications, Inc.

Cress, Daniel and David Snow. 2000. 'The outcomes of homeless mobilization: The influence of organization, disruption, political mediation, and framing.' *American Journal of Sociology* 105: 1063–104.

Creswell, John W. 2003. *Research Design: Qualitative, Quantitative and Mixed Methods Approaches*, 2nd Edition. Thousand Oaks, CA: Sage Publications, Inc.

Creswell, John W. 2009. *Research Design: Qualitative, Quantitative, and Mixed Methods Approaches*, 3rd Edition. Thousand Oaks, CA: Sage Publications, Inc.

Creswell, John W. 2013. *Research Design: Qualitative, Quantitative, and Mixed Methods Approaches*, 4th Edition. Thousand Oaks, CA: Sage Publications, Inc.

Cyr, Darren. 2014. Physical Graffiti and School Ecologies: A New Look at 'Disorder', Neighbourhood Effects and School Outcomes, Doctoral dissertation, McMaster University, Hamilton, Ontario.

Daley, Barbara J. 2004. 'Using concept maps in qualitative research.' Paper presented at the Concept Mapping Conference, Pamplona, Spain (http://cmc.ihmc.us/papers/cmc2004-060).

Davis Kirsch, Sallie E. and Patricia A. Brandt. 2002. 'Telephone interviewing: A method to research fathers in family research.' *Journal of Family Nursing* 8(1): 73–84.

DeCuir-Gunby, Jessica, Patricia L. Marshall and Allison W. McCulloch. 2011. 'Developing and using a codebook for the analysis of interview data: An example from a professional development research project.' *Field Methods* 23(2): 136–55.

Deegan, Mary Jo. 2001. 'The Chicago school of ethnography.' pp. 11–26 in *Handbook of Ethnography*, edited by Paul Atkinson, Amanda Coffey, Sara Delamont, John Lofland and Lyn Lofland. London: Sage Publications, Ltd.

Denzin, Norman K. 1989a. *Interpretive Interactionism*. Newbury Park, CA: Sage Publications, Inc.

Denzin, Norman K. 1989b. *The Research Act: A Theoretical Introduction to Sociological Methods*. Englewood Cliffs, NJ: Prentice Hall.

Denzin, Norman K. and M.D. Giardina. 2010. *Qualitative Inquiry and Human Rights*. Walnut Creek, CA: Left Coast Press.

Denzin, Norman K. and Yvonne S. Lincoln. 2008. *The Landscape of Qualitative Research*, 3rd Edition. Thousand Oaks, CA: Sage Publications, Inc.

Ebbinghaus, Bernard. 2005. 'When less is more: Selection problems in large-N and small-N cross-national comparisons.' *International Sociology* 20: 133–52.

Ellinger, Andrea D. and Baiyin Yang. 2011. 'Creating a whole from the parts: Qualities of good writing.' pp. 115–24 in *Handbook of Scholarly Writing and Publishing* edited by Tonette S. Rocco, Timothy G. Hatcher and John W. Creswell. San Francisco: Jossey-Bass.

Ellis, Carolyn. 1995. 'Emotional and ethical quagmires in returning to the field.' *Journal of Contemporary Ethnography* 24(1): 68–98.

Emerson, Robert M. 1987. 'Four ways to improve the craft of fieldwork', *Journal of Contemporary Ethnography* 16: 69–89.

Emigh, Rebecca Jean. 1997. 'The power of negative thinking: The use of negative case methodology in the development of sociological theory.' *Theory and Society* 26(5): 649–84.

Fern, E. 2001. *Advancing Focus Group Research*. Thousand Oaks, CA: Sage Publications, Inc.

Ferrell, Jeff and Mark S. Hamm. 1998. *Ethnography at the Edge: Crime, Deviance, and Field Research*. Boston: Northeastern University Press.

Fetterman, D.M. 2010. *Ethnography: Step-by-step* (Vol. 17). Thousand Oaks, CA: Sage Publications, Inc.

Fine, Gary Alan. 1993. 'Ten lies of ethnography: Moral dilemmas of field research.' *Journal of Contemporary Ethnography* 22: 267–94.

Firebaugh, Glenn. 2008. *Seven Rules for Social Research*. Princeton, NJ: Princeton University Press.

Gall, M.D., J.P. Gall and W.R. Borg. 2003. *Educational Research: An Introduction*, 7th Edition. Boston, MA: A and B Publications.

Gee, J.P., S. Michaels and C. O'Connor. 1992. 'Discourse analysis in education.' in *Handbook of Qualitative Research*, edited by Margaret D. LeCompte, Judith P. Goetz and Wendy Millroy. New York: Academic Press.

Geertz, Clifford. 1997. 'Spatial practices: Fieldwork, traveling, and the disciplining of anthropology.' pp. 185–222 in *Anthropological Locations: Boundaries and Grounds of a Field Science*, edited by Akhil Gupta and James Ferguson. Berkeley, CA: University of California Press.

Given, Lisa M. 2008. *The SAGE Encyclopedia of Qualitative Research Methods*. Thousand Oaks, CA: Sage Publications, Inc.

Glaser, Barney and Anselm Strauss. 1967. *The Discovery of Grounded Theory: Strategies for Qualitative Inquiry*. Chicago: Aldin.

Goldenberg, Claude. 1992. 'The limits of expectations: A case for case knowledge of teacher expectancy effects.' *American Educational Research Journal* 29: 517–44.

Goldthorpe, John. H. 1997. 'Current issues in comparative macrosociology: A debate on methodological issues.' *Comparative Social Research* 16: 1–26.

Hall, Edward T. 1966. *The Hidden Dimension*. New York: Anchor.

Hammersley, Martyn. 2008. *Questioning Qualitative Inquiry: Critical Essays*. London: Sage Publications, Ltd.

Hammersley, Martyn and Paul Atkinson. 1995. *Ethnography*, 2nd Edition. London: Routledge.

Hart, Chris. 1998. *Doing a Literature Review: Releasing the Social Science Research Imagination*. London: Sage Publications, Ltd.

Hays, Sharon. 1996. *The Cultural Contradictions of Motherhood*. New Haven: Yale University Press.

Hays, Sharon. 2004. *Flat Broke with Children: Women in the Age of Welfare Reform*. New York: Oxford University Press.

Heath, Melanie. 2012. *One Marriage under God: The Campaign to Promote Marriage in America*. New York: New York University Press.

Hennink, M. 2007. *International Focus Group Research: A Handbook for the Health and Social Science*s. Cambridge: Cambridge University Press.

Hennink, M., I. Hutter and A. Bailey. 2011. *Qualitative Research Methods*. London: Sage Publications, Ltd.

Hesse-Biber, Sharlene Nagy and Patricia Leavy. 2010. *The Practice of Qualitative Research*, 2nd Edition. Thousand Oaks, CA: Sage Publications, Inc.

Hochschild, Arlie Russell. 2012. *The Managed Heart: Commercialization of Human Feeling*. Berkeley, CA: University of California Press.

Holbrook, B. and P. Jackson. 1996. 'Shopping around: Focus group research in North London.' *Area* 28(2): 136–42.

Hollander, Jocelyn A. 2004. 'The social context of focus groups.' *Journal of Contemporary Ethnography* 33(5): 602–37.

Holloway, I. and S. Wheeler. 2010. *Qualitative Research in Nursing and Healthcare*, 3rd Edition. Oxford: Wiley-Blackwell.

Horowitz, Ruth. 1986. 'Remaining an outsider: Membership as a threat to research rapport.' *Journal of Contemporary Ethnography* 14: 409–30.

Howells, Stephanie. 2012. *In Search of a Culture of Fear: Understanding the Gap Between the Perception and Reality of School Dangers*. Doctoral dissertation, McMaster University, Hamilton, Ontario.

Humphreys, Laud. 1970. *Tearoom Trade: Impersonal Sex in Public Places*. London: Duckworth.

Hurston, Zora Neale. 1942. *Dust Tracks on a Road*. Philadelphia, PA: J.B. Lippincott.

Jawecki, Gregor and Johann Fuller. 2008. 'How to use the innovative potential of online communities? Netography – an unobtrusive research method to absorb the knowledge and creativity of online communities.' *International Journal of Business Process Integration and Management* 3(4): 248–55.

Jowett, Adam, Elizabeth Peel and Rachel Shaw. 2011. 'Online interviewing in psychology: Reflections on the process.' *Qualitative Research in Psychology* 8(4): 354–69.

Kane, Mary and William M.K. Trochim. 2007. *Concept Mapping for Planning and Evaluation.* Thousand Oaks, CA: Sage Publications, Inc.

Karner, Tracy Xavia. 1995. 'Medicalizing masculinity: Post traumatic stress disorder in Vietnam veterans.' *Masculinities* 3(4): 23–65.

Keizer, Kees, Siegwart Lindenberg and Linda Steg. 2008. 'The spreading of disorder.' *Science* 322: 1681–5.

Khan, M.E. and Lenore Manderson. 1992. 'Focus groups in rapid assessment procedures.' *Food and Nutrition Bulletin* 14: 119–27.

Khan, Shamus Rahman. 2012. *Privilege: The Making of an Adolescent Elite at St. Paul's School.* Princeton, NJ: Princeton University Press.

Knodel, John. 1993. 'The design and analysis of focus group studies: A practical approach.' *Successful Focus Groups: Advancing the State of the Art* 1: 35–50.

Krueger, R. and M. Casey. 2000. *Focus Groups: A Practical Guide for Applied Research*, 3rd Edition. Thousand Oaks, CA: Sage Publications, Inc.

Kuhn, Thomas. 1962. *The Structure of Scientific Revolutions.* Chicago: University of Chicago Press.

Lamont, Michèle. 1992. *Money, Morals, and Manners: The Culture of the French and the American Upper-Middle Class.* Chicago: University of Chicago Press.

Lareau, Annette. 1996. 'Common problems in field work: A personal essay.' pp. 195–236 in *Journeys through Ethnography: Realistic Accounts of Fieldwork*, edited by Annette Lareau and Jeffrey Shultz. Boulder, CO: Westview Press.

Layder, Derek. 1998. *Sociological Practice: Linking Theory and Social Research.* Thousand Oaks, CA: Sage Publications, Inc.

Lee, Raymond M. 2000. *Unobtrusive Methods in Social Research.* Milton Keynes: Open University Press.

Levitt, Steven D. and Stephen J. Dubner. 2009. *Freakonomics: A Rogue Economist Explores the Hidden Side of Everything.* New York: Harper Collins Publishers.

Lewins, Ann and Christina Silver. 2009. 'Choosing a CAQDAS Package.' http://www.surrey.ac.uk/sociology/research/researchcentres/caqdas/files/2009ChoosingaCAQDASPackage.pdf.

Liamputtong, Pranee. 2009. 'Qualitative data analysis: Conceptual and practical considerations.' *Health Promotion Journal of Australia* 20(2): 133–9.

Liamputtong, Pranee. 2013. *Qualitative Research Methods*, 4th Edition. Australia: Oxford University Press.

Lincoln, Yvonna S. and Egon Guba. 1985. *Naturalistic Inquiry* (Vol. 75). Thousand Oaks, CA: Sage Publications, Inc.

Locke, L., W.W. Spirduso and S. Silverman. 2000. *Research Proposals That Work*, 4th Edition. Thousand Oaks, CA: Sage Publications, Inc.

Lofland, John. 1970. 'Interactionist imagery and analytic interruptus.' pp. 35–45 in *Human Nature and Collective Behavior: Papers in Honor of Herbert Blumer*, edited by Tomatsu Shibutani. New Brunswick, NJ: Transaction Books.

Luttrell, W. 2010. '"A camera is a big responsibility": A lens for analysing children's visual voices.' *Visual Studies* 25(3): 224–37.

Luttrell, W., V. Restler and C. Fontaine. 2012. 'Youth video-making: Selves and identities in dialogue.' pp. 164–77 in *Participatory Video Handbook*, edited by E.J. Milne, C. Mitchell and N. de Lange. Lanham, MD: AltaMira Press.

MacQueen, Kathleen M, Eleanor McLellan, Kelly Kay and Bobby Milstein. 1998. 'Codebook development for team-based qualitative analysis.' *Cultural Anthropology Methods* 10(2): 31–6.

Magolda, Peter. 2000. 'Being at the wrong place, wrong time: Rethinking trust in qualitative inquiry.' *Theory into Practice* 39(3): 138–45.

Mahoney, John. 2000. 'Strategies of causal inference in small-N analysis.' *Sociological Methods & Research* 28(4): 387–424.

Maxwell, Joseph A. 2004a. 'Causal explanation, qualitative research, and scientific inquiry in education.' *Educational Researcher* 33(2): 3–11.

Maxwell, Joseph A. 2004b. 'Using qualitative methods for causal explanation.' *Field Methods* 16(3): 243–64.

Maxwell, Joseph A. 2005. *Qualitative Research Design: An Interactive Approach*, 2nd Edition. Thousand Oaks, CA: Sage Publications, Inc.

Maxwell, Joseph A. 2010. 'Using numbers in qualitative research.' *Qualitative Inquiry* 16(6): 475–82.

Maxwell, Joseph A. 2012. 'The importance of qualitative research for causal explanations in education.' *Qualitative Inquiry* 18(8): 655–61.

Maxwell, Joseph A. 2013. *Qualitative Research Design: An Interactive Approach*, 3rd Edition. Thousand Oaks, CA: Sage Publications, Inc.

Mazzei, Julie and Erin E. O'Brien. 2009. 'You got it, so when do you flaunt it? Building rapport, intersectionality, and the strategic deployment of gender in the field.' *Journal of Contemporary Ethnography* 38(3): 358–83.

McCall, George J. 1984. 'Systematic field observation.' *Annual Review of Sociology* 10: 263–82.

McKechnie, Lynne E.F. 2008. 'Reactivity.' pp. 729–30 in *The SAGE Encyclopedia of Qualitative Research Methods*, edited by Lisa M. Given. Thousand Oaks, CA: Sage Publications, Inc.

McKercher, B., B. Law, K. Weber, H. Song and C. Hsu. 2007. 'Why referees reject manuscripts.' *Journal of Hospitality and Tourism Research* 31(4): 455–70.

McParland, Joanna L. and P. Flowers. 2012. 'Nine lessons and recommendations from the conduct of focus group research in chronic pain samples'. *British Journal of Health Psychology* 17: 492–504.

Mears, Ashley. 2013. 'Ethnography as precarious work.' *The Sociological Quarterly* 54: 20–34.

Merriam, S.B. 1998. *Qualitative Research and Case Study Applications in Education*. San Francisco: Jossey-Bass.

Meyer, John W., Patricia Bromley and Francisco O. Ramirez. 2010. 'Human rights in social science textbooks: Cross-national analyses, 1970–2008.' *Sociology of Education* 83(2): 111–34.

Miles, Matthew B. and A. Michael Huberman. 1994. *Qualitative Data Analysis: An Expanded Sourcebook*. Thousand Oaks, CA: Sage Publications, Inc.

Miles, Matthew B., A. Michael Huberman and Johnny Saldana. 2014. *Qualitative Data Analysis: A Methods Sourcebook*, 3rd Edition. Thousand Oaks, CA: Sage Publications, Inc.

Mill, John Stuart. 1843. *A System of Logic, Ratiocinative and Inductive: Being a Connected View of the Principles of Evidence and the Methods of Scientific Investigation, Volume 1.* London: Oxford University Press.

Mills, Melinda C. 2008. 'Comparative research.' pp. 100–3 in *The SAGE Encyclopedia of Qualitative Research Methods*, edited by Lisa M. Given. Thousand Oaks, CA: Sage Publications, Inc.

Mizruchi, Mark S. and Lisa C. Fein. 1999. 'The social construction of organizational knowledge: A study of the uses of coercive, mimetic, and normative isomorphism.' *Administrative Science Quarterly* 44(4): 653–83.

Mohr, Lawrene B. 1982. *Explaining Organizational Behavior.* San Francisco: Jossey-Bass.

Monahan, Torin and Jill A. Fisher. 2014. 'Strategies for obtaining access to secretive or guarded organizations.' *Journal of Contemporary Ethnography* doi: 10.1177/0891241614549834.

Morgan, D. 1997. *Focus Groups as Qualitative Research*, 2nd Edition, Qualitative Research Methods Series, vol. 16. Thousand Oaks, CA: Sage Publications Inc.

Morgan, D. 1998. *Planning Focus Groups.* Thousand Oaks, CA: Sage Publications Inc.

Morgan, D. 2012. 'Focus groups.' in *Approaches to Qualitative Research: A Reader on Theory and Practice*, edited by Sharlene Nagy Hesse-Biber and Patricia Leavy. New York: Oxford University Press.

Morrill, Calvin, David B. Buller, Mary Klein Buller and Linda L. Larkey. 1999. 'Toward an organizational perspective on identifying and managing formal gatekeepers.' *Qualitative Sociology* 22(1): 51–72.

Morrow, Virginia and Gina Crivello. 2015. 'What is the value of qualitative longitudinal research with children and young people for international development?' *International Journal of Social Research Methodology* 18(3): 267–80.

Morse, J.M. 1994. 'Disseminating qualitative research.' in *Foundation of Primary Care Research: Disseminating Research Findings*, edited by E. Dunn, P.G. Norton, M. Stewart, F. Tudiver and M.J. Bass. Newbury Park, CA: Sage Publications, Inc.

Morse, J.M. 2000. 'Researching illness and injury: Methodological considerations.' *Qualitative Health Research* 10(5): 538–46.

Neuman, W.L. 2011. *Social Research Methods: Qualitative and Quantitative Approaches.* 7th Edition. Boston, MA: Allyn and Bacon.

Novak, Joseph D. and Alberto J. Cañas. 2006. 'The theory underlying concept maps and how to construct and use them.' (http://cmap.ihmc.us/Publications/ResearchPapers/TheoryUnderlyingConceptMapsHQ.pdf).

Novak, J.D. and D.B. Gowin. 1984. *Learning How to Learn.* Cambridge: Cambridge University Press.

Odgers, C.L, A. Caspi, C.J. Bates, R.J. Sampson and T.E. Moffitt. 2012. 'Systematic social observation of children's neighbourhoods using Google Street View: A reliable and cost-effective method.' *The Journal of Child Psychology and Psychiatry* 53(10): 1009–17.

Oliver, D.G., J.M. Serovich and T.L. Mason. 2005. 'Constraints and opportunities with interview transcription: Towards reflection in qualitative research.' *Social Forces* 84(2): 1273–89.

Opdenakker, Raymond. 2006. 'Advantages and disadvantages of four interview techniques in qualitative research.' *Forum: Qualitative Social Research* 7(4) (http://www.qualitative-research.net/index.php/fqs/article/view/175/391%3E#g22).

O'Reilly, Karen. 2008. *Key Concepts in Ethnography*. London: Sage Publications, Ltd.

Palys, Ted. 2008. 'Purposive sampling.' pp. 697–8 in *The SAGE Encyclopedia of Qualitative Research Methods*, edited by Lisa M. Given. Thousand Oaks, CA: Sage Publications, Inc.

Patton, Michael Q. 2002. *Qualitative Research and Evaluation Methods*, 3rd Edition. Thousand Oaks, CA: Sage Publications, Inc.

Patton, Michael Q. 2015. *Qualitative Research and Evaluation Methods*, 4th Edition. Thousand Oaks, CA: Sage Publications, Inc.

Persell, C.H. 1985. 'Scholars and book publishing.' in *Scholarly Writing and Publishing: Issues, Problems and Solutions*, edited by M.F. Fox. Boulder, CO: Westview Press.

Photovoice. n.d. 'Participatory photography for social change' (http://www.photovoice.org).

Pink, Sarah. 2001. *Doing Visual Ethnography: Images, Media and Representation*. London: Sage Publications, Ltd.

Ponterotto, Joseph G. 2006. 'Brief note on the origins, evolution, and meaning of the qualitative research concept thick description.' *The Qualitative Report* 11(3): 538–49.

Pratt, Michael G. 2008. 'The good, the bad, and the ambivalent: Managing identification among Amway distributors.' *Administrative Science Quarterly* 45: 456–93.

Pratt, Michael G. 2009. 'For the lack of a boilerplate: Tips on writing up (and reviewing) qualitative research.' *Academy of Management Journal* 52(5): 856–62.

Pullen, Robert, Victor Ortloff, Saundra Casey and Jonathon B. Payne. 2000. 'Analysis of academic misconduct using unobtrusive research: A study of discarded cheat sheets.' *College Student Journal* 34(4): 616.

Ragin, Charles C. 1987. *The Comparative Method: Moving beyond Qualitative and Quantitative Strategies*. Berkeley, CA: University of California Press.

Ragin, Charles C. 2006. 'How to lure analytic social science out of the doldrums: Some lessons from comparative research.' *International Sociology* 21(5): 633–46.

Rainwater, Lee and David J. Pittman. 1967. 'Ethical problems in studying a politically sensitive and deviant community.' *Social Problems* 14: 357–65.

Ray, Raka. 1999. *Fields of Protest: Women's Movements in India*. Minneapolis: University of Minnesota Press.

Reiss, Albert J. 1971. 'Systematic observation of natural social phenomena.' *Sociological Methodology* 3: 3–33.

Richards, Lyn. 2005. *Handling Qualitative Data*. Thousand Oaks, CA: Sage Publications, Inc.

Richards, Lyn. 2009. *Handling Qualitative Data: A Practical Guide*, 2nd Edition. Thousand Oaks, CA: Sage Publications, Inc.

Richardson, L. 1990. *Writing Strategies: Reaching Diverse Audiences*. Newbury Park, CA: Sage Publications, Inc.

Ritchie, Jane and Jane Lewis. 2003. *Qualitative Research Practice: A Guide for Social Science Students and Researchers*. Thousand Oaks, CA: Sage Publications, Inc.

Robert Wood Johnson Foundation. 2014. RWJF homepage (http://www.rwjf.org).

Roberts, Simon, Claire Heaver, Katherine Hill, Joanne Rennison, Bruce Stafford, Nicholas Howat, Graham Kelly, Shuba Krishnan, Penelope Tapp and Andrew Thomas. 2004. 'Disability in the workplace: Employers' and service providers' responses to the Disability Discrimination Act in 2003 and preparation for 2004 changes.' Centre for Research in Social Policy and BMRB International, Department for Work and Pensions (http://webarchive.nationalarchives.gov.uk/20130314010347/http:/research.dwp.gov.uk/asd/asd5/rports2003-2004/rrep202.pdf).

Rocco, Tonette S., Timothy G. Hatcher and John W. Creswell, 2011. *Handbook of Scholarly Writing and Publishing*. Hoboken, NJ: Jossey-Bass.

Rossman, Gretchen B. and Sharon F. Rallis. 2003. *Learning in the Field: An Introduction to Qualitative Research*. Thousand Oaks, CA: Sage Publications, Inc.

Rubin, H. and I.S. Rubin. 2012. *Qualitative Interviewing: The Art of Hearing Data*, 3rd Edition. Thousand Oaks, CA: Sage Publications, Inc.

Saldana, Johnny. 2013. *The Coding Manual for Qualitative Researchers*, 2nd Edition. Thousand Oaks, CA: Sage Publications, Inc.

Salmons, Janet. 2014. *Qualitative Online Interviews: Strategies, Design and Skills*, 2nd Edition. Thousand Oaks, CA: Sage Publications, Inc.

Samet, Jonathan M. 1999. 'Dear author – Advice from a retiring editor'. *American Journal of Epidemiology* 150(5): 433–6.

Sampson, Robert J. and Stephen W. Raudenbush. 1999. 'Systematic social observation of public spaces: A new look at disorder in urban neighborhoods.' *American Journal of Sociology* 105(3): 603–51.

Seawright, Jason and John Gerring. 2008. 'Case selection techniques in case study research: A menu of qualitative and quantitative options.' *Political Research Quarterly* 61(2): 294–308.

Shaffir, William B., Robert A. Stebbins and Allan Turowetz. 1980. *Fieldwork Experience: Qualitative Approaches to Social Research*. New York: St Martin's Press.

Shifman, Limor and Elihu Katz. 2005. '"Just call me Adonai" A case study of ethnic humor and immigrant assimilation.' *American Sociological Review* 70: 843–59.

Silver, C. and A. Lewins. 2014. *Using Software in Qualitative Research: A Step-by-Step Guide*, 2nd Edition. Thousand Oaks, CA: Sage Publications, Inc.

Silverman, David. 2009. *Doing Qualitative Research*, 3rd Edition. Thousand Oaks, CA: Sage Publications, Inc.

Silverman, D. 2011. *Interpreting Qualitative Data: A Guide to Principles of Qualitative Research*, 4th Edition. London: Sage Publications, Ltd.

Skocpol, Theda. 1979. *States and Social Revolutions: A Comparative Analysis of France, Russia, and China*. New York: Cambridge University Press.

Skocpol, Theda and Margaret Somers. 1980. 'The uses of comparative history in macrosocial inquiry.' *Comparative Studies in Society and History* 22: 174–97.

Small, Mario Luis. 2009. *Unanticipated Gains*. New York: Oxford University Press.

Small, Stephen A. and Lynet Uttal. 2005. 'Action-oriented research: Strategies for engaged scholarship.' *Journal of Marriage and Family* 67(4): 936–48.

Snow, David A., Calvin Morrill and Leon Anderson. 2003. 'Elaborating analytic ethnography: Linking fieldwork and theory.' *Ethnography* 4(2): 181–200.

Spradley, James P. 1979. *The Ethnographic Interview*. Belmont, CA: Wadsworth.

Stacey, Judith. 1990. *Brave New Families: Stories of Domestic Upheaval in Late Twentieth Century America*. New York: Basic Books.

Staggenborg, Suzanne. 2001. 'Beyond culture versus politics: A Case study of a local women's movement.' *Gender and Society* 15(4): 507–30.

Stewart, David W., Prem N. Shamdasani and Dennis W. Rook. 2007. *Focus Groups*. Thousand Oaks, CA: Sage Publications, Inc.

Strauss, Anselm L., Leonard Schatzman, Rue Bucher, Danuta Ehrlich and Melvin Sabshin. 1964. *Psychiatric Ideologies and Institutions*. New York: The Free Press.

Sturges, J.E. and K.J. Hanrahan. 2004. 'Comparing telephone and face-to-face qualitative interviewing: A research note.' *Qualitative Research* 4: 107–18.

Tarling, R. 2006. *Managing Social Research*. Abingdon: Routledge.

Taylor, Verta and Leila Rupp. 2003. *Drag Queens at the 801 Cabaret*. Chicago: University of Chicago Press.

Thomson, Rachel, Lucy Hadfield, Mary Jane Kehily and Sue Sharpe. 2012. 'Acting up and acting out: Encountering children in a longitudinal study of mothering.' *Qualitative Research* 12(2): 186–201.

Thorne, S. 2008. *Interpretive Description*. Walnut Creek, CA: Left Coast Press.

Touesnard, Lisa. 2008. 'What's love got to do with it? A study of the effects of infidelity on contemporary couples.' MA Thesis, Department of Sociology and Legal Studies, University of Waterloo.

Trede, Franziska and Joy Higgs. 2009. 'Framing research questions and writing philosophically: The role of framing research questions.' pp. 13–26 in *Writing Qualitative Research on Practice*, edited by Joy Higgs, Debbie Horsfall and Sandra Grace. Rotterdam: Sense Press.

van den Hoonaard, D.K. 2012. *Qualitative Research in Action: A Canadian Primer*. Ontario: Oxford University Press Canada.

Vaughan, Diane. 1986. *Uncoupling: Turning Points in Intimate Relationships*. New York: Oxford University Press.

Vaughan, Diane. 1996. *The Challenger Launch Decision: Risky Technology, Culture, and Deviance at NASA*. Chicago: University of Chicago Press.

Vaughan, Diane. 2004. 'Theorizing disaster: Analogy, historical ethnography, and the *Challenger* accident.' *Ethnography* 5(3): 315–47.

Venkatesh, Sudhir. 2008. *Gang Leader for a Day: A Rogue Sociologist Takes to the Streets*. London: Penguin Press.

Wacquant, Loic. 2002. 'Scrutinizing the street: Poverty, morality, and the pitfalls of urban ethnography.' *American Journal of Sociology* 107: 1468–532.

Warren, Carol A.B. and Tracy Xavia Karner. 2010. *Discovering Qualitative Methods: Field Research, Interviews, and Analysis*, 2nd Edition. New York: Oxford University Press.

Webb, E.J., D.T. Campbell, R.D. Schwartz and L. Sechrest. 1966. *Unobtrusive Measures: Nonreactive Research in the Social Sciences* (Vol. 111). Chicago: Rand McNally.

Weininger, Elliot B. and Annette Lareau. 2014. 'Sleepwalking into neighborhoods: Social networks and residential decisions.' Unpublished manuscript (https://sociology.sas.upenn.edu/sites/sociology.sas.upenn.edu/files/Weininger%20and%20Lareau.Penn%20Oct%2024.Final_.pdf).

Weiss, Robert Stuart. 1994. *Learning from Strangers: The Art and Method of Qualitative Interview Studies*. New York: Free Press.

Westbrook, Laurel and Kristen Schilt. 2014. 'Doing gender, determining gender: Transgender people, gender panics, and the maintenance of the sex/gender/sexuality system.' *Gender & Society* 28(1): 32–57.

Wheeldon, Johannes. 2010. 'Mapping mixed methods research: Methods, measurement, and meaning.' *Journal of Mixed Methods Research* 4(2): 87–102.

Whyte, William F. 1993 [1943]. *Street Corner Society: The Social Structure of an Italian Slum*, 4th Edition. Chicago: University of Chicago Press.

Whyte, William F. 1996. 'On the evolution of *Street Corner Society*.' pp. 9–73 in *Journeys through Ethnography*, edited by Annette Lareau and Jeffrey Shultz. Boulder, CO: Westview Press.

Williams, Hywel C. 2004. 'How to reply to referees' comments when submitting manuscripts for publication.' *Journal of the American Academy of Dermatology* 51(1): 79–83.

Willis, Paul E. 1977. *Learning to Labour: How Working Class Kids Get Working Class Jobs*. Aldershot: Coger.

Wolcott, H.F. 2009. *Writing up Qualitative Research*, 3rd Edition. Thousand Oaks, CA: Sage Publications, Inc.

Wrigley, Julia. 1989. 'Do young children need intellectual stimulation? Experts' advice to parents, 1900–1985.' *History of Education Quarterly* 29(1): 41–75.

Yin, R.K. 2008. *Case Study Research: Design and Methods*, 4th Edition. Thousand Oaks, CA: Sage Publications, Inc.

Zelizer, Viviana. 1994. *Pricing the Priceless Child: The Changing Social Value of Children*. Princeton, NJ: Princeton University Press.

INDEX

Page references to Figures or Tables will be in *italics*, followed by the letters 'f' and 't', as appropriate